Writing: a woman's business

MANCHESTER
UNIVERSITY PRESS

Writing:
a woman's
business

Women, writing and the marketplace

edited by

JUDY SIMONS AND KATE FULLBROOK

MANCHESTER UNIVERSITY PRESS

MANCHESTER AND NEW YORK

distributed exclusively in the USA by St. Martin's Press

Published by Manchester University Press
Oxford Road, Manchester M13 9NR, UK
and Room 400, 175 Fifth Avenue, New York, NY 10010, USA

Distributed exclusively in the USA
by St. Martin's Press, Inc., 175 Fifth Avenue, New York, NY 10010, USA

Distributed exclusively in Canada by
UBC Press, University of British Columbia, 6344 Memorial Road, Vancouver, BC, Canada V6T 1Z2

British Library Cataloguing-in-Publication Data
A catalogue record for this book is available from the British Library

Library of Congress Cataloging-in-Publication Data
Writing: a woman's business : women, writing and the marketplace /
    edited by Judy Simons and Kate Fullbrook
      p.   cm.
    ISBN 0-7190-5280-7. — ISBN 0-7190-5281-5 (pb)
    1. Feminism—Authorship—Marketing.   2. Women authors.   3. Women and literature.   I. Simons, Judy.   II. Fullbrook, Kate.
PN471.W75   1998
808'.02'082—dc21   97-27790

ISBN 0 7190 5280 7 hardback
ISBN 0 7190 5281 5 paperback

First published 1998

01 00 99 98   10 9 8 7 6 5 4 3 2 1

Typeset by Carnegie Publishing, Lancaster
Printed in Great Britain by Bell & Bain Ltd, Glasgow

Contents

Contents

Notes on contributors

Lisa **Appignanesi** is a London-based novelist and writer. Her novels include the best-selling *Memory and Desire* (1991), *Dreams of Innocence* (1994), *A Good Woman* (1996) and *Odd Things We Do For Love*. A former university lecturer in European Studies and founder of the Writers and Readers Publishing Group, Lisa Appignanesi worked throughout the 1980s at London's Institute of Contemporary Arts, first as Director of the prestigious talks programme and then as Deputy Director of the ICA. She initiated and edited the *Documents* series, which includes such titles as *Postmodernism* (1987), *Ideas from France: the Legacy of French Theory* (1989), and *Desire* (1989), as well as the books, *Science and Beyond* (1985) and *Dismantling Truth* (1989). With Sara Maitland, she also edited *The Rushdie File* (1989), the first book to chart the progress of the notorious Salman Rushdie affair. Lisa Appignanesi's other books include *Freud's Women* (1992) (with John Forrester), a critically acclaimed study of Freud's female case histories, ideas on femininity and relations with the women and female analysts in his life; *Simone de Beauvoir* (1988); and a history of literary and political cabaret, *Cabaret* (1994).

As a television producer, Lisa Appignanesi has made, amongst other programmes, *Seductions* and *England's Henry Moore* and worked as a consultant on *Fin de Siècle*. She has also written reviews, articles on various aspects of culture, and has contributed to numerous radio and television programmes. In 1988 she was awarded the *Chevalier des Arts et des Lettres* by the French Ministry of Culture. She lives with her partner, John Forrester, and her two children.

Elisabeth Bronfen is Professor of English and American Literature at the University of Zurich. She was educated at Radcliffe College, USA, at Harvard University and at the University of Munich, where she taught literature from 1984 until 1993. She is Visting Professor of English at Sheffield Hallam University. Her major publications in English include *Over Her Dead Body: Death, Femininity and the Aesthetic* (1992) and the edited collection *Death and Representation* (1993) with Sarah Goodwin. Her book *Hysteria and its Discontents* will appear in 1998 together with her study of Sylvia Plath for the British Council series *Writers and their Work*. Elisabeth Bronfen is currently engaged in extensive research for a new edition of the work of Anne Sexton.

Elisabeth Bronfen's research interests cover feminist and psychoanalytic criticism, and their applications to literature, film and the visual arts. She is on the editorial board of several scholarly journals, including *Literature & History* and

Notes on contributors

Literature, Interpretation, Theory. She has lectured widely in Europe and the USA. In 1993 an international symposium on *Death and the Aesthetic,* devoted to her work, was held at the London Institute of Contemporary Art.

Carmen Callil was born in Melbourne, Australia in 1938 and has lived in London since 1960. She worked in publishing from 1966 and started her own book publicity company in 1972. In that year she also founded the Virago Press of which she was Chairman and Managing Director until 1982, when she was appointed Managing Director of Chatto & Windus and The Hogarth Press, where she remained until 1994, continuing also as Chairman of Virago Press until 1995. She was responsible for the creation and development of the Virago Modern Classics list.

Since 1985 Carmen Callil has been a member of the Board of Channel 4 Television. She is now a critic and writer, working on a book about fiction with Colm Toibin, entitled *The Modern Library: Fiction in English 1950–2000,* to be published in 1998. She has recently published a biographical account of her family in *New Writing 5,* edited for the British Council by Christopher Hope and Peter Porter. She is the joint editor, with Craig Raine, of *New Writing 7,* to be published in 1998.

Carmen Callil is an Honorary Doctor of Letters from Sheffield, York, Oxford Brookes and the Open Universities. She is an occasional broadcaster, a regular book reviewer for *The Daily Telegraph,* and contributes occasionally to many other newspapers and magazines in Britain and Australia. In 1996 she was Chairman of the Booker Prize Judges.

Margaret Drabble was born in Sheffield in 1939, and educated at the Mount School, York, and Newnham College, Cambridge. She is a novelist and critic, author of thirteen novels and editor of the fifth edition of *The Oxford Companion to English Literature* (1985). Her early novels deal largely with the problems and aspirations of educated women struggling to find independence in the 1960s and 1970s. In 1991 she published *The Gates of Ivory,* which is the third part of a trilogy comprising *The Radiant Way* (1984) and *A Natural Curiosity* (1989): the first two volumes are set in Britain of the 1980s, and discuss the new Thatcherite political agenda. Part of the third is set in Thailand, Vietnam and Cambodia, and contrasts the developed and undeveloped world in an age of increasingly sophisticated information technology. Her biography of the novelist Angus Wilson was published in 1995, and her latest novel, *The Witch of Exmoor,* in 1996.

Margaret Drabble has travelled extensively for the British Council and was awarded the CBE in 1980. She is a Fellow of the Royal Society of Literature and is an Honorary Fellow of Sheffield Hallam University. She is married to the biographer Michael Holroyd.

Kate Fullbrook is Professor of Literary Studies and Associate Dean in the Faculty of Humanities at the University of the West of England, Bristol. She studied

Notes on contributors

literature at the Universities of Wisconsin, London and Cambridge. She is the author of *Katherine Mansfield* (1986), *Free Women: Ethics and Aesthetics in Twentieth-Century Women's Fiction* (1990), and, with Edward Fullbrook, *Simone de Beauvoir and Jean-Paul Sartre: The Remaking of a Twentieth-Century Legend* (1993) as well as many reviews and essays. Her and Edward Fullbrook's study of de Beauvoir's philosophical thought, *Simone de Beauvoir: A Critical Introduction*, will appear in 1998. Kate Fullbrook's major interests are in twentieth-century fiction, American literature, and literature and ethics. She has a long-standing commitment to the study of women's fiction and attended both the 1984 and 1995 conferences on women and writing at Sheffield Hallam University.

Maggie Gee was born in Poole, Dorset in 1948. She went to state schools and Somerville College, Oxford, and has three degrees in Literature. Her first novel, *Dying in Other Words*, was published in 1981. The following year she was chosen as one of twenty 'Best of Young British Novelists' and was the Writing Fellow at the University of East Anglia. Her subsequent novels are *The Burning Book* (1983), *Light Years* (1985), *Grace* (1987), *Where Are the Snows* (1991), and *Lost Children* (1994).

In 1989 Maggie Gee was a Booker Prize judge. She is a past member of the Management Committee of the Society of Authors, the writers' trades union, a Fellow of the Royal Society of Literature and a Teaching Fellow in creative writing at Sussex University. She regularly reviews for *The Daily Telegraph* and the *Times Literary Supplement* and lives in London with her husband, the broadcaster Nick Rankin, and their daughter, Rosa.

Clare Hanson teaches twentieth-century literature and feminist theory at the University of Leicester, where she is Reader in English. She read English at Oxford, then did an MA and Ph.D. at Reading University before taking up a post as lecturer at Cheltenham and Gloucester College of Higher Education. Her publications include *Katherine Mansfield* (1981) (with Andrew Gurr), *Short Stories and Short Fictions, 1880–1980* (1984), *The Critical Writings of Katherine Mansfield* (ed.) (1987), *Rereading the Short Story* (ed.) (1989) and *Virginia Woolf* (1994). She has also published articles on a range of women writers and on issues in feminist theory, and is a regular reviewer of feminist literary criticism. She has contributed a chapter on modernism to *An Introduction to Women's Writing*, edited by Marion Shaw (forthcoming) and has also contributed chapters on Angela Carter and Michele Roberts to forthcoming critical collections. She is currently writing a book on 'the woman's novel' in the twentieth century. Other research interests include psychoanalysis, aesthetics and questions of literary value. She confesses to having read 'women's novels' all her life, in a vain attempt to find out, as Brookner puts it, 'what behaviour most becomes a woman'.

Avril Horner teaches at the University of Salford where she is a Senior Lecturer in English and Associate Director of the European Studies Research Institute.

Notes on contributors

She worked previously at the Bolton Institute of Higher Education, Manchester Metropolitan University and the University of Manchester where, together with Sue Zlosnik, she taught several extra-mural courses on women's writing. One of these, entitled 'The Female Gothic', included study of *Rebecca*; teaching du Maurier's work in this context rekindled a shared interest in the author's novels and short stories. Her research interests and publications focus on twentieth-century literature and in particular on modern poetry, women's writing and the Gothic. She is the co-author, with Sue Zlosnik, of *Landscapes of Desire: Metaphors in Modern Women's Fiction* (1990) and *Daphne du Maurier: Writing, Identity and the Gothic Imagination* (1997). Further research projects include a book on comic gothic and further work on the marketing of women's fiction.

Maggie Humm is Professor of Women's Studies at the University of East London, Britain's first full degree in Women's Studies. She was awarded her personal Chair in 1995. She has taught at the University of Massachusetts and has been Visiting Scholar at San Diego State University and at Stanford University and Visiting Professor of Women's Studies at Queen's University, Belfast. Her British Council lecture tours have taken her to universities in Brazil, Bulgaria, Pakistan, Italy and Israel. She was Co-Chair of the British National Association for Women's Studies between 1990 and 1993 and in 1994 was a Fawcett Society Book Prize Judge.

Maggie Humm has published ten books in the area of feminist criticism and theory, including *Border Traffic: Strategies of Contemporary Women Writers* (1991), the best-selling *Feminisms* (1992) and *The Dictionary of Feminist Theory* (1995), whose first edition was named 'Outstanding Academic Book for 1990' by the American Association of College and Research Libraries.

Her chapter in this volume is part of a longer study of *Orlando* in *Feminism and Film* (1997). She is an editor of *The International Encyclopaedia of Women's Studies*, which, with its 1.5 million words, will be the largest data bank in Women's Studies. Currently she is researching Virginia Woolf's photography and aesthetics together with modern visual writing for *Borderline: Feminism and Film* (forthcoming).

Elaine Jordan was born in 1943. She went from a grammar school in Leeds to Somerville College, Oxford, where she was awarded a scholarship to study English Language and Literature. Both institutions were then women-only: a strength, but also, given a mother-and-sister oriented family, something to escape. She graduated in 1964, and after some postgraduate teaching and study, taught for a year at Durham University. She spent the next ten years raising two sons and a daughter, interspersed with varied part-time work in teaching, examining, and later consultancy, and worked for the Open University from its foundation. In 1977 she took a full-time post at Essex University and is now Reader in Literature and Director of the MA in Women's Writing, which considers the question of what it may mean to write and read as a woman.

Elaine Jordan has published *Alfred Tennyson* (1988) and articles or chapters

Notes on contributors

on Jane Austen, Elizabeth Gaskell, Walter Scott, Joseph Conrad, and more recently on Toni Morrison, Angela Carter, and Christa Wolf (1996), and a new essay, 'Getting Heated: Divorce, Democracy and Thermodynamics', in Rebecca Stott's *Critical Reader* on Tennyson (1996).

She is the editor of the *New Casebook* on Conrad (1996), which emphasises recent critical and theoretical approaches. What unifies her work is a concern with gender, sexuality, and feminism, and with history, theory, and cultural representations.

Kadiatu Kanneh is Lecturer in Nineteenth- and Twentieth-Century Literature in the School of English at the University of Birmingham. She has been a lecturer in English at the School of African and Asian Studies and, until recently, in the School of English and American Studies at the University of Sussex. Her BA and MA in English were completed at the University of Southampton, and her Ph.D. at the University of Sussex.

Kadiatu Kanneh's research interests are in post-colonial and feminist theories and literatures, involving literatures of Africa and the Diaspora, histories of race and representation. She has published several scholarly articles, including most recently chapters in *Political Gender: Texts and Contexts* (1994) and 'The Difficult Politics of Wigs and Veils: Feminism and the Colonial Body' in *The Post-Colonial Studies Reader*, Ashcroft, Griffiths and Tiffin (eds) (1995). Her book *African Identities* is forthcoming.

Lyn Pykett was educated at University College and Birkbeck College, London, and is now a Professor of English and Head of Department at the University of Wales Aberystwyth, where she teaches mainly nineteenth-century literature and literary theory. She has published widely on nineteenth-century writing, including *Emily Brontë* (1989), *The Improper Feminine* (1992), and *The Sensation Novel from 'The Woman in White' to 'The Moonstone'* (1994). She is also the author of the chapter on women writers 1830–1880 in *An Introduction to Women's Writing from the Middle Ages to the Present Day*, Marion Shaw (ed.) (forthcoming). *Engendering Fictions: The English Novel in the Early Twentieth Century*, which attempts to rethink the history and the gender of modernism, was published in 1996, and the Longman Critical Reader *Reading Fin de Siècle Fictions* also appeared in 1996. She is currently working on the fiction of May Sinclair and Rebecca West, along with projects on Braddon and on Wilkie Collins. She is a founding member of the Editorial Board and Associate Editor of a new interdisciplinary periodical, the *Journal of Victorian Culture*.

In addition to her scholarly work, Lyn Pykett has published on the institutional organisation and development of English Studies in Britain, areas in which she has also been closely involved through her work with the Council for University English, and more recently the Council for College and University English.

Marion Shaw is Professor of English and Head of the Department of English and

Drama at Loughborough University. Prior to that, she was for many years a member of the English Department at the University of Hull. Her publications include three books on Tennyson, one of which was published in the Harvester-Wheatsheaf *Feminist Readings* series, a series which applied feminist criticism to male canonical writings. She continues to work on Tennyson, not least as editor of the *Tennyson Research Bulletin*. She has also co-authored a book on Agatha Christie's Miss Marple, in the Routledge *'Heroines?'* series, and has edited *Man Does, Woman Is: The Faber Book of Work and Gender* (1995). She is the editor of a forthcoming collection of nine new essays entitled *An Introduction to Women's Literature from the Middle Ages to the Present Day*, and is in the process of completing *The Clear Stream: A Life of Winifred Holtby*.

Judy Simons is Dean of Humanities and Social Sciences at De Montfort University. She was educated in Sheffield and at the University of Manchester, and until recently was Professor of English at Sheffield Hallam University. She has published widely on women's writing from the eighteenth to the twentieth centuries and is a regular reviewer of feminist criticism for scholarly journals. Her books include *Fanny Burney* (1987), *Diaries and Journals of Literary Women from Fanny Burney to Virginia Woolf* (1990), *Rosamond Lehmann* (1992) and, with Shirley Foster, *What Katy Read: Feminist Re-readings of 'Classic' Stories for Girls 1850–1920* (1995). She has written two student guides to Jane Austen and is the editor of *Mansfield Park and Persuasion: A New Casebook* (1997). She is currently working on a study of twentieth-century women's fiction and its use of romance narratives, entitled *Re-Writing the Love Story*, to be published in 1998. Her future projects include a history of women's writing for children.

Among her other research interests, Judy Simons is Director of a long-term research project examining Romantic women's writing in the Corvey literary archive, based at Sheffield Hallam University. From 1993–96 she was Visiting Professor of English at Queen's University, Belfast. She is centrally involved in the politics of English Studies as Chair of the Council for College and University English. She convened the 1995 Sheffield conference 'Literature: A Woman's Business'.

Sue Zlosnik is Head of the Department of English at Liverpool Hope University College. After a brief career as a schoolteacher, she became a research student at the University of Manchester, working on the fiction of George Meredith, and went on to become a lecturer at De La Salle College of Higher Education in 1983. During this period her collaboration with Avril Horner began: they taught courses together in the extra-mural department of the University of Manchester and began work on the book *Landscapes of Desire: Metaphors in Modern Women's Fiction* (1990). In 1987 she moved to the then Liverpool Institute of Higher Education and became Head of its English Department in 1992.

Sue Zlosnik has research interests in nineteenth- and twentieth-century literature and in women's writing and feminist literary theory. She has published articles on the work of Meredith and is co-author with Avril Horner of *Daphne du Maurier: Writing, Identity and the Gothic Imagination* (1997). A graduate in Government from the London School of Economics, she remains interested and involved in politics. Future projects include a book on comic gothic and further work on the marketing of women's fiction.

Acknowledgements

Permission to reproduce stills from *South Riding* (London Films, 1938), in the Winifred Holtby Archive in Hull Public Library, has been kindly given by Kingston upon Hull Leisure Services.

The covers of Daphne du Maurier's *Rebecca* are reproduced courtesy of Penguin: figure 5 (1962, © Virgil Burnett, by permission of the British Library), and figure 8 (1962, © Peter Reddick); Arrow (1992, © Gary Blyth); and Pan Books (1975). The covers of Angela Carter's *Fireworks* are reproduced courtesy of Quartet (1974, © Bob Foulke) and Virago (1987, © Hiroshi Mauabe), and the still from the film *Orlando* is reproduced courtesy of The Sales Company.

Introduction

Judy Simons and Kate Fullbrook

This volume celebrates the professional writing woman and her achieve-ments. It also marks a new, notable, and mature moment in late twentieth-century thinking about women's writing, building at once on the early, delighted discoveries of women's texts by feminist academics in the 1960s, on the theorisation of all aspects of that writerly practice in the 1970s and 1980s, and on the sophisticated and pragmatic diver-sity of feminist thought of the 1990s. Above all, it signals a renewed interest in women's position in the literary marketplace and in our still ambiguous relationship with the structures which allow us access to the public arena. The collection brings together novelists, critics and editors, who, from their differing perspectives, all address the serious topic of the 'business' of writing for and by women. Variously, they consider the issues of consumerism as they affect women's position in a commercial environment, where issues of gender frequently disturb the always fraught transmission from imaginative creation to printed page and to the even more inaccessible terrain of the cinema.

In quite another way this book serves as a commemorative encapsul-ation of a moment in a remarkable historical process. It celebrates not just how far women as conscious analysts of their own complex practice as writers have travelled in the past twenty or so years but also the vigour and excitement of that journey, and, in particular, the way in which it continues to generate vital and diverse debates about women, literature, and cultural value. In 1996, the popular press had a field day publicising the controversy over the Orange Prize, the first lucrative prize for fiction by women (won by the fine poet and novelist Helen Dunmore) and the much hyped 'disappointment' of two of the judges that the standard of entries was so low. Much has been made of Val Hennessy's criticism of the subject matter of the material submitted for the prize, and her complaint that it was 'parochial, small-minded and

1

inward-looking in approach. Too many of the writers were obsessed with trivia and their own psyche'.[1] The occasion also helped to highlight the degree of alienation that confronts women writers in the professional marketplace. Reviewing the 1996 summer season, Iain Sinclair, for instance, in *The London Review of Books*, protested somewhat petulantly about the 'coven of Judys and Louises' who appear to dominate the literary columns, and his perception that quality work by male novelists has been ignored by a conspiratorial sisterhood in favour of books both 'written and reviewed by women who photograph well'.[2]

These remarks strike deep into the heart of the troublesome question of literary evaluation and the traditional tendency of critics to dismiss work by women which focuses on female anxiety or domesticity as inevitably marginal in its appeal. As Virginia Woolf famously remarked in *A Room of One's Own*, satirising the critical establishment of her day, 'This is an important book, the critic assumes, because it deals with war. This is an insignificant book because it deals with the feelings of women in a drawing room. A scene in a battlefield is more important than a scene in a shop' (Woolf, 1929: 74). Commenting on the Orange affair, the *Times Literary Supplement* observed that amongst all the fuss there does stand a valid objection to the promotion of a 'delegate culture, the miserable idea that writers only represent their particular groups, for readers also from those groups'.[3] Even today, it appears, there is an assumption that women authors write exclusively for women readers, while male authors continue to have 'universal' appeal, and that certain subjects offer inadequate means for dealing with the general human condition.

Whether or not there should be a separate literary prize for women is certainly highly controversial – Margaret Drabble confronts the issue head-on in her chapter – but what the media interest in the matter demonstrates more than anything else is that literary debates remain inextricably entwined with the politics of gender. Further, the subtext of the Orange Prize affair is economic: the source of abrasion underlying the journalistic furore regarding the supposedly suspect quality of women's writing is the audacity of women daring to award one of their number the serious money and attendant publicity of the £30,000 prize itself. Women/writing/business: this is still a potentially scandalous union of terms which retains its power to shock.

But then, the visibly public association of women working seriously in concert to address their own interests has always been simultaneously shocking, difficult, and an occasion for celebration. Academic work of a feminist cast is, at the moment, a respected part of many universities' teaching and research portfolios. This happy state of affairs is, however, scandalously recent, and historically still in its infancy. As few as ten years ago, hospitable conditions for feminist work in literature in British universities were still rare and subject to considerable contention. National links between feminist scholars were unformed, or insecure, or extremely limited.

In 1984 a group of women academics from the two universities in Sheffield decided to mount the first national conference devoted to women's writing. It is now extraordinary to recall that at that time such a gathering was something of a novelty. It is also important to remember that feminist literary criticism itself was a response to the huge burst of creative energy from women writers and editors which characterised the 1970s. It was this rapidly growing popularity of women's literature, both in academic circles and in publishing, which exerted its hold over the minds of female scholars, students and general readers, and which was already having a dramatic impact upon traditional university curricula, that made the need for such a conference so pressing. That conference, held in September 1984, at what is now Sheffield Hallam University, represents a milestone in the development of literary feminism in the United Kingdom. It attracted sixty academics from forty institutions of higher education and generated thirty scholarly papers on subjects ranging from Fanny Burney to Colette. It drew together the diverse institutional hierarchies of publishers and teachers, authors and critics, whose mutual allegiances had never before been acknowledged or articulated quite so publicly. Keynote speakers included Carmen Callil, then chairman of Virago Press, the influential feminist critics Cora Kaplan and Lorna Sage, the experimental writer Nicole Ward-Jouve and the poet Ann Stevenson. For many delegates the conference was a happy revelation of the numbers of other women who shared their commitment to the study of women writers.

It is only since the late 1970s that literature about and produced by women has become explicitly acknowledged as big business. In the revised intellectual climate of the last quarter of the twentieth century, deeply affected by the impact of feminism and responsive to the demands of women students and teachers in universities, studies of women's writing have developed as a discrete part of the international curriculum. Undergraduate and postgraduate courses in women and literature, in gender studies, in women's history and in feminist theory have emerged as central to the understanding of cultural and literary production in all its forms. Meanwhile it is reported that research on Angela Carter and Toni Morrison have each, separately, overtaken the entire sixteenth, seventeenth, and eighteenth centuries in the popularity stakes as topics for doctoral students making grant applications to the British Academy. Indeed, the 'Angela Carter syndrome' is, in itself, a remarkable manifestation of the changed status accorded women's writing by the current generation of literary scholars, and is addressed, and to some extent explained, by Elaine Jordan's fascinating analysis of Carter's publishing history in this volume.

The academic market is a key example of the changed public recognition of the importance of feminist debates. And the level and vitality of current activity in that market reflects the demands of a culture which now insists on claiming a significant, permanent, and prestigious space for women's writing both in academia and beyond. Hard evidence for this shift can be found in the most cursory glance at what, precisely, publishers find it in their interest to print and promote. Academic publishers' lists, with their hundreds of titles dealing with women, have demonstrated the strength of a market for rigorous analysis of women's writing which was formerly disregarded. The first Sheffield conference played a part in crystallising this new readerly public. The collection of papers which emerged from that conference, published under the title *Women's Writing: A Challenge to Theory*, edited by Moira Monteith, is now recognised as a key work which defended its eclecticism with conviction, and which has never been out of print since its original appearance (Monteith, 1986). The 1984 conference also succeeded in fostering the solidarity of a growing and organised group of women university teachers of literature who founded Network, an organisation whose official membership now numbers 250 (with an unofficial membership of at least three times that figure), and whose meetings have provided an important testing ground for some of Britain's leading feminist critics, several of whom are contributors to this present volume.[4] Indeed this collection is in itself something of a testament to the strength of that first invigorating occasion which sparked a fertile interchange of ideas and opened up new ways of thinking about texts and interactions between those with an interest in their production.

The chapters in this volume were for the most part originally delivered as papers in Sheffield in March 1995 at a second conference which at once celebrated the legacy of the previous decade, and embodied the dynamic interplay of debates regarding women as producers and consumers of text. This conference, 'Literature: A Woman's Business', focused on the industry that feminist criticism has become, and on the commercial factors which affect and in some cases determine the success of women's writing. Both a pleasing anniversary occasion and a place for recognition of the success of its programme, as well as a forum for bringing into focus some of the central debates of the late 1990s regarding women and literature, the conference teasingly resurrected Robert Southey's notorious advice to Charlotte Brontë that 'Literature cannot be the business of a woman's life' as a basis for examining the often startling successes of women who have both made literature their business and forcefully alerted others to that fact. From Carmen Callil, the most significant editor of her generation in Britain, who virtually single-handedly proved that women's publishing is not only a viable enterprise but one that recognises the importance of the niche market of women readers and writers in a stunningly successful way, to Marilyn Butler, Rector of Exeter College, Oxford, who, with a series of ground-breaking critical studies, has revolutionised attitudes to thinking about women's writing as fundamentally rooted in contemporary intellectual and political debate, the speakers at this simultaneously commemorative and initiatory event demonstrated how women's writing can never be isolated from issues surrounding its production and reception.

The dazzling array of contributors to 'Literature: A Woman's Business' demonstrates both the oppositional and the mutually supportive emphases of the present business of women's writing. As Linda Fildew, a senior editor with Harlequin Mills & Boon, observed at a conference session on 'romance reading', the latest figures show that there are approximately twenty-four million women over the age of fifteen in the UK, all of them potential or actual readers.[5] Together they form a substantial consumer base in which publishers and authors alike have a vested interest. Mills & Boon, of course, represents one extreme of the market, its name having passed into the vocabulary – and into the Oxford Dictionary – as synonymous with romantic fiction and the popular, and accordingly discredited by the traditional literary establishment. Yet it was revealing how many distinguished academics and delegates at Sheffield (not all of them women) confessed, often guiltily, to a predilection for reading such novels. Several more confessed to having attempted to write them. The seductive nature of this genre gives pause for thought. One of the most consistently articulated themes of this volume (and an emergent and powerful topic for debate at the conference) is the need for more systematic enquiry into the problematic relationship between literary categorisation, commercial success and critical estimation, the need to combat the common prejudice that popular writing cannot also be writing of quality.

The predominance of fiction as the favourite 'female genre' is a well rehearsed subject and this predilection is reflected in the essays which follow. The Sheffield conference, however, also gave space to those iconoclastic voices of women who break out of the expected confines into new and adventurous territory. The author Kathy Lette spoke wittily but with feeling on the thorny issue of women and humour, and described the hostility she has encountered from male audiences when her comedy has targeted subjects previously taboo for women, such as machismo or sexual posturing. The cartoonist Jacky Fleming, in a quick-fire exhibition of her work, described the incomprehension with which men greet feminist satire, a self-evident contrast to the audience of women, helpless with laughter, whom she addressed. From a totally different (but ultimately related standpoint, the Shakespearean scholar Ann Thompson examined the exclusion of women from 'bardbiz', the industry of Shakespearean scholarship, over the centuries. In reviewing the revisionist readings of Shakespeare by later twentieth-century feminist critics, she exposed the difficulties women have encountered, and to some extent overcome, in staking claims to a dominant cultural product which is traditionally perceived as a male preserve. Together, these discussions, coming from polarised points on the literary map, help to re-focus the debates about gender and genre which affect women's imaginative and critical practice alike.

It is deeply regrettable that for reasons of space not all of the conference contributions could be included in this published collection, with its particularly modern bias. The volume does, however, concentrate a number of pressing questions which absorb women's interest. Despite the lively diversity of the chapters which make up this collection, they are united in their challenge to still-prevailing notions regarding the inadequate competence of women in the literary marketplace. They show the vigour and dedicated professionalism of women's writing in the modern period, without neglecting serious and repeated concerns about the production and marketing of women's writing and the pressures which determine its direction. Taken as a whole, the chapters are sensitive not only to the conditions governing women's literary and cinematic production, but to issues of reception and to the ways in which women writers and film-makers are taken up and marketed in the ever-shifting cultural and intellectual climate of the modern and post-modern periods. The chapters identify a series of recurrent issues, which, in essence, locate central questions regarding women and textual production and distribution as well as the reception of that work at the end of the twentieth century.

For, although collectively the chapters that follow challenge any vestigial notions of women's exclusion from the literary marketplace, they also repeatedly illustrate the continuing difficulties women confront in establishing a serious presence in an industry which, until recently, has been determinedly male-dominated. We refer, of course, not to the industry of writing itself (which women have always embraced with enthusiasm), but to the economic power base of publishing and the crucial promotional policies which support it. In particular, this volume explores women writers' conscious awareness of their own marketability as products and the extent to which gender is a factor that can be exploited profitably by publishing houses in targeting readership. A number of chapters address the tension between the 'serious' and the 'popular' as literary and market categories, and the way that many women writers tend to be associated only with the latter term, with the consequent intellectual devaluation of their work. In the process, the chapters question whether or not there is such a phenomenon as the 'woman writer' and consider the various ways in which that blanket term has been used. The highly acclaimed novelist Maggie Gee for one, as she argues here, doggedly resists any such attempt to classify her work. Her fiction continually experiments with modes, voices, and subjects in ways which confound both critics and editors who struggle to pigeonhole her as an author.

Several of the contributors document women writers' disquiet with a manipulative marketplace that can simultaneously trumpet their achievements while consigning their work to the women's columns of the review sections in national newspapers or literary supplements. In her contribution to a panel discussion at the Sheffield conference, the distinguished literary editor and biographer Claire Tomalin provided fascinating insights into contemporary reviewing practices. She also spoke from her own position as a biographer about the genesis of *The*

Invisible Woman, her biography of Ellen Ternan, the intimate friend of Charles Dickens. As she wryly observed, despite the fact that Dickens appears only as a minor character in her narrative, acquaintances still refer to her 'Dickens book', an ironic illustration of the still-presumed insignificance, if not utter invisibility, of women as subject matter in the eyes of many readers.

Tomalin's example remains paradigmatic. For, despite the solidity, ambition, and often brilliance of the last twenty years' discussion of women and literature, the position of women's writing in relation to the market remains underanalysed and, therefore, not well enough understood. This is, in turn, curious, following the 1980s, a decade which had, as its distinguishing characteristic, an obsession with consumption and manipulation of economic markets of all kinds (though scarcely curious at all, given the conservative cast of that decade). In Britain, there were several significant attempts to bring the question of women's experience of the literary market into focus. The Women in Publishing group's *Reviewing the Reviews* of 1987, which considered women as publishers, editors, booksellers, librarians, and authors, was one significant attempt to survey the complex forces governing the production and reception of women's writing. Similarly, the earlier *Rolling Our Own: Women as Printers, Publishers and Distributors* of 1981 from the Minority Press Group provided a wealth of information on areas of the production of women's texts. Jean Radford and Helen Taylor's work in the final years of the 1980s on women's reception of romance writing opened another, insufficiently followed path to understanding the dynamics of women's relationship to literary production. Nicci Gerrard's troubled meditation of 1989 on the state of feminism and its relationship to publishing in *Into the Mainstream: How Feminism Has Changed Women's Writing* asked questions which still demand to be addressed more widely. In the United States, *The Women's Review of Books'* publication in 1994 and 1995 of many of the thoughtful, and sometimes agonised papers presented at their 1993 conference, 'Women reviewing/Reviewing Women', demonstrates the tenacity of the classic problems facing women who write when they enter the marketplace. And amongst a number of revisionist studies of the literary canon, Jayne E. Marek's trenchant study *Women Editing Modernism* has unveiled the wealth of both individual and collaborative contributions of women editors and publishers to the emergence of literary modernism and its most eminent male exponents.

Introduction

As Gaye Tuchman's study of nineteenth-century publication conditions *Edging Women Out: Victorian Novelists, Publishers and Social Change*
made clear, the discrediting of women's writing has a lengthy history
in which economic factors have played the major part. Well over a
century ago, influential editorial policies determined a rank order for
manuscripts submitted for publication, ranging from the so-called 'high
prestige' manuscripts at the top of the list to the 'women's specialities'
at the bottom. The major parameters shaping the debates relating to
gender, economics and cultural value, as Lyn Pykett's analysis of 'sensation fiction' included in this volume indicates, can be thus traced back
over a hundred years. And, as Jayne E. Marek pointed out, women's
editorial vision and influence has rarely merited serious consideration
in the authorised version of aesthetic history.

The chapters which form this collection pick up and extend this
discussion of the woman writer's relation to the market, which is, by
its nature, exceptionally multivocal and diverse. We have divided the
chapters into a number of loose categories. Those in the first category
consider the implications of marketing women's fiction from a broadly
historical perspective. Second come chapters which theorise the
strategies adopted by writers and critics as they negotiate the calculated
commercial environment in which women must both present themselves and be marketed as commodities. Finally, a selection of personal
reminiscences by practising authors and editors on their experience of
the publishing industry in the late 1990s makes an important contribution to the recorded history of women's position as literary practitioners
in the previous two decades. These overlapping sections all address the
interaction between the literary subject and the twentieth-century
development of a consumer culture in which women figure centrally
as both writers and readers. By bringing together academics, novelists,
and editors in this way, the collection as a whole provides a unique
dialogue between the critical, creative, and professional voices of
women who are actively engaged with the processes of writing and its
distribution.

Certain themes emerge as pivotal in the collection. Taken together, a
number of the chapters trace the growth of popular fiction written for
and by women in modern times, from the 'sensation' novels of the late
Victorian period through to the contemporary blockbusters of a writer
such as Lisa Appignancsi. Recalling Robert Southey's thankfully
ignored advice to Charlotte Brontë, Lyn Pykett's chapter puts the entire

concept of 'woman's business' under scrutiny by exploring the tensions between the 'unwomanly' profession of literature and the supposedly 'proper duties' for women at a significant moment in late nineteenth-century women's cultural history. These tensions are recognised, too, in the contributions of Marion Shaw and Clare Hanson on the under-rated achievements of the hugely popular novelists of the mid-twentieth century, Winifred Holtby and Elizabeth Taylor, and the source of their distinctive appeal. Placed side by side with the original statements of the contemporary authors, which close the volume, they illustrate the con-tinuity of subject and approach throughout the century as novels by women are shown to provide alternative versions of the family romance, combining a serious interest in psychology with an interrogation of cultural definitions of femininity. In analysing the undoubted attraction of writing which continues to charm successive generations of women readers – evidenced by the huge success of the Virago Modern Classics reprint series – these chapters point to the hybridity of such texts and discuss ways in which they draw on already available cultural nar-ratives. The interest in issues of readership and in the reception of middle-brow novels for women is a recurrent motif in many of the chapters. Shaw and Hanson's contributions, for example, are com-plemented by Avril Horner's and Sue Zlosnik's account of the marketing of Daphne du Maurier's *Rebecca*, which examines details of the publish-ing practices and sales figures attending one of the best sellers of all time. Elaine Jordan's chapter on Angela Carter, which concludes the first section, advances the boundaries of the discussion so as to focus explicitly on the scholarly industry of women's writing, which must now be acknowledged as an additional, serious market force in the revised literary climate of the 1990s.

If close attention is paid in this collection to the paradoxical issues surrounding the marketing and the reception of women's writing as simultaneously popular and unnatural, another instance of common-ality threads through Part II concerned with the artistic presentation of women writers' subjectivity in terms of performance, textuality, and the market. Maggie Humm's analysis of the gendered politics of identity, as both represented and challenged by the postmodernist cinematic practice of Sally Potter in her film of *Orlando*, as it is in Woolf's original text, stresses questions regarding the self, its stability and its display as key themes in women's artistic production. Elisabeth Bronfen's essay on the marketability of women's public performance of hysteria structures her account of Anne Sexton's poetry readings in ways which take account of both recent psychoanalytic theory and classic expectations of women as embodiments of the irrational. The lessons learned during Simone de Beauvoir's first, and spectacularly unsuccessful, attempts to enter the literary marketplace, and their impact on her subsequent writing about women and as a woman, form the focus of Kate Fullbrook's exploration of the market's altogether too familiar marginalisation, on gendered grounds, of even one of the greatest philosophers of the century. Kadiatu Kanneh considers the case of Alice Walker as a woman writer of colour whose public reception has been dominated by expectations of kinds of literary performance limited by conventional figurations of subjectivity associated with both gender and race. Interestingly, these same issues surface again in the personal discussions of artistic and editorial practice, based on market experience, from those who are actively engaged in the business of producing imaginative literature, Margaret Drabble, Maggie Gee, Lisa Appignanesi, and Carmen Callil.

There is, then, a recurrent interlocking series of issues addressed by the chapters in this collection which persistently return to questions about the literary representation of women's subjectivity and experience, and to the seriousness and worth of these factors in a publishing market which oscillates between hostility, doubt, and receptiveness to the business of breaking the conventional boundaries for the public presentation of women, whether as subjects, as historical agents, or as commodities. Although this volume concentrates on these issues as they affect twentieth-century literature, the 1995 Sheffield conference also demonstrated that attention to the topic of women writers and their marketing is by no means confined to the modern and postmodern eras. The seventeenth-century scholar Helen Wilcox described how women first made an impact on the 'business' of literature through autobiographical writing in the early modern period, using textuality to explore identity. In delineating a seventeenth-century marketplace where the very definition of the feminine was interconnected with materiality, money and the body, she showed how these early texts developed strategies of self-representation which projected their subjects as marketable items. Equally, Marilyn Butler's keynote lecture on 'Romantic Women and Literary Professionalism' challenged preconceptions about women's marginalisation in a male-dominated eighteenth-century marketplace. Butler's incisive account of the literary debuts of three famous figures of the 1790s, Mary Wollstonecraft, Maria Edge-worth and Jane Austen, emphasised the self-conscious artistry of these writers as they simultaneously acknowledged their debt to élite literary forms and subverted these for their own, more popular, purposes. It thus provided an enhanced focus for the conference's continuing dis-cussion of women writers' relationship to high culture and to the popular. Helen Wilcox's and Marilyn Butler's accounts of the concerns of women writers since the seventeenth century link seamlessly with the issues outlined by the contributors analysing the situation of women writing in our own time. Understanding this continuity is most definitely the business of those of us who are women writing now.

We hope that *Writing: a woman's business* contributes to that necess-ary understanding not only by providing fascinating insights into the complex relationship between women and writing but also by implicitly identifying a number of large and urgent questions about women and the literary market which need further and close attention. More work is needed on the place of women as literary economic agents, both as writers and as consumers of writing. Next, it is telling that the majority of the chapters in the collection focus on fiction, as, indeed, does much of the current research into women's writing, although this can to some extent be explained by its popularity as a genre. Much remains to be said about the constraints on women's entry to the economically difficult and expensive art forms of the cinema and the theatre, and on their place in the often enclosed publishing field of poetry. The intriguing question of the ambivalence of women in welcoming or rejecting the label of 'woman writer' invites much more attention. Feminism's com-plicated relation to popular literary art forms, including journalism, and its often unspoken distrust of women's success in them demands much more overt discussion. Finally, the need for more research on the details of women's financial circumstances at every point of the publishing process is imperative. For, as much as the essays in this collection demonstrate that writing has been, is, and will be a woman's business, the further development of understanding of all aspects of precisely just what that might entail can only help in the business of more women securing a place in the market for their writing.

Notes

1 Val Hennessy quoted in the *Times Literary Supplement*, 19 April 1996, p. 16.

Introduction

2 Quoted in the *Sunday Times*, 25 August 1996, Section 7, p. 2.
3 *Times Literary Supplement*, 1996.
4 For further information about Network, the association of Women Teachers of English in Higher Education, contact Dr Vivien Jones, School of English, University of Leeds, Leeds, LS2 9JT, England.
5 Figures taken from the survey *Books and the Consumer*, by Book Marketing Limited (1995), extracts from which appeared in *The Bookseller*, February 1995.

References

Gerrard, Nicci (1989) *Into the Mainstream: How Feminism Has Changed Women's Writing*, London: Pandora Press.

Marek, Jayne E. (1995) *Women Editing Modernism: 'Little' Magazines & Literary History*, Lexington: University Press of Kentucky.

Minority Press Group (1981) *Rolling Our Own: Women as Printers, Publishers and Distributors*, London: Minority Press Group.

Monteith, Moira (ed.) (1986) *Women's Writing: A Challenge to Theory*, Brighton: Harvester Wheatsheaf.

Radford, Jean (ed.) (1986) *The Progress of Romance: The Politics of Popular Fiction*, London: Routledge & Kegan Paul.

Taylor, Helen (1989) *Scarlett's Women: Gone With the Wind and its Female Fans*, London: Virago Press.

Tuchman, Gaye (1989) *Edging Women Out: Victorian Novelists, Publishers and Social Change*, London: Routledge.

Women in Publishing (ed.) (1987) *Reviewing the Reviews: A Woman's Place on the Book Page*, London: Journeyman Press

'Women Reviewing Women' (1994–5) *Women's Review of Books*, 11–12 (March 1994–June 1995).

Woolf, Virginia (1929) *A Room of One's Own*, repr. 1975 Harmondsworth: Penguin.

I

Women, fiction
and the reading public

1

Women and the sensation business

Lyn Pykett

This chapter explores the sensation novel of the 1860s as a revealing episode (perhaps even a defining moment) in the complex history of the connections between women, writing and the marketplace which is the subject of this collection. Both the sensation novel and the contemporary response to the sensation phenomenon in general were complexly and inextricably intertwined with attitudes to the business of a woman's life, to the business of writing in the mid-nineteenth century, and to changes in the literary marketplace and in women's place within it. I will begin with a well-known example of an authoritative view on the subject of women and writing from the early Victorian period, the response (in March 1837) of the Poet Laureate, Robert Southey, to Charlotte Brontë's request for advice about how best to realise her literary aspirations:

> It is not with a view to distinction that you should cultivate this talent, if you consult your own happiness. I, who have made literature my profession ... and have never ... repented of the deliberate choice, think myself, nevertheless, bound in duty to caution every young man who applies as an aspirant ... against taking so perilous a course. You will say that a woman has no need of such a caution; there can be no peril in it for her. In a certain sense this is true; but there is a danger ... the day dreams in which you habitually indulge are likely to induce a distempered state of mind; and, in proportion as all ordinary uses of the world seem to you flat and unprofitable, you will become unfitted for them without becoming fitted for anything else. Literature cannot be the business of a woman's life, and it ought not to be. The more she is engaged in her proper duties, the less leisure she will have for it, even as an accomplishment and a recreation. To those duties you have not yet been called, and when you are you will be less eager for celebrity.[1]

Fortunately, the woman writer whose ambitions as a poet were rebuffed by Southey (re)turned to the novel. However, the terms in which

Southey's advice to Charlotte Brontë was couched were repeated over and over again in the nineteenth century. They figured with particular prominence in the debates about the sensation novel in the 1860s, especially in the way in which those debates focused on female writers, readers, and fictional protagonists. Southey's warnings to Charlotte Brontë about the dangers of daydreaming, especially for women, were replicated in numerous reviews which rehearsed the potentially danger-ous moral and psychological effects of sensation writing and reading. For example an article on 'Our female sensationalists' in the *Christian Remembrancer* in 1863 took up Southey's theme on the distempering powers of fantasy by warning against the sensation novel's tendency, 'willingly and designedly [to] draw a picture of life which ... make[s] reality insipid and the routine of ordinary existence intolerable to the imagination'.[2] Youthful readers were considered to be particularly vulnerable to 'the utter unrestraint in which the heroines of this [fiction] are allowed to expatiate and develop their impulsive, stormy, passionate characters, and to question the customary social checks on feeling'.[3] A fictional version of the Southey doctrine can be found in Charlotte Riddell's autobiographical novel *A Struggle for Fame* (1883) which tells the story of a woman writer's struggles in the literary marketplace in the 1860s. Lacere, the husband of Riddell's heroine, the aspiring novel-ist Glen Wesley, takes a view of women's writing which differs from Southey's only in its slightly more patronising tone:

> There never yet lived a wise man who wished women to turn artists, or actresses, or authors; and Mr Lacere, theoretically at least, was a wise man. By some subtle intuition he knew Glen would be far happier if she never gained a hearing – if she laid aside her manuscripts as a child lays aside its toys which have pleased it a while, and betook herself to *the business of life, as such business usually presents itself to her sex, taking her pleasure while she could, mixing with other young people, going to places of amusement; then being loved and loving; then marrying and ruling her husband's household* (my emphasis).[4]

The plots of sensation novels, especially (although not exclusively) those written by women, invariably focus on the business of a women's life, but they often problematise those conventional feminine roles and 'proper duties' of a woman which appear to be so incontrovertibly self-evident to Southey and Lacere. The rise of sensation fiction and the critical furore it generated were also complexly and inextricably bound up with both the business of the woman writer and the business of writing. The sensation phenomenon was the means of launching several women as career writers, enabling them to support families and dependent male relatives with their earnings from writing, and/or to acquire fame (or notoriety) as prominent authors of best sellers. In short it was a vehicle by means of which writing or 'literature' became a business for women, and which allowed them to dominate (or, at least, give the impression of dominating) the fiction market. Perhaps even more significantly, sensation fiction was also closely associated with contemporary perceptions that writing or literature was becoming a business. Indeed, one of the most interesting aspects of the sensation debate is the way in which reviewers read these novels as symptoms of the commodification of literature, a process which was represented in contemporary critical discourse as one of feminisation.

Charlotte Brontë's reply to Southey's strictures on the impropriety of women taking up writing might almost have been devised by Mary Elizabeth Braddon, one of the queens of the sensation novel, for her secretive governess protagonist, in *Lady Audley's Secret* (1863):

> I thought it ... my duty, when I left school, to become a governess. In that capacity I find enough to occupy my thoughts all day long ... without having a moment's time for one dream of the imagination. In the evenings, I confess, I do think, but I never trouble any one else with my thoughts. I carefully avoid any appearance of preoccupation and eccentricity, which might lead those I live amongst to suspect the nature of my pursuits. Following my father's advice ... I have endeavoured not only attentively to observe all the duties a woman ought to fulfil, but to feel deeply interested in them. I don't always succeed, for sometimes when I'm teaching or sewing I would rather be reading or writing; but I try to deny myself.[5]

Brontë's apparently prim acceptance of Southey's version of a woman's proper duties not only displays an ironic awareness (or so I like to think) of the specific conflict between a socially ascribed feminine role and the imaginative life of the aspiring woman writer, but it also has the effect of foregrounding the sources of (some) women's more general dissatisfactions with a woman's proper duties. It is in precisely such dissatisfactions with socially defined femininity, and in their attendant strategies of masking and concealment, that many sensation narratives have their origin. Indeed Charlotte Brontë, herself the creator of several secretive governesses, might be argued to have produced a prototype of the sensation novel. *Jane Eyre* (1848) contains many of the elements

19

which Mary Elizabeth Braddon was later to rework in *Lady Audley's Secret*. Brontë's female protagonist, like Braddon's, is the liminal figure of the governess who is discontented with her lot, although, significantly, that discontent takes almost diametrically opposed forms in the two novels, as Lucy Audley is only too eager to conform outwardly to the feminine ideal and to occupy the role of icon of conspicuous consumption, both of which positions are vehemently rejected by Brontë's governess-heroine. Both novels contain a bigamy plot (Braddon reverses Brontë's gender pattern by making the central female character her bigamist). In both narratives a violent and unstable wife chooses fire as her instrument of vengeance. Perhaps one of Braddon's most interesting variations of the pattern lies in the fact that in her novel the mad woman inhabits the drawing room, rather than the attic.

It is not simply a particular female character, dissatisfied with or failing to conform to the proper duties of a woman's life, who provides the central narrative impulse of the typical sensation plot, but also the disputed category of femininity itself. As Braddon's narrator observes of the heroine of *Aurora Floyd*:

> [I]f she had been faultless, she could not have been the heroine of this story; for has not some wise old man of old remarked, that the perfect women are those who leave no histories behind them, but who go through life upon such a tranquil course of quiet well-doing as leave no footprints on the sands of time; only mute records hidden here and there, deep in the grateful hearts of those who have been blest by them.[6]

It is interesting to speculate that at the end of the sensation decade the attentive reader of *Middlemarch* might well have recalled these last-quoted words when reading George Eliot's concluding elegiac comments on the 'incalculably diffusive' but unrecorded virtue of her heroine's life: 'for the growing good of the world is partly dependent on [the] unhistoric acts' of those 'who lived faithfully a hidden life and rest in unvisited tombs'.[7]

It is worth dwelling for a moment on these parallels between *Aurora Floyd* and *Middlemarch* and *Jane Eyre*, for to do so will serve to remind the reader of the ambiguous history of the sensation novel's relationships with more mainstream fiction, and of its role in defining the category of the literary. For many nineteenth-century critics the sensation novel marked the boundary between high culture and popular culture, and the critical discourse on sensationalism was a way of policing that boundary. In practice, however, there was a remarkable continuity between the preoccupations and narrative patterns of the high culture (or literary) novel and the popular sensation novel, as some contemporary commentators were aware. Thus, in her 1867 article on sensation novels, Margaret Oliphant used the category 'sensational' as a means of drawing the line between the literary novel and inferior popular productions, while, at the same time, pointing out the sensation novel's continuities with Brontë's work.[8]

By the 1860s the sensation novel had not only taken over what Oliphant described as *Jane Eyre*'s 'protest against the conventionalities in which the world clothes itself',[9] but it was also busily exploring and problematising the business of a woman's life. In the 1860s the sensation novel also became the chief (if extremely problematic) exemplum of the fact that literature not only could be the business of a woman's life, but was a business in which several women were astoundingly successful. The moral panic about sensationalism in the 1860s was generated in large part by the perception that sensation fiction was a feminine phenomenon, a symptom of a pervasive and invasive feminisation of literature and culture. The sensation debate also focused on *women* – as writers, readers and subjects: anti-sensationalists deplored the fact that women were disproportionately represented among both the writers and readers of the genre; that the sensation effect was likely to have particularly adverse effects on its female readers; and that sensation novels foregrounded female characters, most commonly the 'wrong sort' of female – that is to say ambitious, assertive, devious and deviant women.

One of the notable features of the sensation phenomenon was its generation of, or association with, a group of women writers for whom writing was the *business* of their lives: Mary Elizabeth Braddon, Mrs Henry Wood, Rhoda Broughton, Ouida (Marie Louise de la Ramée) and other writers less well-known to modern readers such as Charlotte Riddell. All of these women enjoyed considerable commercial success in the 1860s. Two of them (Braddon and Wood) produced two of the best selling novels of the century, and several (with varying degrees of commercial success) enjoyed very long careers as novelists and journalists. A number of the women sensationalists who came to prominence in the 1860s were also closely associated with other important developments in the fiction market in that decade, most notably with the rise of inexpensive illustrated fiction magazines for the middle classes.

Charlotte Riddell was part proprietor of *St James's Magazine*; Wood edited the *Argosy* from 1867; and Braddon edited *Belgravia* from 1866 as well as being a prolific supplier of tales for the popular penny magazines which flourished in the sixties. Those women whose selling-power survived the decade were also involved in subsequent innovations in the marketing and distribution of fiction, such as newspaper syndication. For example, in 1873, one of Braddon's novels was serialised simultaneously in eight provincial newspapers.

The rise of the sensation novel was also associated with perceptions about the state of fiction and the fiction market at the mid-century. The sensation vogue was seen by many commentators as a symptom of cultural decline, of the process by which literature became commodified in a mass culture. Reviews such as Henry Mansel's in the *Quarterly Review* in 1863 represented the sensation novel as a formulaic, mechanistic, commercial article which was mass-produced for mass distribution to feed the craven appetites of its audience. Sensation fiction, Mansel asserted, was produced according to the 'market-law of supply and demand', and was thus tainted by 'a commercial atmosphere ... redolent of the manufactory and the shop'.[10] Margaret Oliphant wrote about the sensation novel as a work of art in an age of mechanical reproduction. In her account, sensation novels endlessly recycle the same plots and representational formulae, and she accused Braddon of copying herself and of stealing her plots from others.[11] Some of the sensationalists appeared to share their critics' views of these matters. Braddon, for example, was disarmingly frank about her penchant for recycling, as she confided in a letter to the editor at *Temple Bar*: 'it seems you want the right-down sensational; ... I will give the kaleidoscope ... another turn, and will do my very best with the old bits of glass and pins and rubbish.'[12] Always alive to the possibilities of satirical affront, Braddon also brazenly appropriated the charges of her critics to her own purposes. Thus she writes of the hero of *Birds of Prey*: 'He had been brought up among people who treated literature as a trade as well as an art; and what art is not more or less a trade? He knew the state of the market and what goods were likely to go off briskly, and it was for the market he worked.'[13]

Sensation fiction can also be connected with another aspect of the commodification of culture in the mid-nineteenth century, which Thomas Richards analyses in *The Commodity Culture of Victorian England*. Richards argues that the sensation phenomenon is 'a specific form of capitalist representation', a symptom of 'the Victorian taste for spectacle ... [which] consisted primarily of a rhetorical mode of amplification and excess that came to pervade and structure private and public life in the nineteenth century'.[14] Richards's main interest is in the growth of advertising and the development of forms of display and spectacle. However, the sensation novel, itself a spectacular mode of representation which deploys the strategies of an emergent culture of advertising, can be seen as another component of this emergent commodity culture. Sensation novels (particularly those by women) incorporate in their mode of representation many elements of the semiotic codes of the magazines in which they were first published, and of other illustrated magazines of the period.[15] Like the illustrated women's magazines of the 1860s, sensation novels were addressed to 'domestic' women and designed as entertainment to be consumed in the home. The women sensationalists often focus, as the contemporary middle-class magazines do, on the homes and gardens of the upper middle classes. They mobilise desirable consumer objects in a display of the lavish domestic settings of their heroines, and also, interestingly, focus on the fragility of the middle-class or upper middle-class home. As I have argued elsewhere, several of the novels of Braddon and Wood offer their readers a literary equivalent of visiting stately homes.[16]

As well as making a spectacle of the middle-class home, sensation novels also made a spectacle of femininity. They put on display the lavishly clothed and decorated body of the upper middle-class female (or the woman who aspires to or apes that particular lifestyle). This form of representation owes something to current art styles, notably to Pre-Raphaelitism in the case of Braddon, and something to contemporary magazine and advertising culture. The women's sensation novel, like magazines for women in the late 1860s, was 'meeting a heightened demand for romantic fiction, advice about dress and the "toilette"'.[17] The descriptions of beautiful female characters in sensation novels (particularly those by Braddon) often function as the written equivalent of the fashion-plate which was a regular feature of magazines such as the *Englishwoman's Domestic Magazine* (1852–79) and *The Queen* (1861–63).[18] This taste for feminine spectacle had been developed and catered for in the lavishly illustrated annuals, a sort of Victorian coffee table book which enjoyed considerable success between the 1820s and the 1850s (the last edition of the *Keepsake*, one of the best-known of the annuals, appeared in 1857). It was satirised by Dickens in *Bleak House*

(1852–53) in his comments on the 'Galaxy Gallery of British Beauty' series with which Weevle decorates his room:

[A] choice collection of copper-plate impressions from that truly national work, The Divinities of Albion, or Galaxy Gallery of British Beauty, representing ladies of title and fashion in every variety of smirk that art, combined with capital, is capable of producing. With these magnificent portraits ... he decorates his apartment; and as the Galaxy Gallery of British Beauty wears every variety of fancy dress, plays every variety of musical instrument, fondles every variety of dog, ogles every variety of prospect and is backed up by every variety of flower-pot and balustrade, the result is very imposing.[19]

As Anne Cvetkovich has argued, an enterprise such as the 'Galaxy Gallery' series

reveals mass culture's power to sensationalize capitalism by using female display as a vehicle for representing consumer culture. Erotic fetishism is set in motion to produce commodity fetishism. A prototype of advertisements ... [&] the gossip magazine ... [it] demonstrates mass culture's power to combine 'art and capital', selling the products by selling the life-styles with which they are associated.[20]

A similar process of the blending of erotic and commodity fetishism can be seen in the representation of the female body and its *mis en scène* in the sensation novel, especially in novels by women.

If representations of femininity were at the centre of sensation novels, much of the contemporary discussion of both sensation fiction and the female sensationalists focused on their 'unwomanliness'. E. S. Dallas, writing of the increased prominence of women novelists in the 1860s, noted 'it is curious that one of the earliest results of an increased feminine influence in literature should be a display of what in woman is most unfeminine'.[21] Margaret Oliphant objected that:

What is held up to us as the story of the feminine soul as it really exists underneath its conventional coverings, is a very fleshly and unlovely record ... [T]he dreaming maiden waits ... now for flesh and muscles, for strong arms that seize her, and warm breath that thrills her through, and a host of other physical attractions, which she indicates to the world with a charming frankness ... [W]ere the sketch made from the man's point of view, its openness would at least be less repulsive. The peculiarity of it in England is ... that this intense appreciation of flesh and blood, this eagerness of physical sensation, is represented as the natural sentiment of

English girls, and is offered to them not only as the portrait of their own state of mind, but as amusement and mental food.[22]

There was much speculation by reviewers about the lives of the women who offered their readers such 'intense appreciation of flesh', and women sensation novelists discovered for themselves the force of the judgement of the writer in the *Westminster Review* who asserted that the woman artist must 'sacrifice maiden modesty or matronly reserve' and be 'stared at, commented on by [an] unmannered audience who forget the woman in the artist'.[23] The unconventionality of the lives of the women sensation novelists – Rhoda Broughton's youthful escapades, Ouida's exoticism and colourful private life, Braddon's racy past in the professional theatre and the irregularity of her domestic establishment as the mistress of the publisher John Maxwell and mother of his five illegitimate children – were all referred to in coded terms in contemporary reviews. These aspects of writers' private lives became a matter of more open interest in subsequent discussions of their careers in obituaries and memoirs, in the personal interviews which became a prominent feature of newspapers and magazines later in the century, and in subsequent attempts to recuperate some literary reputations, such as Michael Sadleir's essays on Braddon and Rhoda Broughton in *Things Past*. One of the most well-known of the contemporary *ad feminam* reviews is Henry James's 1865 essay 'Miss Braddon' in *The Nation*:

> She knows much that ladies are not accustomed to know, but that they are apparently very glad to learn. The names of drinks, the technicalities of the faro-table, the lingo of the turf, the talk natural to a crowd of fast men at supper, when there are no ladies present but Miss Braddon.[24]

James's comments are symptomatic of a more widespread approach to the female sensationalists – an apparent need to explain what were perceived to be the excesses of the genre in terms of the excesses and irregularities of its authors' lives, and, in particular, their failure to conform to the proper duties of a woman's life. The quiet, conservative, dully domestic Mrs Henry Wood (as described by a disappointed Mrs E. M. Ward)[25] is the exception that proves the rule, but even she had an intriguingly dysfunctional family in the shape of an incapacitated and economically ineffectual husband, as did several other sensation novelists.

The hapless Mr Henry Wood, and his numerous counterparts, is a key figure in the discourse on the women sensation writers. As is so often the case in connection with writing by women, this is a double or contradictory discourse. On the one hand, as Catherine Gallagher has pointed out, the woman writer, or indeed anyone who wrote for profit, was figured as a whore. Gallagher notes the common links made in the nineteenth century 'between a certain kind of female literature, inflation, dishonest retailing, and usurious exchange ... [which] easily called to mind the woman of pure exchange ... the prostitute'.[26] Alternatively the woman writer was (inevitably) figured as the madonna or 'angel in the house'. Several commentators, in the twentieth century as well as in the Victorian period, have attempted to link the 'unwomanly' professionalism of the women sensationalists with a woman's proper duties, or perhaps to erase the one by reference to the other. In some of the female sensationalists' letters and interviews, and in the accounts of their apologists (or critics), there is a repeated emphasis on the way in which women's practice of the profession of writing was not a *denial* or *refusal* but rather an *extension* of their proper duties as women. Their involvement in the business of writing was represented as an act of feminine self-sacrifice undertaken in order to provide for their children and other dependent relatives, and especially weak, incompetent or incapacitated husbands. In this discourse, women were figured as entering the public sphere of authorship and commerce in order to secure and maintain the private, domestic, affective sphere. Such writing undertaken by women as an extension of a woman's proper domestic duties left them little time for either the 'feminine' daydreaming or the 'masculine' artistic ambition against which Southey warned Charlotte Brontë. Instead, those women who made literature the business of their lives spent their time, according to their contemporary critics, in feeding and also creating the daydreams of others. They did not court 'celebrity' so much as financial success, and in achieving the latter they often gained notoriety rather than celebrity.

The peculiar combination of self-sacrifice and commercialism which set the terms on which the women sensationalists participated in the literary marketplace was used by themselves and others as both an explanation of and an excuse for their supposed inferiority as artists. For example, Mary Elizabeth Braddon, who wrote constantly in the 1860s both to support Maxwell's children and to prop up his ailing publishing business, confessed in a letter to her mentor Bulwer-Lytton: 'I know that my writing teems with errors, absurdities, contradictions and inconsistencies, but I have never written a line that has not been written against time and sometimes with the printer waiting at the door. I do an immense deal of work which nobody ever hears of, for halfpenny and penny journals'.[27] For George Eliot, the supposition that women took to the fiction business as an extension of those 'proper duties' which were the business of a woman's life was the only legitimate excuse for the offences aginst art and sense committed by the silly lady novelists in the pre-sensation decade of the 1850s:

> We had imagined that destitute women turned novelists, as they turned governesses, because they had no other 'lady-like' means of getting their bread. On this supposition, vacillating syntax and improbable incident had a certain pathos for us, like the extremely supererogatory pincushions and ill-devised nightcaps that are offered for sale by a blind man. We felt the commodity to be a nuisance, but we were glad to think that the money went to relieve the necessitous, and we pictured to ourselves lonely women struggling for a maintenance, or wives and daughters devoting themselves to the production of 'copy' out of pure heroism – perhaps to pay their husband's debts, or to purchase luxuries for a sick father. Under these impressions we shrank from criticising a lady's novel: her English might be faulty, but, we said to ourselves, her motives are irreproachable ... Empty writing was excused by an empty stomach, and twaddle was consecrated by tears.[28]

Kate Flint's [29] demonstration of the self-conscious literariness of some of the women sensation novelists suggests that Braddon protests too much about her illiteracy. Nevertheless, confronted with the apparently unending supply of commercially successful sensation fiction in the 1860s, reviewers were frequently much more unforgiving of faulty syntax and formulaic plots and characters than George Eliot was of the silly novels by the lady novelists of the 1850s. The adverse judgements of the reviewers of the 1860s were echoed even by those who later wished to rescue the reputations of those women writers who had first achieved fame as sensationalists in the sensation decade. Thus Thomas Seccombe's entry for Mrs Wood in the *Dictionary of National Biography* praises her work with faint damns: 'Overpraised at the time of their first appearance, Mrs Henry Wood's novels have since been unduly depreciated ... A careless writer and an incorrigible contemner both of grammatical and legal accuracy ... Mrs Henry Wood is nevertheless in her way an artist.' [30] Mary Elizabeth Braddon did not gain entry to the DNB, but Michael Sadleir later attempted to rescue her from critical obloquy, by constructing a fantasy version of the writer she might have become had she not been ensnared into 'potboiling' by economic necessity and by her early success as a sensationalist:

> The history of English novel writing during the period of 'branded' fiction offers no more complete example than Miss Braddon, of a writer owing to a single too successful book, not only reputation and fortune, but also the partial atrophy of a real and distinguished talent. It was Mary Braddon's destiny (both fortunate and unfortunate) to become known the world over as the author of *Lady Audley's Secret*. Her long life of seventy-seven years was one of ceaseless but unflagging toil as a writer of stories ... none knew better than she what is meant by 'writing for one's life'; few were subject to anything approaching the obloquy which she suffered from critics and moralists ... Luckily ... she had that peculiarly feminine quality of resilient but unostentatious courage which smiles through adversity.[31]

From the point at which they entered the literary marketplace until their recent recuperation by feminist critics, the women sensation novelists have been adversely judged on account of their 'professionalism', in other words, because they made literature a business. The female sensationalists were castigated for writing too much and too quickly (and sometimes for too lengthy a period), solely in order to feed the appetites of their readers and supply the demands of the market. No matter how great their commercial success, they were merely literary journeywomen, or 'female drudges' to use Nigel Cross's phrase.[32] They did not have an artistic vocation, nor, as mere women writing novels about women and for women, could they have – at least according to a number of influential reviewers, some of them women. Moreover, as I have suggested, for many commentators the women sensationalists were always women first and novelists second. The two most successful of the women sensationalists, Braddon and Wood, were both memorialised by their sons, each of whom is at pains to point out that his mother's familial and domestic duties were never compromised by her professional literary labours. 'No home duty', wrote Charles Wood in 1894, 'was ever put aside for literary labours'.[33] Similarly, Braddon's son, William Maxwell, marvelled at the way in which his mother 'got through her immense amount of work as if by magic. She never seemed to be given any time in which to do it. She had ... no part of the day to be held sacred from disturbance and intrusions.'[34] Even when writing was only *a business* it could not, by common consent, be *the* business of a woman's life.

Women and the sensation business

Notes

1 T. J. Wise and J. A. Symington (eds), *The Brontës, Their Lives, Friendships and Correspondence* (Oxford, Blackwell, 1933), 4 vols, vol. 1, pp. 155–6.
2 'Our Female Sensation Novelists', *Christian Remembrancer*, 46 (1863), pp. 209–36, p. 212.
3 *Ibid.*
4 Charlotte Riddell, *A Struggle For Fame* (London, R. Bentley and Son, 1883), vol. 2, pp. 133–4.
5 Wise and Symington, *The Brontës*, vol. 1, pp. 157–8.
6 Mary Elizabeth Braddon, *Aurora Floyd* (London, Virago, [1863] 1984), p. 330.
7 George Eliot, *Middlemarch* (Oxford, [1871–72] 1988), p. 682.
8 Margaret Oliphant, 'Novels', *Blackwood's*, 102 (1867), pp. 257–80.
9 *Ibid*, p. 258.
10 Henry Mansel, 'Sensation Novels', *Quarterly Review*, 113 (1863), pp. 481–514, p. 483.
11 Oliphant, 'Novels', pp. 264–5.
12 Quoted in Winifred Hughes, *The Maniac in the Cellar: The Sensation Novel of the 1860s* (Princeton, Princeton University Press, 1980), p. 121.
13 Mary Elizabeth Braddon, *Birds of Prey* (London, Ward, Lock and Tyler, 1867), p. 139.
14 Thomas Richards, *The Commodity Culture of Victorian England: Advertising and Spectacle, 1851–1914* (London, Verso, 1991), pp. 1, 54.
15 See 'Nineteenth Century Women's Magazines', in Ros Ballaster, Margaret Beetham *et al.* (eds), *Women's Worlds: Ideology, Femininity and the Woman's Magazine* (London, Macmillan, 1991), pp. 75–107.
16 See Lyn Pykett, *The Improper Feminine: The Women's Sensation Novel and the New Woman Writing* (London, Routledge, 1992), pp. 111–12.
17 Cynthia White, *Women's Magazines, 1693–1968* (London, Joseph, 1970), p. 53.
18 See Margaret Beetham in Ballaster *et al.* (eds), *Women's Worlds*.
19 Charles Dickens, *Bleak House*, Chapter 18.
20 Anne Cvetkovich, *Mixed Feelings: Feminism, Mass Culture and Victorian Sensationalism* (New Brunswick, New Jersey, Rutgers University Press, 1992), p. 69.
21 E. S. Dallas, *The Gay Science* (London, Chapman and Hall, 1886), vol. 2, p. 298.
22 Oliphant, 'Novels', p. 259.
23 'Women artists', *Westminster Review*, n. s. 14 (1858), pp. 163–8, p. 164.
24 Henry James, 'Miss Braddon', *The Nation*, 9 November 1865, p. 594.
25 Mrs Ward recalled that Mrs Wood was 'a very nice woman, but hopelessly prosaic. Calling upon her one day when she was alone I hoped that she would reveal some hidden depth yet unseen. But alas! the topics she clung

to and thoroughly explored were her servants' shortcomings, and a full account of the cold she had caught.' Quoted in Charles Wood, *Memorials of Mrs Henry Wood* (London, R. Bentley and Son, 1894), p. 245.

26 Catherine Gallagher, 'George Eliot and *Daniel Deronda*: The Prostitute and the Jewish Question', in Ruth Bernard Yeazell (ed.), *Sex, Politics and Science in the Nineteenth-Century Novel* (Baltimore and London, Johns Hopkins University Press, 1990), p. 44.

27 Letter from Braddon to Edward Bulwer-Lytton, in Robert Lee Wolff, 'Devoted Disciple: The Letters of Mary Elizabeth Braddon to Sir Edward Bulwer-Lytton, 1862–1873', *Harvard Library Bulletin*, 22 (1874), p. 10.

28 George Eliot, 'Silly Novels by Lady Novelists', *Westminster Review*, 1856, repr. in *George Eliot: Selected Critical Writings* (Oxford, Oxford University Press, 1992), pp. 297–8.

29 Kate Flint, 'The Woman Reader and the Opiate of Fiction: 1855–1870', in J. Hawthorn (ed.), *The Nineteenth-Century British Novel* (London, Edward Arnold, 1986). See also the chapter on the sensation novel in Flint's *The Woman Reader, 1837–1914* (Oxford, Oxford University Press, 1993).

30 *Dictionary of National Biography*, ed. Sidney Lee (London, Macmillan, 1909), vol. 24, p. 827.

31 Michael Sadleir, *Things Past* (London, Constable, 1944), p. 69.

32 Nigel Cross, *The Common Writer: Life in Nineteenth Century Grub Street* (Cambridge, Cambridge University Press, 1985).

33 Charles Wood, *Memorials*, p. 228.

34 W. B. Maxwell, *Time Gathered* (London, Hutchinson, 1937), p. 281.

2

The making of a middle-brow success: Winifred Holtby's *South Riding*

Marion Shaw

I recently asked a group of students how they would define a 'middle-brow' book. They said that it was the kind of book one would not be ashamed to be seen reading on a beach. It would be relaxing but not too popular, serious but accessible, not canonical but might become so and then it would cease to be middle-brow. It was also, they said, the kind of book their mothers read. Since some of the students were mature women in their forties and fifties and others were young students of nineteen or twenty, the motherliness of the middle-brow category is obviously not fixed to a particular age but is rather a type of reading one has left behind as a student. It belongs to a homely world, familiar, unthreatening, sensible, moral and life-revealing, as one's mother should be.

The terms high-brow and low-brow seem to have gained currency during the inter-war period. Arnold Bennett's comment, in his 1929 review of Virginia Woolf's *A Room of One's Own*, is typical: '... she is the queen of the high-brows; and I am a low-brow. But it takes all sorts of brows to make a world, and without a large admixture of low-brows even Bloomsbury would be uninhabitable' (Majumdar and McLauren, 1975: 258). One would not now class Bennett as a low-brow but as one of the other brows[1] he mentions, a middle-brow perhaps, but this precise term does not seem to have gained currency at the same time as its counterparts. There was, however, a very strong sense of a middle ground between popular and élite literature, and an equally strong desire to stratify readers and writers into identifiable levels. Julian Symons did this in his depiction of the political-artistic movement of the

1930s as a pyramid, with the audience at the base, the artists at the apex, and in the middle:

> the most interesting part of the pyramid, for in its members were the seeds of the shifting pattern of the decade, and even of the post-war Welfare State. Since these people had in many cases the practical ability and organising energy that artists lack, they played a large part in making the theatre and the novel, and to a less degree painting and music, vehicles for social propaganda. It was from this middle part of the pyramid, rather than from the artists themselves, that there came all those exhortations about moving out of the ivory tower of the imagination into the market place. In the sense that all artists are to some extent concerned with the form of their work ... these people were enemies of art, since they were almost always impatient of merely formal considerations; but ... they were, at this time of social flux a powerful energising force. Let us call them the Pragmatists ... ideally all readers of the *New Statesman* [they] will boil away like geysers, frothing anger at the Audience for its smug liberalism and at the Artists for their social inadequacy. (Symons, 1973: 37–8)

At the time, few were as cheerful as this about cultural divisions. I. A. Richards had sounded the alarm bells in the 1920s in his prophecy in *Principles of Literary Criticism* (1924) and *Practical Criticism* (1929) of social and cultural chaos arising from a vastly increased, unstable and ill-educated reading public, 'the masses', whom the supposedly educated classes were poorly equipped to control. This anxiety was developed by F. R. Leavis in, for example, *Mass Civilisation and Minority Culture* (1933) and *For Continuity* (1933). A traditional reliance on a minority to guide the nation was challenged in the inter-war period by the masses (or 'the herd', to use W. Trotter's term in his influential *Instincts of the Herd in War and Peace* (1916)), creating, in Chris Baldick's words, 'an oppositional language subversive of cultural authority' (Baldick, 1983: 169), a low-brow cultural language associated particularly with the cinema, the radio, the thriller and detective story, and other forms of mass popular culture. The increasing use of derogatory labels for erstwhile cultural authority was also a symptom of a widening gulf between the masses and the intelligentsia. Leavis singles out the sneering use of the term 'high-brow' in this respect: '"High-brow" is an ominous addition to the English language. I have said earlier that culture has always been in minority keeping. But the minority is made conscious, not merely of an uncongenial, but of a hostile environment' (Leavis, 1933: 38).

The book which above all summarised the issues was Q. D. Leavis's

The making of a middle-brow success

Fiction and the Reading Public (1932), the most thoroughgoing contemporary British investigation of reading habits. Her despairing view was of a society 'so decisively stratified in taste that each stratum is catered for independently by its own novelists and journalists'. The general reading public, she believed, had not even a glimpse of 'the living interests of modern literature' which are left in the sole charge of a critical minority which is 'isolated, disowned by society and threatened with extinction' (Leavis, 1965: 35). At the other extreme from the high-brow were what Leavis considered to be low-brow and degenerate forms, like the detective novel, the thriller, the romance, and the oriental story such as E. M. Hull's *The Sheikh*. In between are 'respected middling novelists of blameless intentions and indubitable skill, "thoughtful", "cultured", impressive, but lacking interest for the "high-brow" reader, who complains that ... they bring nothing to the novel but commonplace sentiments and an out-worn technique' (Leavis, 1965: 36). This divided culture is contrasted with that of previous ages when a novel by Defoe, Smollett or Dickens was highly popular and also 'the best literature of its own day' (Leavis, 1965: 235).

This line of thought was explored with some political rigour by Marxist critics during the 1930s, perhaps most clearly articulated in the exchanges between Walter Benjamin and Theodor Adorno. Benjamin's nostalgia, in *The Work of Art in the Age of Mechanical Reproduction* (1936), for a past aesthetic unity, and his belief in the progressive potential of popular art, particularly the cinema, stand accused of romanticism by Adorno, whose letter of riposte contains the famous sentence about the separateness of avant-garde and popular art: 'Both are torn halves of an integral freedom, to which however they do not add up.' The passage in which this sentence occurs is worth quoting at greater length:

> Both bear the stigmata of capitalism, both contain elements of change (but never, of course, the middle-term between Schönberg and the American film). Both are torn halves of an integral freedom, to which however they do not add up. It would be romantic to sacrifice one to the other, either as the bourgeois romanticism of the conservation of personality and all that stuff, or as the anarchist romanticism of blind confidence in the spontaneous power of the proletariat in the historical process – a proletariat which is itself a product of bourgeois society. (Bloch, 1977: 123)

In very different ways, Leavis and Adorno condemn the middle-brow ('middling' and 'middle-term', as they respectively call it) to conservatism

33

and inanition: 'commonplace sentiments and outworn techniques' is Leavis's description, and to Adorno the middle-term contains no elements of change.

It is in relation to this debate that I want to discuss a quintessentially middle-brow novel, Winifred Holtby's *South Riding* (1936), and in particular to take into account a gender perspective which neither Leavis nor Adorno addresses. As my students' comments suggest, there is an assumption that middle-brow reading is women's territory. Men, it seems, and fathers in particular, read technical books, books about hobbies, sci-fi, newspapers, or nothing at all. But mothers, with their presumed greater leisure and relative indifference to journalism, are the ones who borrow novels from the library and buy the occasional paperback. This is a generalisation which had considerable validity during the inter-war period. As Nicola Beauman has suggested, the middle-brow reader of the inter-war period is resonantly represented on the stage and in film by a woman such as Laura Jesson in Noel Coward's play *Still Life* (1935) and the film based on it, *Brief Encounter* (1945). She is a doctor's wife, 'a respectable married woman with a husband and a home and three children' (Beauman, 1983: 1), who goes shopping in the local town every week, has lunch, perhaps goes to the cinema and then changes her library books. The library would be a subscription library – Boots, W. H. Smith's or the more expensive Times Book Club – and the books she brought home would be middle-brow novels by women. A less idealised version of the figure of the middle-brow reader is Miss Sigglesthwaite in *South Riding* who writes to Sarah Burton describing her new life since she was persuaded to retire from Sarah's school: 'I am installed as daily companion to an old lady living here who is almost blind. [I] read to her ... You would be amused at her literary tastes, and so am I. I shall soon become quite an expert in the works of Ruby M. Ayres, Pamela Wynne and Ursula Bloom. Do you know any of these novelists? I assure you that they have opened up a new world to me' (*South Riding* (hereafter *SR*) 393). The image is intriguing: the blind old lady and the 'blind', failed, spinster teacher, who could have had a distinguished career as a biologist had it not been for family burdens, looking into the new worlds that the middle-brow novel brought them. Holtby could, of course, have added her own novels to Miss Sigglesthwaite's list.

Holtby's list of novelists suggests another feature of the middle-brow novel – Nicola Beauman's instancing of Noel Coward's play notwithstanding – which was that it was frequently written by women. Characteristically, the middle-brow novel was thus written for and by middle-class women, and could be stigmatised, to use Adorno's term, as a middle-class, bourgeois activity. This is not to say that its subject matter nor even its actual readership was always middle-class but rather that it had middle-class fictional agendas relating to the family, education, sexuality, and progress. To present these agendas, it used familiar literary and social discourses; the new worlds revealed to Miss Sigglesthwaite in her reading would not have alienated her and her old lady by a highly experimental style. Alison Light has commented on the fact that middle-brow books showed no obvious cleverness of manner in regard to the reader, that they succeeded in addressing a heterogeneous audience in a homogeneity of style, and with an 'apparent artlessness and insistence on … ordinariness [which] made [them] peculiarly resistant to analysis' (Light, 1991: 11). For many readers, Light argues, the middle-brow novel, with its own kind of cultural pretensions, was 'symbolic capital … a means of achieving prestige and displaying position', defining its own terms of reference, as Arnold Bennett had suggested, in relation to other 'brows'; 'the middlebrow is impossible in a culture that has no highbrow' (Light, 1991: 137). Light's concern is with conservative middle-brow writers like Agatha Christie, Daphne du Maurier, and Ivy Compton Burnett, and their often nostalgic evocation of Englishness. But there was another kind of middle-brow novel of the period, written by women, which offered a progressive view of English society, which looked not backwards to Christie's villages, du Maurier's romances or Compton Burnett's Victorian domestic tyrannies but forwards to a future of a fairer and more imaginative society, particularly a society of greater opportunities and responsibilities for women. This kind of middle-brow novel shared the stylistic ordinariness of its conservative counterparts but it did so for different political ends. The 'symbolic capital' the progressive middle-brow novel offered its readers was the not unsatisfying one of an awareness of the possibilities of social and sexual reform.

South Riding was Winifred Holtby's last novel; she was to die before it was published and its passage through the press was undertaken by her friend Vera Brittain, with some opposition from Holtby's mother who thought that the book was both libellous and vulgar. Holtby had written novels before, and short stories, none of which was high-brow but which could best be characterised as the progressive middle-brow fiction I have described, particularly in regard to their feminism. Her fiction brought her only a small income. She lived off lecturing and off journalism, for which she was best known during her life. As a prolific reviewer with eclectic tastes she was very conscious of the distinctions between middle-brow and high-brow fiction, and it was with an appreciation of their differences that she wrote the first critical book in English on Virginia Woolf, choosing as an intellectual challenge 'the writer whose art seemed most of all removed from anything I could ever attempt, and whose experience was most alien to my own' (Brittain, 1980: 308). Surprisingly, *Virginia Woolf* (1932) sold 500 copies within the first three months of publication, more than any of Holtby's novels to date, perhaps because it supplied a need to have high-brow fiction explained, particularly by someone with Holtby's clarity, unpretentiousness and accessibility.

This modest achievement was, however, as nothing compared with the success of *South Riding*: 'critics and public alike acclaimed it as a masterpiece, a classic, a picture of England' (Brittain, 1980: 409). Within five days of publication 16,000 copies were sold, 40,000 in the first year in the UK at 8 shillings a copy, and nearly 20,000 in America. It was the English Book Society choice in March 1936, and the next year it was awarded the James Tait Black prize. The film rights were bought immediately by Victor Saville and the novel was made into a film in 1938. By the provisions of Holtby's will, Somerville College, Oxford, where she had been a student, received, via the Dorothy McCalman Fund,

> the profits on any manuscripts unpublished at the time of her death, which should subsequently be published. In accordance with her wish the income from royalties thus received was used in the first instance to endow a scholarship commemorating the name of Dorothy McCalman (1922–25),[2] limited to candidates who have been earning their living for a period of three years or more before applying for admission to the College, and who could not enter without financial assistance. (Somerville Council minutes 14, 21)

The history of the bequest to Somerville is complicated, with more than one fund and scholarship becoming established. It is sufficient in indicating *South Riding*'s enduring marketability to say that to date the college has received just over £291,000 from Holtby's bequest. *South Riding* has never been out of print and has had several bursts of popularity, usually coinciding with transmission in other media. For example, there was a BBC radio dramatisation of it in 1949, it was BBC Radio 4's Book at Bedtime in 1971, and it was again dramatised in five episodes on radio on Sunday evenings in 1973. In 1970 all Holtby's books were reissued by Cedric Chivers of Bath at the request of the London Home Counties Branch of the Library Association. In 1974 Yorkshire Television serialised the novel and in September of that year, to coincide with the serialisation, Fontana brought out a paperback reprint of 250,000 copies at 60p each. The novel's popularity may be gauged by a comparison with the sales in the same year of one of the best selling novels of all time, Agatha Christie's *Murder on the Orient Express*, 500,000 copies of which were issued at 35p each, timed to coincide with the film adaptation starring Albert Finney as Poirot. Finally, Virago Press acquired *South Riding* in 1988, to complete their publishing run of Holtby's fiction, and since that date have sold 32,000 copies of the novel. All through its history it has made its way as a genuinely marketable product on its own appeal with very little institutional patronage; it has never been a a set text for English A-level exams, nor has it featured very often on university syllabuses.

The novel has, then, been a considerable commercial success and in this basic sense bears the stigmata of capitalism in that it has been unusually profitable for those who have benefited from its sales; it has entered the marketplace in a discernible way and in a manner which confirms its middle-brow credentials. That is, it is not stylistically innovative or formally experimental; it is not difficult to read nor puzzling in its conclusions; it employs familiar literary and social discourses, such as the romance plot and a concern with community, which align it with the novels of the nineteenth century. In these respects *South Riding* as a middle-brow novel is conservative, but is this quite the same as saying that it contains no elements of change, that it expresses only commonplace sentiments and that its techniques are outworn? To answer this question one must ask other questions: *Change for whom? Commonplace to whom? Outworn for which readership?*

South Riding draws on many of Holtby's own experiences: a failed heterosexual relationship, an admiration for her mother, a longing to write again of the East Riding of Yorkshire,[3] particularly the crisis in farming at this time, and the failure of a traditional farming culture. It also has local relevance in its geography, and in its reference to the opening of a new mental hospital which was one of her mother's favoured schemes, and in its narrative dynamic which depends to some extent on a version of an actual land purchase fraud which scandalised Hull in the early 1930s. In a way which is still important to those who live in the East Riding,[4] it spoke to the community of its specific concerns; it was not afraid to be a regional novel, 'second-rate' though these were often considered to be, as Holtby herself acknowledged. Its wider relevance derives political impetus from the 1932 Local Government Act[5] with its empowerment of local democracy as 'the first-line defence thrown up by the community against our common enemies – poverty, sickness, ignorance, isolation, mental derangement and social maladjustment' (SR xi). It also draws strength from inter-war feminism with its interest in education and welfare provision for women, particularly in maternity and contraceptive services. Its protagonist, Sarah Burton, like its author, is a pragmatist of the middle band of Symons's pyramid, in whom lay 'the seeds of the shifting pattern of the decade and even of the post-war Welfare State'.

The novel draws, then, on progressive forces in society and alludes to many 'elements of change' of the period. But at first reading the novel appears conformist, even 'commonplace', in its reassurance and familiarity, binding together its many characters, sentiments and plot lines in an overarching thematic development in which differences and diversity are accommodated within a benevolent unity. It is subtitled 'An English Landscape' and it does confirm a stereotype of Englishness (even of Yorkshireness), particularly in its stress on practical compromise and a muddle-through philosophy which purportedly were to become the saving qualities against German mechanistic efficiency in the 1939–45 war. The pastoral suggestion in 'Landscape' is fulfilled in the novel's agricultural concerns, and its focus on the small town of Kiplington, which is about the size of Middlemarch. Above all, the ending celebrates George V's Silver Jubilee of 1935 with the citizens of Kiplington united for the occasion, their differences temporarily reconciled, huge Union Jacks fluttering from the town's buildings. It is a heartening scene, and the thoughts of Sarah Burton summarise the message the book has advanced: 'we are members one of another. We cannot escape this partnership. This is what it means – to belong to a community; this is what it means, to be a people' (SR 491).

This homogeneity is, however, perceived as something of a delusion, and the achievement of whatever compromise is reached at the end of the novel is recognised as perhaps excessively costly. The undermining of its own outer conformism begins early in the novel, when the nostalgia evoked by 'An English Landscape' is rapidly dispelled in the first two scenes in the novel, that of a Council meeting, followed by that of Midge Carne looking at the 'dull landscape' from the decaying mansion she shares with her father. Both scenes end with the resounding defeat of the Carnes, the Conservative gentleman-farmer Robert Carne losing the election for the position of Alderman to the revolutionary Socialist Joe Astell, and Midge Carne collapsing into hysteria. The battle lines between capital and labour, between tradition and reform, paternalism and free enterprise, privilege and equality of opportunity are drawn up and it seems that the forces of English conservatism are to be routed. But even here there is no certainty and the novel mocks revolutionary pretensions right from the very start in the melodramatic responses of the young reporter Lovell Brown, as he watches the Council meeting: 'Here was World Tragedy in embryo. Here gallant Labour, with nothing to lose but its chains, would fight entrenched and armoured Capital. Here the progressive, greedy and immoral towns would exploit the pure, honest, elemental and unprogressive country. Here Corruption could be studied and exposed, oppression denounced, and lethargy indicted' (SR 3).

The chief character in the novel, Sarah Burton, brings to this 'English Landscape' a progressive, practical feminism which will complicate the various and conflicting political and social forces which the Council meeting has announced. Sarah too has an extremist's imagination, a fighting belief in 'the power of the human intelligence and will to achieve order, happiness, health and wisdom' but this is channelled into faith in her ability as a teacher to 'equip the young women entrusted to her ... for their part in that achievement' (SR 48). At the end, Carne is dead and Astell dying, two of the many deaths the novel features, and the centre ground of Kiplington is left to Sarah Burton and her ageing mother-figure, Mrs Beddows. Joe Astell writes from Clydeside, 'I'm a militant again, thank God, quit of compromise ... we can't build anything permanent on these foundations' (SR 482). But he is a finished man and has to recognise that change may come more from 'the bricks and mortar' of Sarah's type of good citizenship, which he despises, than the 'bloody, brutal prospect' of revolution. If South Riding is an English landscape, it is an England in which revolution is denied, and the opposing forces of Left and Right – Astell and Carne – are becoming, and perhaps even ought to become, extinct. Carne's angina pectoris and Astell's tubercular lungs function as symptoms, in their respective ways, of fatigued or wasted energies. It is not without significance that these figures from the extreme Right and Left are men.

At an earlier point in the novel, Astell and Sarah Burton talk about the relationship between politics and education and she describes the three kinds of girls she teaches: those to whom ideas of love, marriage and children are all-sufficient; those who have not thought seriously about what they want; and those to whom 'the words exploitation, injustice, slavery, and so on start the wheels going round'. 'I don't think you can change the first and third groups much', she says.'The middle group you might alter a bit – but many women, like many men, never grow up' (*SR* 104). Holtby herself belonged to the third group but *South Riding* is addressed to the first two groups, in particular the middle group of women whom Holtby wanted to help to grow up. It is a strongly didactic novel and its educational drive is towards the middle-brow, middle group whose opinions and lives as *women* are still capable of being altered 'a bit'.

South Riding is a radical text in relation to this middle group of women in several respects but the most important has to do with Sarah as a model of singleness and independence, and the novel's consequent refutation of the claims of romantic love as the only satisfactory destiny for a woman. Sarah's unmarried, lonely state is not taken lightly; she is not unattractive to men nor unattracted by them, she has been engaged to be married three times, she falls unexpectedly and violently in love with her political opponent, Carne. But although there are echoes of *Jane Eyre* in the novel, there will be no Ferndean at the end of the story. The husband loves only his mad wife, who outlives him, and even a modern revision of the romance element, in which an adulterous affair might have intensified the relationship, is thwarted by the heart attack Carne suffers when he visits Sarah's room. If the novel eschews a happy ending, it also skirts a tragic one; Carne dies because his horse rears on the cliff path, not because he commits suicide; Sarah thinks after his death that she wishes to die but as her plane threatens to crash she realises this is a false wish. Although Sarah, the character, makes an extreme statement about romantic love – 'I tell you here and now that I would have given all I have for one night – one hour ... I should not have cared what happened to me afterwards' (*SR* 468) – the text carries her on beyond this towards a 'serene old age' of usefulness and public service, and, in the figure of the elderly Mrs Beddows, to 'gaiety ... kindliness [and] valour of spirit'. At a time when women still outnumbered men by a million and a half, and when many of these 'superfluous' women must have had memories of unfinished love affairs and frustrated sexual passion, *South Riding* offered an alternative model for life. Sarah Burton's is not the spinsterhood of rejection and defeat – 'she knew herself to be desirable and desired, withheld only from marriage by the bars of death or of principle' (*SR* 49) – but a transcendant second best. In the total scheme of the novel, what Sarah will do outweighs the loss of Carne and even of personal happiness and its narrow satisfactions. 'I shall build up a great school here', she says; 'I shall make the South Riding famous'.

I am irresistibly reminded at this point of my own mother, who first recommended *South Riding* to me. Her promotion of it must have been strong because I can remember reading it when I was about twelve, and her talking about how much she had enjoyed it. For me it is the essential, motherly, middle-brow novel, with a particular resonance in that my mother, a docker's daughter, trained as a teacher, was widowed when she was in her late thirties, and then returned to the teaching she had been forced to retire from on marriage. Like Sarah Burton, she became a headmistress. There is, of course, no simple correlation between the model of single life offered in *South Riding* and my mother's life, except that both are expressions of profound change in the lives of women, and represent a revolution at the heart of things, in the bricks and mortar of women's life in the community.

Just how potentially changeful and even threatening *South Riding* was in the context of its time is illustrated in the changes the film version introduced. The novel's immediate success had persuaded Alexander Korda, through Victor Saville, to buy the film rights for £3,000 within a month of its publication. Like the novel, the film also was successful, bringing popular as well as critical approval: 'a scrupulous, authentic picture of English life for the first time on any screen', said the *Daily Mail*, and even the *New Statesman* thought it 'something positively real' (quoted in Richards and Aldgate, 1983: 32). But the film's construction of English life owes very little to Holtby's novel. The initial image, accompanying the opening credits, is one of rolling farmland with a team of horses ploughing. Superimposed on scenes like these is a tribute to Holtby's purpose in the novel: '. . . she strove to preserve for us a part of the changing England that is typical of the whole'. This is not at all what the novel does, nor, to be fair, does the film which shows, albeit to a lesser degree, the end of the gentleman-farmer, feudalistic way of life of the Carne family. The film does, however, save Robert Carne from death, although it teaches him a lesson or two in the process, particularly about abandoning his aristocratic pretensions and instead forming an unlikely alliance with the Socialist Joe Astell, both of them motivated by commitment to the community and in opposition to unscrupulous businessmen like Snaith, Huggins and Tadman. It is a curious political conclusion, reminiscent of Disraeli's *Sybil* in its linking of aristocracy and worker against commerce and trade as the means to save England. The film's alliance between Carne and Astell is echoed in the equally unlikely friendship that grows up between Midge Carne and the working-class scholarship girl, Lydia Holly (see figures 1 and 4).

But if the film ties together class elements in a conservative solution at odds with the novel's radical uncertainty regarding class distinctions, it neutralises yet more thoroughly the sexual politics of the novel. The film is glamorised by the presence, in flashback, of Carne's mad wife, played by Ann Todd, whose wild beauty and imperious manner create some of the dominant images of the film. In the film, an incident related

1 From the 1938 film of *South Riding*, produced and directed by Victor Saville. The men look at each other over the woman's head as the alliance between landed interest and labour is forged between Robert Carne (Ralph Richardson) and Joe Astell (John Clements). Visually, as well as thematically, Sarah Burton acts as intermediary.

2 Robert Carne looks yearningly at Sarah Burton. In this scene in the film, he kisses her and tells her how much she means to him. The novel unromantically concludes with Sarah registering 'the bleak repulsion of his sombre enmity'.

briefly by a servant in the book, in which Muriel Carne forces her horse to go upstairs, is given full scope (in a scene which foreshadows a similar episode in the box-office success *Gone with the Wind* of 1939), and the servant's humorous conclusion to the tale, in which the terrified horse had urinated on the bedroom floor, causing a permanent stain on the ceiling of the room below, is entirely omitted. Carne has no shadow of heart disease in the film, and though he is tempted to commit suicide in order to pay his debts, he is roused from this by Sarah, to whom he has already declared his love (see figure 2). She tells him of the plot to buy land fraudulently and on the strength of this he routs the dishonest upstarts at the next Council meeting (see figure 3). Muriel Carne, in the mean time, has conveniently died.

The film does acknowledge some of Sarah's 'new woman' qualities: she cares about her school, she is outspoken and unprudish (though by no means as sexually liberated as her counterpart in the novel), and Carne is enough of a new man to admire her progressiveness, even allowing Maythorpe Hall to become the new buildings for the girls' grammar school (not the mental institution it becomes in the novel) on the payment of the mortgage. But the pre-eminence of love in a woman's life is upheld, death, age and indifference have no part in the lovers' story, and Sarah herself is silenced at the end, except as sustainer of the man and his adoring companion in the singing of 'Land of Hope and Glory'. There is no such singing at the end of the novel, but instead a speech of exhortation by Sarah to her schoolgirls to 'Question everything ... Question every one in authority ...'

Vera Brittain saw the film on its opening night and later commented that 'A more realistic film could be made today, showing Sarah Burton and Robert Carne as the star-crossed middle-aged semi-lovers whom Winifred created, and depicting Mrs Beddows as a patriarchal seventy-four instead of the glamorous sixty-six presented by young-looking Marie Lohr' (Brittain, 1980: 188). Odd, to describe Mrs Beddows as 'patriarchal', but otherwise an interesting recognition that the film spoke to and of its own time with far more conventional reassurance than the novel. Indeed, the film seriously misreads the novel in the interests of compromise, traditional values, and unity across class divides; these interests are best served by the presentation of heterosexual love as victorious and as a regenerative and purifying force in society. To recall some of the events occurring at the time Holtby's novel was published

3 Robert Carne, Sarah Burton and Joe Astell ranged against the upstart, corrupt businessman Dolland who stands for Council election against Carne.

4 The film's unlikely friendship between Robert Carne's daughter Midge (Glynis Johns) and Lydia Holly, the girl from the slum settlement, the Shacks.

and the film produced is to understand how great the need was for consolidation of national identity along traditional, even nostalgic, class and gender lines. In 1935 Italy invaded Abyssinia; in 1936 German troops entered the Rhineland, the Spanish Civil War was fought and Franco was recognised by Germany and Italy; 1937 was the year of Guernica and of Italy leaving the League of Nations, and it saw the beginning of the Mosley anti-Jewish marches; in 1938 there was the Munich crisis. In this year, the year of the film of *South Riding*, stunned by the 'sudden crescendo of international tension' (Brittain, 1979: 194), Vera Brittain made plans to evacuate her children to America in the almost certain knowledge, which all shared, that war was coming again to Europe. Ever since its inception, British (and American) cinema had tended to be a conservative medium and never more so than in the years before the outbreak of the 1939–45 war. At such a time, no popular film, or even serious middle-brow film, could refuse to endorse the message of national consensus and therefore of love between the sexes as legitimately triumphant.

But the middle-brow novel in the inter-war period was a different matter, and in the particularly female milieu in which it flourished, it represented a force with profound implications. It grew from the gulf between the torn halves of high-brow and low-brow, contained within capitalism, yet containing within itself far-reaching elements of change. *South Riding*'s enduring marketability stigmatises it both as a stable and profitable commodity in a market economy, yet also, within these constraints, as a vehicle for change, a medium of exchange between old and new ideas and ideologies in the lives of women.

Notes

I am grateful to Somerville College for information on income accruing to the College from *South Riding*, and for publishing figures from Virago Press.

1 'Brows' used in this sense probably derives from nineteenth-century phrenology. The OED gives the first instance of the use of 'high-browed' in a letter written by George Eliot on 23 November 1848. As a noun, 'high-brow' is cited as first used in 1908, 'low-brow' in the USA in 1906.
2 Dorothy McCalman was a teacher 'who went late to Somerville after earning her living ... and died after only a year as a tutor at the Oxford Training College' (Brittain, 1979: 145).
3 She had already written of the East Riding in her first novel, *Anderby Wold*, 1923.
4 The area ceased to be called the East Riding more than twenty years ago and became part of 'North Humberside'. It has now reverted to the previous name. There never was, of course, a South Riding; it was Holtby's name for that part of the East Riding which runs from Beverley to the coast down to Spurn Point, encompassing Hull.
5 It is, as far as I know, the only novel to be 'about' local government. Its eight books are named after fictional local government committees – 'Education', 'Highways and Byways', 'Finance', and so on – and each is prefaced by a quotation from committee minutes. It is an ingenious way of giving an appearance of structure to a long and sprawling novel, with a listed cast of more than 160 characters, and at the same time keeping the social concerns of the novel to the fore.

References

Baldick, Chris (1983) *The Social Mission of English Criticism 1848–1932*, Oxford: Oxford University Press.
Beauman, Nicola (1983) *A Very Great Profession: The Woman's Novel 1914–39*, London: Virago.
Bloch, Ernst *et al.* (1977) *Aesthetics and Politics*, London: NLB.
Brittain, Vera ([1957] 1979) *Testament of Experience: An Autobiographical Story of the Years 1925–1950*, London: Virago.

The making of a middle-brow success

Brittain, Vera ([1940] 1980) *Testament of Friendship: The Story of Winifred Holtby*, London: Virago.

Holtby, Winifred ([1936] 1988) *South Riding*, London: Virago.

Leavis, F. R. (1933) *For Continuity*, Cambridge: Cambridge University Press.

Leavis, Q. D. ([1932] 1965) *Fiction and the Reading Public*, London: Chatto & Windus.

Light, Alison (1991) *Forever England: Femininity, Literature and Conservatism Between the Wars*, London and New York: Routledge.

Majumdar, Robin and McLauren, Allen (1975) *Virginia Woolf: The Critical Heritage*, London: Routledge & Kegan Paul.

Melman, Billie (1988) *Women and the Popular Imagination in the Twenties*, London: Macmillan.

Richards, Jeffrey and Aldgate, Anthony (1983) *The Best of British: Cinema and Society 1930–1970*, Oxford: Blackwell.

Symons, Julian ([1960] 1973) *The Thirties: A Dream Revolved*, Connecticut: Greenwood Press.

3

'Extremely valuable property':
the marketing of *Rebecca*

Avril Horner and Sue Zlosnik

During the fifty-seven years since Daphne du Maurier's *Rebecca* first appeared, it has never been out of print. Published originally by Victor Gollancz in 1938, it has subsequently appeared in a range of editions which reflect the various ways in which it has since been categorised or, indeed, has eluded categorisation. Such categorisation is particularly interesting in relation to the concept of the 'woman writer'. However, the female authorship of *Rebecca* does not appear to have been foregrounded in its early marketing or reception. Rather, it was recognised from the outset as a potential best seller with a wide appeal and comparisons were made with the work of earlier and contemporary male writers.

In a letter to Michael Joseph dated 28 July 1947, Victor Gollancz notes that his publishing firm 'received the manuscript of *Rebecca* on April 21st 1938, and published on August 5th. How quick production was in those days!'[1] Things did, indeed, move fast. By 26 April 1938, Norman Collins (recruited from the *News Chronicle* in 1933 and deputy chairman at Victor Gollancz Ltd. since 1934) had written a report on the novel. He immediately recognised it as a best seller: 'The new Daphne du Maurier contains everything that the public could want ... the whole thing has all the marks of a really rollicking success'. As well as giving a plot summary, the report describes the novel as 'sentimental in a haunting and melancholy way' and likens it to both *Peter Ibbetson* (the best seller written by Daphne du Maurier's grandfather and published in 1892) and le Fanu's *Uncle Silas*, published in 1864 (particularly in the characterisation of Mrs Danvers, who is compared to the 'terrifying' old woman in Le Fanu's novel). Collins placed *Rebecca* firmly within the modes of suspense/sensation writing and melodrama (a word he uses three times in the report): 'There is superb melodrama of the "she-didn'tdrown,-I-shot-her" type, and the whole book is held together by the entangling and unbreakable web of Daphne's imagination. I don't know any author who imagines so hard all the time.' Collins's reservations concerned spelling ('there is another full weekend's work to do on the book before it goes to the printer'), length (about 160,000 words), the puzzling (to him) nature of the novel's opening (which presents the narrator and Maxim apparently penniless and in exile), and a certain rawness of plot: 'In outline the story sounds crude, and the melodrama *is* crude, but little touches, such as the way in which the character of Rebecca which appears at first sight to be that of the divinely gifted and beautiful wife is shown under analysis to be that of a depraved and remorseless creature, are extremely brilliant.' Du Maurier's novel, then, was placed by Collins within both the tradition of late nineteenth-century popular fiction (*Peter Ibbetson*) and that of the Victorian sensation novel;[2] it was also, it seems, being obliquely linked to the vogue in the 1920s and 1930s for films and books which had, as a central character, a wilful and 'depraved' woman.[3] Interestingly, there is no mention in the report of the influence of *Jane Eyre* (something immediately picked up by American reviewers when it was published in the United States) nor (perhaps not surprisingly at this time) to a tradition of women's writing. Collins's reference to du Maurier is also revealing: 'If you are writing to the girl, you might ask whether she means to use "Jasper" or "Jaspar".' (Du Maurier was, at this time, thirty-one years old and married with two children.)

Victor Gollancz was immediately persuaded by Collins's report. Whilst du Maurier's first three novels (*The Loving Spirit, I'll Never Be Young Again* and *The Progress of Julius*) had all been published by Heinemann, Victor Gollancz had brought out, between 1934 and 1937, *Gerald: A Portrait, Jamaica Inn* and *The Du Mauriers*, all of which sold reasonably well. On 3 May 1938, he sent a letter to the book trade announcing the imminent publication of *Rebecca* and proclaiming his faith in the novel as a best seller:

> This is only the third or fourth time in the ten years history of my firm that I have written a personal letter to booksellers about a new novel, but having finished reading Daphne du Maurier's new novel REBECCA last night, I cannot lose a moment in writing to the trade to say what a winner this book is going to be. I do not indeed remember ever having read a book which contains so obviously, every single one of the essential qualities of a 'best-seller'.

Much of Collins's report is incorporated into this letter, including the comparisons with *Peter Ibbetson* and *Uncle Silas*, but Victor Gollancz added another dimension to the description of *Rebecca*: 'it contains an exquisite love story in which the emotion is heightened by drama'. Du Maurier herself, however, saw it as a 'rather grim' study in jealousy and not as a love story (Forster, 1993: 137). The length of the novel, which worried Collins, was presented positively by Gollancz as rather voguish: 'The book is written on the grand scale, and in line with the current fashion, is long, but not excessively so. It will be published at the price of 8/6d, and *I confidently believe that it is going to be "The Citadel" of 1938.*' *The Citadel*, by A. J. Cronin, published by Victor Gollancz in 1937, had 'shattered every record in the nine years of the firm's existence' (Sheila Hodges, 1978: 71). According to *The Publishers' Circular* of 20 October 1937, it had sold 40,083 copies in nine days in 1937, a bookselling record indeed (Joseph McAleer, 1992: 56). In his letter of 23 April 1938, enclosed with the manuscript of *Rebecca*, Gollancz asked Collins to look at it 'from the possibility of turning it into this year's Cronin'. As Ruth Dudley Edwards points out, the publishing firm of Victor Gollancz was at this time more reliant than most on its best-seller list:

> Where Longmans and Macmillan were virtually impregnable financially by virtue of their educational lists, Victor had failed to invest the time and money required in that area, and Gollancz's venture into education during the thirties was too half-hearted to get off the ground. Other publishers found security in reprinted classics that were out of copyright, but Victor needed the excitement of live authors and new books. The firm was therefore more precariously based than some of its serious competitors: to keep its profits up it depended on regular new books by such authors as Daphne du Maurier, A. J. Cronin or Dorothy L. Sayers, along with the bestsellers that Victor found or created from year to year. (Edwards, 1987: 331)

Victor Gollancz had an additional reason for wanting to keep the profits up: he had launched the Left Book Club (led by a committee comprising John Strachey, Harold Laski and Gollancz himself) on 29 February 1936. According to Sheila Hodges, by 1936 Victor Gollancz felt his firm was financially secure enough (it had by now an excellent list of writers) for him to 'at last carry out his ambition to breach the barrier which made the large-scale distribution of left-wing books so difficult' (Hodges, 1978: 123). From 18 May 1936 the club published political books of a socialist and Fabian nature. Although it brought six million books to press between 1936 and 1946 (Edwards, 1987: 396), its most active years were from May 1936 to September 1939. Since his best-seller list guaranteed a secure financial base for his left-wing publishing activities, Victor Gollancz had every reason for wanting to promote and market du Maurier's *Rebecca* as effectively as possible. Well known in the world of publishing for his bold and adventurous publicity and marketing campaigns,[4] he swung into action.

Du Maurier herself was slightly bemused by Gollancz's excited response to *Rebecca* and somewhat appalled by the thought of the publicity and marketing strategies both he and Collins suggested. In a letter written on 12 May 1938 to Norman Collins she comments on the novel: 'It seemed ghastly to me when I read it through, and I was quite prepared for you and V. G. to write and say the whole story must be re-written! What a relief that you both pass it.' He responded immediately by letter congratulating her on 'a superb piece of work' and commenting that the novel 'is head and shoulders above anything else you have done'. For Victor Gollancz, the timing of publication was crucially important: the prospect of war, imminent in 1938, would bring slumps in book-buying and the threat of paper rationing (a reality by March 1940). Thrown into a panic by a letter from du Maurier's literary agent, Spencer Curtis Brown, which suggested accepting a magazine offer for serialisation rights – a step which would mean delaying publication of *Rebecca* until the spring of 1939 – Victor Gollancz wrote at length to the author on 27 May 1938. He set out to persuade her against Curtis Brown's advice, arguing that, given sufficient publicity and 'a really good press', serialisation offers would follow publication anyway and that newspaper serialisation *after* publication would help books sales more than magazine publication *before*. Stating that he was 'horribly alarmed' by the idea of postponing publication till the following year, he listed points in defence of his position:

1. To begin with, I myself am thoroughly worked up about the book, and am eager to launch it: God only knows what may happen between now and a year hence. The whole thing, so to speak, goes into cold storage.
2. I sent you a copy of that letter we sent out to the booksellers. As a result of it the travellers are subscribing the book exceedingly well and the book-sellers themselves are sending in their orders. Any long postponement means, of course, that the effect of that letter is completely thrown away – and I can't repeat a letter of that kind.
3. As part of the campaign I have already started working up advance

interest. See, for instance, the enclosed proof of an advertisement that is to appear in this week's 'Sunday Times'. I should have to drop this too.

He went on to assure du Maurier that he had 'a hunch' that June or July would be exactly the right time for publication 'and I honestly believe that the final result in *earnings*, even if the American serial offer is big, will be every bit as satisfactory to you (in my view more satisfactory) than if the book is postponed'. To confirm his belief in the book – and as incentive for du Maurier to agree to early publication – Gollancz also suggested an increase in the advance: 'if I am given *carte blanche* to publish the book in June or July I will increase the advance on REBECCA from £1,000 to £1,500'. The letter concludes with a postscript informing du Maurier that Gollancz is negotiating to get the book made a Book Society choice 'which is extremely useful for *launching* a book'. (*Rebecca* became, in the event, the choice of the Book Society for August.)

To his relief, du Maurier shared Gollancz's enthusiasm for quick publication: 'It's absurd to think of postponing book publication until next March, for the sake of £400 from that rather dreary magazine I never read. As you say, anything may happen by then.' She modestly refused, however, the offer of a larger advance: 'I think that offer of yours very generous but dont [*sic*] think you should make it. The sales of my last books (barring Gerald) don't warrant it, and I think my £1,000 advance is fair and just. If Rebecca does go with a boom, that extra £500 will come along soon enough. It its [*sic*] a flop, it'll just mean I didn't deserve it anyway!' (Undated letter from Daphne du Maurier to Victor Gollancz.) As Margaret Forster notes, the huge success of *Rebecca* meant that the money did, indeed, pour in during the second half of 1938 (Forster, 1993: 140), but du Maurier was not to know that when she refused the increased advance. As chief breadwinner for the family – her husband's army pay did not meet his expensive tastes and his father's money had been lost in the 1929 stock market crash (Forster, 1993: 96) – she was always keen to know how much money her novels had made: a letter of 10 October 1938 to Victor Gollancz asks for 'a rough estimate of what I've earned (if anything!) in excess of any advance on "Rebecca", up to date. It would help me in budgeting expenses for the coming winter.' (Victor Gollancz's answer was £3,000, of which £1,000 she had already had by way of the advance.) She was, in fact, proud of her money-making capacity as an author. Her refusal to accept any increase in the agreed advance was certainly not, therefore, made out of the sense that money was somehow a vulgar consideration in the pursuit of her craft. Sheila Hodges, a key figure at Gollancz for many years, remarking on the modesty and scrupulousness of Elizabeth Bowen and Elizabeth Jenkins as authors (both published by Gollancz), suggested that the 'combination of diffidence and immense pains is a characteristic that seems to be a particular gift or curse – whichever way one looks at it – of women writers' (Hodges, 1978: 90).

Du Maurier was not so amenable, however, to the marketing and publicity strategies Gollancz had in mind. Less confident than Gollancz and Collins of the novel's success ('My personal feeling is that it's a bit too much on the gloomy side to be a winner, and the psycological [sic] side of it may not be understood'), she was nevertheless appalled by the thought of having to enter the glare of publicity herself in order to promote it. She complied willingly enough with signing sheets for both English and American 'signed' editions, but took some persuading to attend Foyle's Literary Lunch and vowed never to attend such a function again. She also had quite specific ideas concerning the cover design: 'can I beg you again for no blurb on the jacket ... And I have a childish fancy for the title "Rebecca" to be written on the cover in a long thin pointed handwriting! Will this be possible. Incidentally, I'm surprised that the book is long enough for 8/6.'[5] There is no record of Victor Gollancz's reply to this request, but in the event the cloth cover of the first edition carried, in the top left-hand corner, the name 'Rebecca' in slanting, if not particularly 'long', 'thin' and 'pointed', handwriting.[6]

Although the literary reviews were rather mixed, *Rebecca* was an instant publishing success in commercial terms. In Britain, the novel sold 50,000 copies by 15 October 1938 and 72,000 copies by 25 May 1939.[7] In the United States, where the book had been published by Doubleday, Doran and Company in September 1938, it topped 'virtually every city's bestseller list' by December 1938;[8] it had sold 150,000 copies by 31 January 1939 (excluding book club sales) and over half a million copies by 17 January 1941. In the UK, it was the Literary Guild choice for October 1938 and several articles on du Maurier appeared both in the quality and the popular press during the autumn and winter of 1938/9. By early 1939 the American Booksellers' Association had voted it their favourite novel for 1938. Gollancz kept the novel in the public eye by a number of means. For example, he produced a special presentation edition of 200 copies in November 1938. In a letter to du

Maurier dated 11 November 1938 he explains that these are being sent out as 'a kind of "appetizer" to the principal Rajahs of the Book Trade. Receiving a special copy always flatters them a great deal, and this is the first time we have ever produced a special edition.' In the United States, Malcolm Johnson of Nelson Doubleday orchestrated similar campaigns, including a telephone interview of du Maurier by Clifton Fadiman, described in a letter from Johnson to du Maurier dated 3 February 1939 as 'one of America's most distinguished book critics, and incidentally a great admirer of REBECCA'; this was broadcast in the United States on 14 February 1939.

However, despite such marketing and publicity campaigns, British sales of *Rebecca* had fallen quite dramatically by May 1939. By now, war was imminent and the original excitement about the book was beginning to evaporate. In a letter to du Maurier dated 25 May 1939, Victor Gollancz, whilst making it clear that the novel was in the top league in terms of sales figures ('not more than a dozen books have had such a sale since the war'), remarked that sales were now down to a couple of hundred copies per week. Timing was once again crucial:

> *When* one should publish a cheap edition is always a moot point. My own view is that when a book has been a real best seller one should publish the cheap edition round about a year after the original date of publication, provided that the sales have become small. I believe this to be the right policy because the cheap edition has a much better chance, and gets a much better sale, if the excitement of the book's 'best selling' is vividly in the public mind.

In the event, the cheap Gollancz hardback edition was published on 24 July – a few days before the anniversary of its first publication – 'so that we can get the advantage of the August Bank Holiday and general summer holiday sales' (unpublished letter from Victor Gollancz to du Maurier, 5 June 1939). A similar strategy was adopted in the United States, where Doubleday brought out a $1.39 edition of the novel in the summer of 1939. Interestingly, however, there is no reference to falling sales on either side of the Atlantic after the summer of 1939, despite the onset of war. The rise in sales figures in the United States (from 150,000 by 31 January 1939 to over half a million by January 1941) is particularly striking. This upturn in sales figures was no doubt due to the huge impact of the film, *Rebecca*, starring Laurence Olivier as Maxim de Winter, Joan Fontaine as the young wife and Judith

Anderson as Mrs Danvers. Made in the United States with David Selznick (who had also been responsible for *Gone with the Wind* in 1939) as producer and Alfred Hitchcock as director, it was released in 1940 when it won several Academy Awards. The publicity surrounding Selznick's massive talent hunt for the film's leading actors brought du Maurier's novel sharply back into public focus, as did the success of the film itself. Furthermore, the timing of the picture's release had been handled very carefully, according to Nelson Doubleday, so as not to clash with other films which were proving hugely popular, such as *Gone with the Wind*.[9] Pleased with the film, which he considered very true to the book, Nelson Doubleday used it to boost sales of du Maurier's novel. The American publishing firm issued a paperback 'Motion Picture edition' of *Rebecca* which sold for 69¢ and which contained sixteen pages of black-and-white stills from the film. Listing a sales total of over 400,000 *before* the release of the film, and targeted at a vast cinema-going audience, it promised, as Nelson Doubleday noted, greatly to increase sales of the book once the film was out. The huge upturn in the American sales of the novel between January 1939 and January 1941 would suggest that he was right.

Since then, *Rebecca* has become firmly established as a best seller and has never been out of print. In November 1958, Walter Allen, who was researching a book on twentieth-century international best sellers, wrote to Victor Gollancz, noting that *Rebecca* 'had sold more than 2,358,000 copies in the U. S. alone by 1955', and asking for the British sales figures. Victor Gollancz replied the following month that *Rebecca* had sold, to date, approximately 900,000 hardback copies and commented that 'we have never allowed the book to go into the paper-backs' ... since [it] is still in big daily demand in its hard-cover form'. (Interestingly, when giving her permission for the figures to be released to Allen, du Maurier commented that she had no idea what they were.) In 1978, Sheila Hodges noted that the Gollancz edition of *Rebecca* 'has sold nearly a million copies, quite apart from America, paperback editions, and translations into twenty-four languages' (Hodges, 1978: 94).

From the early 1950s, Gollancz allowed *Rebecca* to appear in other hardback editions in the UK and in soft and hard cover abroad. Negotiations concerning rights and royalties (split 50/50 with du Maurier) were always rigorously conducted, Victor Gollancz frequently pointing out to other publishers the uniqueness of du Maurier's novel: 'REBECCA is probably one of the most valuable literary properties in the world' (unpublished letter to Studio Publications, Toronto, 19 June 1952); 'REBECCA is ... as you must realize, extremely valuable property' (unpublished letter to J. G. Ferguson Publishing Company, New York, 5 February 1969). However, Gollancz frequently refused other publishers licence to issue du Maurier's novel, the most common reason for refusal being the likelihood of sales competition with Gollancz's own hardback edition in the UK and the Commonwealth. Nevertheless, *Rebecca* did go into many issues and editions. The way in which the book was perceived in terms of genre and literary status, and the manner in which it was subsequently produced and marketed, tell us much about post-war cultural perceptions of popular fiction in general and du Maurier's novel in particular. It would seem, for example, that by the late 1950s *Rebecca* was being perceived as a *Jane Eyre* for less able pupils in the UK. Longman wanted to include the novel in an abridged series 'suitable for secondary modern pupils' (unpublished letter from Curtis Brown to Victor Gollancz, 13 August 1959) but permission for this was refused on commercial grounds. There were also requests from European publishers who wished to add it to their annotated schools editions series, J. B. Wolters of Groningen, for example, wishing to include it in their 'The Unicorn Library' series aimed at Dutch secondary and grammar schools (unpublished letter dated 23 May 1960). Frequently the novel was perceived as suitable reading matter for older children or young adults and advertised as such; in 1961, for example, it appeared in Longman's Modern Reading Series, issued for school and college use, along with titles such as *Fair Stood the Wind for France* and *The Snow Goose*. In a letter written to Oriel Malet in 1962, Daphne du Maurier indicates that she was well aware of this trend: 'Of course it was old-fashioned in 1938 when it was written – I remember critics saying it was a queer throwback to the 19th-century Gothic novel. But I shall never know quite *why* it seized upon everybody's imagination, not just teenagers and shop girls, like people try to say now, but *every age, and* both sexes' (Malet, 1993: 131). Brockhampton Press also wrote to Gollancz in 1963 asking for permission to include it in their 'Twentieth Century Classics' series which featured novels such as *The Scarlet Pimpernel* and *Finn the Wolfhound* (the terse reply was 'I'm afraid we should hate to see REBECCA in your Twentieth Century Classics'). This pattern continues, with Longman issuing it in 1986 within their Simplified English series alongside titles such as *The Coral Island, Dr. Jekyll and Mr. Hyde, Kidnapped, A Journey to*

the Centre of the Earth, The Prisoner of Zenda, Pride and Prejudice and *Jane
Eyre.* These series for younger readers tend to comprise a range of texts
that embrace adventure, mystery and love interest. Sometimes *Rebecca*
would be placed within one of these categories: the introduction to the
1992 Longman simplified edition, for example, whilst noting that it 'is
different from the usual novel of this sort', relates it to 'many romantic
novels [which] tell the story of two women'.

Until recently, however, *Rebecca* was often perceived, in the spirit of
Norman Collins's original reader's report, more as a novel of suspense
than of romantic interest; the Reader's Digest Book Club of New York,
for example, included it in their 1968 'Modern Classics of Suspense, a
single volume comprised of condensations of six outstanding mystery
titles' (authors included Dashiell Hammett, Eric Ambler, Helen Mac-
Innes, Andrew Garve, and Mary Roberts Rinehart). In the same year,
Gollancz issued a new edition of the novel 'putting it back into the
original 1938 setting' in terms of print format – presumably on the
assumption that book sales might benefit from the 1960s nostalgia for
the 1930s. In 1969 J. G. Ferguson approached Gollancz for licence to
issue *Rebecca* within their 'Twentieth Century Classics' series which
included *Gone with the Wind, Lord Jim, The Robe, Mutiny on the Bounty,
Of Human Bondage* and *Grapes of Wrath*. In 1977, Heinemann added it
to their 'Heinemann Guided Reader Series' (which retold novels in
simpler English than the original and included illustrations): others in
the series included *Of Mice and Men, Bleak House, The Man of Property,
The Olympic Games, The Great Ponds* and *The Cinema*. Interestingly, in
the early 1980s, The Franklin Library of New York included it in two
separate series, 'The Collector's Library of Great Mystery Classics' (in
which it was grouped with novels such as *Dr. Jekyll and Mr. Hyde, The
Day of the Jackal* and *The Maltese Falcon*) *and* in its 'Romance Library'.
Rebecca has, therefore, been grouped with both 'classic' and 'middle-
brow' texts, romance and mystery, canonised works and novels which
have sunk into oblivion.

However, it is *Rebecca's* transition from hardback to Penguin paperback in 1962 which marks perhaps the most interesting moment in its
publishing and marketing history. The transition was not an easy one,
since Victor Gollancz's hostility to the paperback revolution, which he
saw as part of a decline in cultural standards, bedevilled his authors'
transference into paperback: 'For almost twenty years after the foundation of Penguin Books Victor had stoutly refused to sell any of his list

to the hated "paper-cover affairs": authors could reap the benefits of his paperback royalties only by reclaiming their rights when Victor failed to reprint' (Edwards, 1987: 680). For various reasons, by the late 1950s his attitude to paperback publishing had softened somewhat, but since du Maurier was still one of his best selling novelists he was not at all keen to sell the paperback rights to her work, particularly those of *Rebecca*. In her recent biography, Margaret Forster describes the nego-tiations between du Maurier and Gollancz concerning Penguin publication of her work as constituting the only 'serious difference' she had with her publisher. Victor Gollancz was, apparently, 'appalled at the idea' and told her that he had '75,000 copies of various books of hers in stock and could not see how he would ever sell these if they went into paperback' (Forster, 1993: 320). Du Maurier was adamant, however, having become convinced that she was entitled to benefit, like other authors, from the attractive financial deals offered by paperback publishers. Gollancz held out for some time, occasionally using emo-tional blackmail by, for example, reminding her of what he had done for her career and commenting on the enormous amount of work Sheila Bush had had to put into editing the manuscript of the book on Branwell Brontë (Forster, 1993: 320–1). According to Ruth Dudley Edwards, Gollancz fell out with several of his authors during the early 1960s, often because of his refusal to let their work go into paperback. She comments that 'Even the devoted Daphne du Maurier was upset by Victor's refusal to let her books go to Penguin, and Spencer Curtis Brown became almost hysterical over what he termed first Victor's "dog-in-the-manger" attitude and then his "avarice"' (Edwards, 1987: 713). Gollancz was, apparently, particularly incensed by the proposed division of the paperback advance which was to be 60 per cent to du Maurier and 40 per cent to Gollancz, instead of the usual 50/50 split (Forster, 1993: 321). However, he did eventually capitulate but, according to Ruth Dudley Edwards, 'only because du Maurier appealed to him with a face-saving formula for his climbdown' (Edwards 1987: 713) – pres-umably a reference to du Maurier's offer to produce a new novel about her French ancestors, *The Glass-Blowers*.[10]

Seven of du Maurier's novels appeared as Penguin reprints in 1962, several of the covers featuring restrained but imaginative pen and ink drawings. The cover for *Rebecca* (which sold for 4 shillings) is particularly interesting: the faint image of a woman's face is partially obscured by two interlocking twisted trees (suggestive of the wild bleakness of much of the Cornish landscape). The face, unattached to a body, has something of a dream-image about it; the mouth is wide and sensual, and the hair, which flares up and around the face in wild curls, is rather Medusa-like (see figure 5). Whereas most jacket covers of *Rebecca* portray the nameless heroine (the 1975 Pan and 1992 Arrow issues are characteristic in this respect, see figures 6 and 7), the Penguin edition successfully suggests the sensual, haunting and slightly threatening presence of Rebecca herself. Penguin also played down the element of melodrama in du Maurier's writing and played up its relationship to canonical works: thus the jacket blurb of *Jamaica Inn* describes the novel as transferring 'the world of the Brontës ... to the Cornwall of the early nineteenth century'. This particular emphasis had a clear impact on the reviewing community: several re-assessments of du Maurier's work, debating its literary worth and its debts to the Brontës' novels, appeared during 1962. Ronald Bryden's dismissal of *Rebecca* as 'a Cornish Gothic resetting of *Jane Eyre*' in a review article published in the *Spectator* on 20 April 1962, for example, was countered in the *Times Literary Supplement* on 19 October 1962 by an uncredited piece (by Margharita Laski) entitled 'Archangels Ruined', which claimed that *Rebecca* had been denied a fair critical appraisal. The article, which sets out to evaluate the seven du Maurier novels reprinted in Penguin editions, pays particular attention to *Rebecca* and *The Scapegoat;* dismissing the other five as 'poor', the writer defends these two works as fine examples of the 'demoniac' novel. Du Maurier's invention of the character Rebecca is described as 'brilliant'; her portrayal of the 'mousy' heroine's inadequacies is seen as astute, 'anti-romantic, and ... very clever' ('social insecurity is not necessarily trivial and may be the proper stuff of nightmares'); Ronald Bryden is taken to task for not taking sufficient account of the 'puzzling' opening. The time may well have been ripe for a re-assessment of du Maurier's status as a novelist, but it was the Penguin imprint which brought her into the focus of the literary critic. Interestingly, however, those same reviewers ignored the fact that Penguin had placed *Rebecca* firmly within a tradition of writing of particular importance to the *adult woman* reader: 'There are said to be three books that every woman reads: *Jane Eyre, Gone With the Wind,* and *Rebecca.* And who can say how many men have read them all?' (blurb on back of jacket shown in figure 8). It was not until the mid-1980s, by which time the advent of feminism and cultural studies had made consideration of popular fiction respectable in academic circles, that critics began to pay serious attention to du Maurier's work and to assess its significance in relation to class, historical moment, gender and writing.[11]

More recent publishing and marketing strategies have, however, implicitly shifted *Rebecca* back into the categories of popular writing and women's romantic fiction. The latter is a category which, as Alison Light has pointed out, 'became more narrowly specialised between the wars, coming to signify only those love-stories, aimed ostensibly at a wholly female readership, which deal primarily with the trials and tribulations of heterosexual desire, and end happily in marriage' (Light, 1991: 160). *Rebecca*, with a plot that focuses as much on murder as love-story, and with an opening which forestalls any simple sense of a 'happy' ending, does not fit neatly into this category, as du Maurier herself realised. Nevertheless, several publishers who bought the paperback rights for *Rebecca* commissioned covers for the novel which suggest that the targeted reader was one who enjoys women's romantic fiction. For example, in 1992 Arrow brought out its paperback edition of *Rebecca*

5 Cover of Daphne Du Maurier's *Rebecca*, by Virgil Burnett (Penguin, 1962).

6 Cover of *Rebecca*, by Gary Blyth (Arrow, 1992).

with a cover featuring the nameless narrator, looking young and vulnerable, with Manderley behind her, staring into the distance in a state of what appears to be sadness and emotional confusion. Interestingly, both her hairstyle and her clothes can be 'read' as belonging to a much earlier period than the between-the-wars setting of du Maurier's novel – unlike the Pan edition which, although it also features the narrator looking hurt and confused (her brow is furrowed and she, too, looks anxiously into the distance), has her sporting a neat 1930s hairstyle and wearing a 'Peter Pan' blouse suggestive of the period. The historical vagueness of Arrow's cover, together with the representation of Manderley as a rather mysterious-looking building in the background, hint at the Gothic genre, although the words 'Her world-famous bestseller of romantic suspense', printed on the front cover, ensure that the notion of romance (in the more modern sense of the love story), as well as that of suspense, is foregrounded. Arrow's covers for their editions of du Maurier novels are clearly designed to appeal to the reader of popular

7 Cover of *Rebecca* (Pan, 1975).

8 Cover of *Rebecca*, by Peter Reddick (Penguin, 1962).

fiction: each cover carries the title in black or white wording, but the author's name is given more visual prominence, being picked out in larger gold letters which are edged in white or blue. The reader, it is hoped, will – like the reader of Victoria Holt or Danielle Steele – move on from one du Maurier title to the next and be quick to both recognise and pick up another of her works from a bookshop shelf or station stand. Arrow also adopt the common practice of bringing other works by the same author to the reader's attention on the last page or so: their edition of *The Rendezvous and Other Stories* (1994), for example, advertises *Mary Anne, Rebecca, Frenchman's Creek* and *My Cousin Rachel*, amongst other du Maurier novels. However, accuracy of description gives way to formulaic cliché in the rather poorly written 'trailer' for *Rebecca*:

> 'Last night I dreamt I went to Manderley again ...'. One of the most appealing heroines in all of fiction, with a special magic that enthrals every reader.
> *Rebecca* is known to millions through its outstandingly successful stage and screen versions; and the characters in this timeless romance are hauntingly real ...

The notion of the novel as 'timeless' is open to debate as, indeed, is the idea that its narrator is 'one of the most appealing heroines in all of fiction' (many young women readers, in our experience, find her intensely irritating as a character although they may well identify with her state of emotional insecurity).

Rebecca, like many works by women writers, is a generically hybrid novel, although publishing and marketing strategies have sometimes confined it to a particular generic category. Indeed, it has probably been the intrinsic hybridity of the novel itself which has allowed different publishers to inflect their marketing strategies so successfully, according to their particular publishing mission. This, in turn, has occasionally influenced critical reception and understanding: Sheila Holland (whose pen-name is 'Charlotte Lamb'), in her obituary for du Maurier (published in the *Guardian* in April 1989), described *Rebecca* as 'the archetypal romantic novel' (Light, 1991: 158). However, it is clear, as more discerning readers such as Alison Light have established, that du Maurier's fiction is anything but archetypal romance. Interestingly, more recent re-assessments of du Maurier have cautiously included her in the canon of modern literature by categorising her as a writer of the Gothic. Andrew Michael Roberts, for example, in his recent survey of the modern novel, defines her primarily as a Gothic writer (Roberts, 1993: 136). This perception of du Maurier's authorial standing and writing identity probably owes as much to the recent upsurge of interest in the Gothic within academic circles as to inherent elements of the Gothic in du Maurier's writing.

The public identity of the woman writer, then, is constructed through the reception of her work. This itself, however, is subject to a complex set of inter-relating forces which are constantly changing. Amongst these must be counted marketing and publishing strategies, which exert no little influence over the way her work is perceived, and over which she may have little control. As she grew older, du Maurier herself became more aware of the power and influence of these strategies, commenting, for example, in a letter written to Oriel Malet in 1962 that:

> Publishers are all the same. They think of nothing but sales, and unless they've made a whack out of a book, it just gets wiped off and forgotten, no matter how good the reviews. I don't think I had any bad reviews for my Branwell, but right from the start I know old V. G. was bored by the thought of it, and he never made any effort to push it after it was published ... Now, of course, he's all over me again, because he hopes *The Glass-Blowers* will do well. (Malet, 1993: 138) [12]

The case-history of *Rebecca* is one which clearly illustrates how far publishing and marketing strategies influence reader response and critical reception. Daphne du Maurier's identity as a writer continues to develop as her work is revisited with the new perspectives offered by the changing nature of literary scholarship. The progress of du Maurier's most famous novel suggests that the marketing of books is an important element in the 'making' of a literary text, and one which no modern-day critic can afford to ignore.

Notes

1 We would like to thank Jane Blackstock of Victor Gollancz Ltd for allowing us access to letters and documents held by the publishing company. Unless attributed otherwise, all letters and documents referred to in this chapter are held by Victor Gollancz Ltd. We are also grateful to Barbara Smith of Doubleday (London Office) for sending us copies of letters concerning the publication of *Rebecca* in the United States. Thanks are due to Curtis Brown, literary agents for the estate of Daphne de Maurier, for permission to quote from published and unpublished letters, and to Lloyd Dorfman, who allowed

access to unpublished correspondence between Daphne du Maurier and Meaburn Staniland of Penguin

2 Lyn Pykett lists the following as the main elements of the mid-Victorian sensation novel: 'the construction and unravelling of an intricate, cross-word puzzle plot; the atmospheric scene; the mysterious, prophetic dream; obsessive and disordered mental states; overtly respectable villains; and bold, assertive and/or devious and scheming heroines and villainesses'. She adds that 'Secretiveness is not only the structuring principle of the sensation plot, it is also its origin, and its subject' (Pykett, 1994: 14). Since *Rebecca* would seem, superficially at least, to have much in common with the sensation novel, it is not surprising that Collins perceived it in this way.

3 Cf. Alison Light's comment on the rise of an 'erotic literature written by women for a female audience' between the wars, which she describes as drawing on other, often more aggressive, cultures 'in order to imagine female pleasure'. She gives, as a primary example, E. M. Hull's *The Sheikh*, published in 1919, which allows its transgressive heroine to go unpunished and which, in so doing, affronted contemporary bourgeois sensibility (Light, 1991: 175). In 1926 the book was made into the famous film which starred Rudolph Valentino as the sheikh.

4 See Sheila Hodges, who claims that Gollancz excelled at publicity campaigns (Hodges, 1978: 72), and John Sutherland, who describes Gollancz as displaying 'a new flair in publicity' in the 1920s 'with imaginative "stunts", bold advertising and the famous eyecatching yellow covers' (Sutherland, 1981: 25). See also Ruth Dudley Edwards (1987: 168). Writing to Norman Collins on 31 January 1939, Malcolm Johnson (of Doubleday in the United States) notes that the Gollancz Book Catalogue for New Year 1939 is 'as interesting as a book ... I wonder if all the rest of us aren't missing a bet, and an important one, by clinging to more pedestrian forms' (unpublished letter held by Doubleday's London Office).

5 She was not the only one to have reservations about the Gollancz book jackets: 'The jackets were, however, unpopular with many of the booksellers, who also disliked them (as did the librarians) because the "blurbs" often failed to fulfil their function of providing much indication of what the book was about' (Hodges, 1978: 36).

6 Despite du Maurier's own insistence on the significance of Rebecca's handwriting, it is only recently that critics have become interested in the symbolic significance of Rebecca's handwriting in du Maurier's novel. See, for example, Allan Lloyd Smith (1992) and the chapter on *Rebecca* in Horner and Zlosnik (1997).

7 Norman Collins and Victor Gollancz refer to 'English' sales when quoting figures for *Rebecca* in correspondence with, for example, Malcolm Johnson of Doubleday in the United States; it is not clear to us, however, whether these refer to sales within England or the UK.

8 Information contained in an unpublished letter, dated 6 December 1938,

from Malcolm Johnson to du Maurier. The letter is held by Doubleday (London Office).
9 Information contained in an unpublished letter from Nelson Doubleday to du Maurier, dated 12 March 1940 and held by Doubleday (London Office).
10 See Forster (1993: 321).
11 See, for example, Alison Light (1984) (later revised and incorporated in *Forever England*, 1991) and Roger Bromley (1986).
12 'Branwell' here refers to *The Infernal World of Branwell Brontë* published by Gollancz in 1960; *The Glass-Blowers* was published by Gollancz in 1963.

References

'Archangels Ruined' (1962) *Times Literary Supplement*, 3, 164 (19 October), 808.
Bromley, Roger (1986) 'The gentry, bourgeois hegemony and popular fiction: *Rebecca* and *Rogue Male*' in Humm, P. , Stigant, P. and Widdowson, P. (eds), *Popular Fictions: Essays in Literature and History*, London, Methuen.
Edwards, Ruth Dudley (1987) *Victor Gollancz: A Biography*, London, Victor Gollancz.
Forster, Margaret (1993) *Daphne du Maurier*, London, Chatto & Windus.
Hodges, Sheila (1978) *Gollancz: The Story of a Publishing House*, London, Victor Gollancz.
Horner, Avril and Zlosnik, Sue (1997) *Daphne du Maurier: Writing, Identity and the Gothic Imagination*, London, Macmillan.
Light, Alison (1984) '"Returning to Manderley": Romance Fiction, Female Sexuality and Class', *Feminist Review*, 16 (Summer).
—— (1991) *Forever England: Femininity, Literature and Conservatism between the Wars*, London, Routledge.
Malet, Oriel (1993) *Letters from Menabilly: Portrait of a Friendship* (edited selection of letters written by Daphne du Maurier to Oriel Malet), London, Weidenfeld and Nicolson.
McAleer, Joseph (1992) *Popular Reading and Publishing in Britain 1914–1950*, Oxford, Clarendon Press.
Pykett, Lyn (1994) *The Sensation Novel: From 'The Woman in White' to 'The Moonstone'*, Plymouth, Northcote House in association with the British Council ('Writers and their Work' series).
Roberts, Andrew Michael (1993) *The Novel*, London, Bloomsbury.
Smith, Allan Lloyd (1992) 'The Phantoms of *Drood* and *Rebecca*: The Uncanny Reencountered through Abraham and Torok's "Cryptonomy"', *Poetics Today*, 13: 2 (Summer), 285–308.
Sutherland, John (1981) *Bestsellers: Popular Fiction of the 1970s*, London, Routledge & Kegan Paul.

4

Marketing the 'woman writer'

Clare Hanson

The term 'woman writer' is a profoundly problematic one. The qualifier 'woman' suggests a concentration on the feminine sphere, which is generally construed as the private, the domestic and, perhaps, the everyday. To be classed as a woman writer is thus to have one's broader (or 'universal') artistic status compromised. Writers who have been classified in this way have responded in varying ways to this difficulty. Some, such as Margaret Drabble, have accepted the term bravely and in a positive spirit. In 1973 she wrote: 'I think I hold the position that as there is nothing wrong with being a woman (a bold enough statement in some ways) so there is nothing wrong with being a woman writer' (Drabble, [1973] 1983: 156). Others, such as Drabble's sister, A. S. Byatt, have resisted the term. In a 1986 review, while welcoming in general terms the 'resuscitation of women's novels', Byatt warned against the dangers of over-valuing such books. Her remarks are interesting because she links this revival of women's novels with 'the flowering of Virago and the rehabilitation of the library novel and good read' (Byatt, [1991] 1993a: 268). Some of the novels which I want to consider in this essay are exactly the kind of fiction Byatt is referring to. They are archetypal Virago Modern Classics, novels which sold well in their day and which are having a repeat success with a readership very similar in composition to their first readership. Byatt's remarks are the more interesting because she herself is classed in the category of the 'woman writer' in Hilary Radner's essay on the middle-brow novel which I'll be turning to in a moment. In warning against 'the woman writer', Byatt might seem to be warning against herself. Why should this be so?

I want to return to Byatt at the end of this chapter, but my immediate focus is on women writers of the period 1930–60, that is, in the period immediately after modernism. The modernist period was a difficult one for women writers: critics such as Janet Wolff and Elizabeth Wilson have discussed at some length the social factors which contributed to women's exclusion from the modernist avant-garde.[1] In a recent article Bridget Fowler has made the further point that gender was a key term in underwriting the modernist distinction between high art and mass culture (Fowler, 1995: 91). The boundary between these two, she suggests, could be reinforced by such measures as 'the stigmatization of the kitsch women read'. (She cites Flaubert's stigmatisation of the romance-reading Emma Bovary: one could equally well cite Joyce's representation of Gerty McDowell in *Ulysses*.) For Fowler, it was the association of women with mass culture which had the effect of marginalising them within modernism. The fact that women were marginalised can be confirmed by even the most cursory reading of such critical studies as Bonnie Kime Scott's anthology *The Gender of Modernism*, or Suzanne Clarke's *Sentimental Modernism*. Yet it was in the period immediately after this that 'the woman writer' re-emerged as a powerful and distinct phenomenon.

'The woman writer' is defined by Radner as an educated middle-class woman writing for women like herself (Radner, 1995: 106). In the light of this definition, I want to argue that the rise of 'the woman writer' after modernism can be attributed in part to the rapid increase in the female middle-class reading public in the 1930s and 1940s. This increase was caused by a combination of wider educational opportunities and changing patterns of leisure. Nicola Beauman has stressed too the importance of the circulating library in bringing books to women readers (Beauman, 1983: 9–10). The turnover of the circulating library gives some impression of the level of demand: 25 million volumes were exchanged among Boots libraries in 1925 and 35 million by the time of the outbreak of the Second World War. Different libraries served different class interests, with Boots catering for the 'middle-brow' reader, smaller libraries like Mudie's or Day's for such 'high-brow' readers as Virginia Woolf. The rise of 'the woman writer' can then be linked with social and demographic changes and with the growth of new markets. However, Bridget Fowler also makes the point that we should take into account the 'refugee' factor in the creation of 'the woman writer'. She suggests that because women writers were rejected by the serious literary world in the modernist period, many potentially 'serious' writers turned to popular forms. She shows that among twentieth-century women writers of the Gothic and of romance, a much higher proportion than might be expected had a university education: 33 per cent of British writers, 72 per cent of American writers. Such writers had some 'cultural capital', she argues, but, failing to gain entry to the legitimate literary world, transferred their skills to the popular market. Male writers in a similar position would be less likely to do this, as the mass markets were so strongly associated with a devalued femininity. While Fowler is considering writers of popular rather than middle-brow texts, her argument perhaps applies with even more force to writers of the latter, amongst whom 'women writers' must be counted.

In her essay 'Exiled from Within: The Woman's Novel'(1989), Radner offers a definition of the 'woman's novel' as a specific category. She begins by distinguishing between canonical and popular texts, which she suggests are read in contrasting ways. Canonical literary texts, like Barthes's writerly texts, demand an active and initiated reader who decodes them. She argues that this represents a kind of 'obsessional' reading: 'By analyzing the text, the reader dissects, reworks, and re-writes the narrative, each time recreating anew another narrative in his own image – reinscribing the enigma in his own terms as a sign of his position of mastery' (Radner, 1989: 254). Popular texts, on the other hand, invite a 'hysterical' reader, who takes pleasure in the textual experience (or symptom) for its own sake. Such texts often involve repetition, as in formula romance, which the reader does not read for the plot but for the pleasure of reading as process. 'The process has no ostensible goal except its own replication' (Radner, 1989: 253). Having made this distinction (which is as much to do with reading practices as with textual features), Radner goes on to argue that one genre which challenges this distinction is the woman's novel:

> This novel stubbornly rejects the status of high art. It is adamantly not against interpretation and demands to be understood in terms of its content. The woman's novel says, by and large, what it means to say, refusing to reveal its secrets under the scrutiny of the analyst by displaying these last for all to see, literati and nonliterati alike. Yet the richness of its language, the subtlety of its arguments, and its undeniable intelligence and self-consciousness defy the classification of popular culture. (Radner, 1989: 256)

The woman's novel invites, simultaneously, two kinds of reading. On the one hand it offers the pleasure of interpretation and decoding by virtue of its representation of social and pychological issues, its grounding in historical and political reality and so on. On the other, it offers the kind of identificatory reading pleasure most reminiscent of the romance.

Obviously, this definition is not exhaustive, but it offers a starting point for discussion of a cultural form which has been overlooked in critical debate. In view of the historical context, it is worth noting Radner's point that the woman's novel confounds the categories of high modernism – perhaps it reacts to these categories? It is also significant that Radner illustrates her argument through discussion of a novel by Rebecca Goldstein entitled *The Mind-Body Problem: A Novel* (1983). Goldstein wrote this novel as a narrative reply to 'the impossibility of a philosophical epistemology that would resolve the ontological paradox of the mind-body problem' (Radner, 1989: 258–9). This was the topic of Goldstein's own doctoral dissertation, and it is also that of the novel's heroine. The novel attempts to bring together the analytic framework of philosophy and experience that cannot be understood within academic discourse. The novel thus represents, Radner suggests, a point of intersection between dominant or masculine discursive practice and occulted or feminine discursive practice. The heroine of *The Mind-Body Problem* moves between these two poles, between a discourse which does not represent her and experience which it is difficult to represent. Such experience is often the daily experience of the body – precisely the kind of experience which was occulted in modernist texts by women. Nicola Beauman has pointed to this lack of representation of the bodily in modernist texts by women. As she suggests: 'We would be enchanted to find a novel written in the 1920s or 1930s which actually told us how a woman organised contraception. How did Mrs Dalloway hold up her stockings? What did the breast-feeding mother do about milk leaking on to her dress?' (Beauman, 1983: 98). In representing the quotidian experience of women, Goldstein's novel challenges such an occluding of the female body. The fact that her heroine is a female academic allows her to represent a woman who can deploy both the masculine discourse of mastery and a feminine discursive practice.

Radner sees women's novels as posing an interpretive problem because they cannot be read either as canonical or as popular texts. She argues that the woman's novel thus always remains 'out-of-category', a position which she sees negatively. The hybridity of the form prevents any satisfactory narrative resolution: 'In other words, the "out of category" romance in the form of the woman's novel tends to reproduce its position as out-of-category for its reader – who is thus confirmed in her "exile"' (Radner, 1995: 114). I would suggest instead that the hybridity of the form and its lack of narrative resolution are integral to the challenge which it offers to the divisions between high and low culture, masculine and feminine, the transcendent and the bodily. I want to explore this argument first in relation to earlier twentieth-century women writers, before returning to contemporaries such as A. S. Byatt. The earlier writers I have in mind are such writers as Rosamond Lehmann, Elizabeth Bowen, Antonia White and Elizabeth Taylor. These were all educated and professional writers working in the realist mode, whose writing, while it does not have canonical status, does not fit into the category of popular literature either. Their novels sold well and achieved a wide circulation, often through being reprinted as Book Club or Reprint Society editions within a year or two of first publication. They were also favourites at circulating libraries. They were, then, widely read, mainly by middle-class women.[2] The initial success of many of these novels was repeated when they were reprinted by Virago during the 1970s and 1980s, finding a new readership of educated, middle-class women.

Considerations of space prevent me from looking in sufficient detail at more than one of the writers mentioned above. The novelist I want to focus on is Elizabeth Taylor, whose work is in many ways exemplary. Taylor (1912–75) was first published in the 1940s, winning discriminating praise from contemporaries and friends such as Elizabeth Bowen and Ivy Compton Burnett. Her novels and short stories began to be republished by Virago in the 1970s, and are still widely available. Taylor is especially interesting for my purposes because she so clearly identified herself as a 'woman writer'. For example, in a rare autobiographical sketch, she seems as much concerned to place herself within the conventional narrative of femininity as to stake out her artistic territory. In the first two paragraphs of her article she spends considerable time documenting her position as a representative middle-class wife and mother, stressing her ordinariness and her love of the domestic and the everyday:

> I was married in 1936 and we live now in the village of Penn in Buckinghamshire. We have two children – a son, Renny, who is sixteen, and a daughter, Joanna, who is twelve. I am always disconcerted when I am asked for my life story, for nothing sensational, thank heavens, has ever

happened. I dislike much travel or change of environment, and prefer the days (each with its own domestic flavor) to come round almost the same, week after week. Only in such circumstances can I find time or peace in which to write. I also very much like reading books in which practically nothing ever happens. (Taylor, [1945] 1988: v)

Taylor thus identified herself with, rather than repudiating, the 'feminine' sphere, and it seems to have been this identification with femininity which annoyed early critics of her work. In his memoir, *Elizabeth and Ivy* (1986), Robert Liddell recalls that around the time of publication of *A Wreath of Roses* ([1949] 1950), Taylor roused the hostility of some women reviewers: 'It was about this time that Elizabeth's growing reputation began to attract the envy and malice of reviewers. "Feminine, feminine!" cried the manlier sort of lady novelist' (Liddell, 1986: 39). Some years later, in a review of her collection *The Blush and Other Stories*, a male reviewer, Anthony Quinton, took Taylor to task for being able to write for such diverse outlets as the *New Yorker* on the one hand and *Woman's Own* on the other. Of Taylor's stories he wrote:

For the popular mass-circulation women's magazines she provides either their usual pabulum most competently dressed up (as in a story of a man making a last painful visit to the child-garnished woman he loves where they are unable to speak of their great renunciation) or variations on well-established themes (the plain girl at the dance). Satirical matter is reserved for more selected audiences. (Quinton, 1959: 70)

Robert Liddell astutely comments that this reviewer, while finding Taylor's stories penetrating and subtle, 'could not forgive Elizabeth for her good fortune in being able to please the simple as well as the highbrow reader. This is enviable good luck, and financially profitable' (Liddell, 1986: 76). Several things seem to come together here. It is felt that it is in some sense Taylor's concentration on the 'feminine' sphere which makes her work appeal to a wide audience. The 'feminine' is again linked with the popular, and the novels become contaminated because of the connection with mass culture and also, perhaps, because of the financial success which they bring for their author.

Taylor's novel *A Wreath of Roses* ([1949] 1950) foregrounds such problems, anxiously exploring the status of Taylor's 'feminine' art. The central character is Frances Rutherford, an elderly painter who has come to doubt herself and her life's work. She feels that she has, perhaps, failed to explore the violence which is at the core of life, and has retreated instead into a ladylike 'sentimentality'. In this mood, she thinks despondently about her paintings. It is worth quoting the passage in full, because it is so relevant to Taylor's own project:

> She closed her eyes and bunches of roses were printed for an instant, startlingly white upon the darkness, then faded, as the darkness itself paled, the sun from the window coming brilliantly through her lids. Trying to check life itself, she thought, to make some of the hurrying everyday things immortal, to paint the every day things with tenderness and intimacy – the dirty cafe with its pock-marked mirrors as if they had been shot at, its curly hat-stands, its stained marble under the yellow light; wet pavements; an old woman yawning. With tenderness and intimacy. With sentimentality, too, she wondered. For was I not guilty of making ugliness charming? (Taylor, [1949] 1950: 45–46)

Here Frances presents a text-book description of 'the woman writer', transposed into the terms of visual art. Frances's paintings focus on the everyday and the evanescent, the 'hurrying' things which must be seen not dispassionately but from a perspective which acknowledges the painter's own knowledge of and complicity with them. Her paintings also accommodate the dirty, the 'stained' and 'pock-marked', and the ageing female body – 'an old woman yawning'. What Frances does is to 'make ugliness charming' to the extent that she shows the messily contingent to be both acceptable and meaningful. Compare Radner on what she calls a sub-category of 'the woman's novel', the dissertation novel: 'as a dirty genre, the dissertation novel produces an imperfect discourse that actively engages in the messiness, the "out of category" nature of the quotidian experiences of its readers' (Radner, 1995: 108).

The roses Frances sees at the beginning of the passage quoted are the roses on her bedroom wallpaper, which she is beginning to detest, perhaps because they remind her of her paintings. The image of the roses is seamed through the text and occurs also in the epigraph, which is a quotation from Virginia Woolf's *The Waves*: 'So terrible was life that I held up shade after shade. Look at life through this, look at life through that; let there be rose leaves, let there be vine leaves – I covered the whole street, Oxford Street, Piccadilly Circus, with the blaze and ripple of my mind, with vine leaves and rose leaves.' This haunting epigraph could be read as endorsing Frances's view of the inadequacy of her 'woman's art', but I would suggest that it functions in a more complex way. In citing Woolf, Taylor is claiming 'canonical' or 'high-brow' antecedents for her work, a move which Radner sees as typical of 'the woman's novel'. But she is also, perhaps, offering a critique of the canonical and of Woolf. After all, the passage quoted comes from the section in *The Waves* in which Rhoda foresees her death, which is, of course, a death by suicide. By the end of Taylor's novel there are clear indications that Frances is also in a suicidal state. (An abortive painting, for example, is compared to Ophelia's 'last terrible gesture but one'.) We could thus read Frances's jaundiced view of her art as the product of despair, and her desire to move beyond such art – like Woolf's desire to move beyond the mundane and contingent? – as similarly founded on despair. Taylor's novel could then be seen as articulating and measuring the differences between two kinds of art. One would be that produced by Woolf, striving for transcendence and a disavowal of the 'terrible' aspects of life. The other would be that practised by Frances, an art of acceptance which accommodates the contingencies of life and death.

In the novel, the argument for Frances's kind of art is put by a character called Morland Beddoes, a film director and another artist working in the medium of the contingent, who has been inspired by Frances's paintings. As he thinks of her work, his point of view merges with that of the narrator:

> There are great paintings which are for everybody, and then there are lesser pictures which will reflect light only here and there, rather capriciously, to individuals. Life itself shifts round a little, and what we had thought all whiteness, or all darkness, flashes suddenly, from this new angle, with violet and green and vermilion. So that old picture of Liz sitting on the sofa, seen through the rain-washed window, turned life a little under his very eyes, put beauty over the people in the streets, the dwarf, and a woman with dyed hair standing in a doorway. (Taylor, [1949] 1950: 130–1)

I think that what Taylor is doing here is to articulate a painful distinction between her own art and that of the canonical texts of high modernism. Taylor is aware of all the attractions of this 'high' art, which haunts her text through the allusions to Woolf. Reluctantly, however, she distances herself from it in favour of an art which will be seen as lesser but which is more faithful to the contingent, to the ugly, to 'the dwarf and a woman with dyed hair'. *A Wreath of Roses*, like many other novels written by women in this period, thus offers a critique of the transcendent art of modernism which, as I suggested earlier, presents particular problems for the woman artist because of its occulting of the female body. Identified with the desired/feared body, how could a woman artist ever achieve the state of transcendence necessary to the production of 'great' art?

Taylor did not like *A Wreath of Roses*, according to Robert Liddell; A. S. Byatt does not much like 'women's novels'. There is a good deal of anxiety, among those who have 'cultural capital', about the decision to write 'women's novels' which combine intellectual seriousness with a commitment to the feminine sphere. The refusal of writers like Taylor to relinquish their 'feminine' status is precisely what has made them unpopular among some feminist critics – Elizabeth Wilson, for example, has written disparagingly about Lehmann, Bowen and Taylor.[3] I would argue, however, that there is a critical and even radical element in the representation of feminine experience in the fiction of these writers. As I have suggested above, the daily, contingent, bodily experience of women is elided in modernist texts by women. Woolf herself acknowledged in 'Professions for Women' (1931, in Woolf 1942) that she had failed to solve the problem of 'telling the truth about my own experiences as a body'. The 'dirty genre' of the woman's novel tells such truths, critically examining the consequences of women's entrapment in bodies which are endlessly interpreted in ways outside their control. In consequence, I want to suggest that marketing the woman writer can be viewed as an ideologically sound practice, even for a feminist publishing company such as Virago. In other words, to borrow terms from Rosalind Coward's well-known article, women's novels can indeed be feminist novels. Coward argues that 'woman centred' novels have no necessary relationship to feminism, and also that 'feminism can never be the product of the identity of women's experiences and interests' (Coward, [1980] 1986: 238). The first of these claims rests on a rather narrow definition of feminism, and the second is extremely problematic. While many recent interventions in feminist theory have usefully drawn attention to the different ways in which women may experience oppression, there is a danger, as Kate Soper has pointed out, that the postmodern emphasis on difference will destroy feminism as a political movement. Like any other politics, Soper argues, feminism has implied a banding together of women 'who are linked by perhaps very little else than their *sameness* and "common cause" as women' (Eagleton 1996: 364). If

Soper is right, then it could be argued that the woman's novel performs a particularly valuable function in articulating experiences, longings and fears which are gender-specific and which cut across differences of class, of sexuality and perhaps even of nation. The middle-class woman's novel might be seen, then, as offering a 'protected space' in which topics which do not feature in any other form of artistic production can be explored. Of particular importance are issues relevant to the life of the female body and the ways in which that body is interpreted. In relation to such issues, the woman's novel has a role to play both in passing on information (Doris Lessing suggests in her introduction to *The Golden Notebook* that we read mainly in order to find things out) and in offering a critique of existing artistic and social practices.

I want to finish by examining, briefly, two contemporary writers. A. S. Byatt is an exemplary 'woman writer' in Radner's terms, having every possible academic and literary credential while also being committed to the realist mode and concentrating primarily on women's experience. The text I want to focus on is *The Matisse Stories*. This collection of stories was published by Chatto and Windus in 1993, and has been strongly marketed as a 'high' cultural text. The cover reproduces three paintings by Matisse on a blue ground, and even incorporates Matisse's signature in the title design. The book thus advertises its affiliations with high culture, yet it also offers, perhaps unwillingly, a critique of such culture. The first story in the collection, 'Medusa's Ankles', opens with a description of Matisse's *Le Nu Rose*, which catches the eye of the central character when she sees a reproduction of it hanging on the wall in a hairdressing salon. The painting is represented as a great painting, statuesque, universal: 'The rosy nude was pure flat colour, but suggested mass. She had huge haunches and a monumental knee, lazily propped high. She had round breasts, contemplations of the circle, reflections on flesh and its fall' (Byatt, 1993b: 3). Intimations of decay and mortality are held within the harmony of the painting, which thus offers transcendence. As the story progresses, however, a very different female figure comes into view, the figure of the middle-aged narrator, who has 'trusted' the hairdresser with her own physical deterioration. The story documents her slow rage over her own disintegration, and her sense of incredulity, her inability to reconcile her sense of self and her body: 'And this, too, now, she wanted to accept for her face, trained in a respect for precision, and could not. What had left this greying skin, these flakes, these fragile stretches with no elasticity, was her, was her life, was herself' (Byatt, 1993b: 19). She feels betrayed by her body, or rather by the ways in which it is interpreted. All her sense of self, her talents and experience, can be negated because of their embodiment in a middle-aged woman: 'She was in a panic of fear about the television, which had come too late, when she had lost the desire to be seen or looked at. The cameras search jowl and eye-pocket, expose brush stroke and cracks in shadow and gloss. So interesting are their revelations that words, mere words, go for nothing, fly by' (Byatt, 1993b: 19–20). I do not think that Byatt intended her story to function as a critique of Matisse's work. Nonetheless, the abiding impression left by this story is one of rage, which is partly bound up with a sense that the experience which it documents is not, in any sense, allowed into the world of Matisse's art. Indeed, I would argue that throughout Byatt's fiction we see a tension between the claims of 'high' art and the claims of daily life and bodily experience which cannot be represented in it. This is true of *Still Life*, I would sugggest, and also of the other stories in *The Matisse Stories*. 'Art Work', for example, offers a richly comic contrast between the painstaking and abstract(ed) male painter, Robin Dennison, and the cleaning lady who turns out to be an artist too. An interviewer tells us that her work, which is literally made out of rubbish, is: 'full of feminist comments on the trivia of our daily life, on the boredom of the quotidian, but she has no sour reflections, no chip on her shoulder, she simply makes everything absurd but sur-prisingly beautiful with an excess of inventive wit' (Byatt, 1993b: 83). In 'The Chinese Lobster', the last story in the collection, the transcend-ent, universal power of Matisse's art is strongly asserted, but we are given an alternative point of view through the figure of a feminist art student who is preparing a critique of his work. While her perspective is emphatically not endorsed by Byatt, it is profoundly disruptive, largely because the student's dislike of Matisse, and of his representations of the female body, is linked with her anorexia. The anorexia functions as a disturbing reminder of the real dangers attendant on cultural idealisa-tion of the female form. Almost against her will, it seems, Byatt thus occupies the middle ground of the woman writer, worrying at the dis-tinction between 'great' art and the art of everyday life.

Anita Brookner is another contemporary woman writer to occupy this ground, less reluctantly than Byatt. Brookner has declared that 'the women novelists I really admire in the English tradition are Rosamond Lehmann and Elizabeth Taylor' (Brookner, 1985: 71). She writes novels in this tradition: they are well-crafted and serious, but also sell widely. Their hybrid status is often explicitly signalled and acknowledged within the text. In the Booker Prize-winning *Hotel du Lac*, for example, the heroine, Edith Hope, bears a physical resemblance to Virginia Woolf (which is frequently mentioned) but writes romantic fiction. Brookner's text inhabits the space between these two extremes. Brookner does not offer the happy ending which invariably characterises Edith Hope's novels, but nor does she claim the universality of statement of great literature. In an interview, she makes an interesting comment on the 'truths' of great literature which might have implications for her own work: 'I think the lessons taught in great books are misleading. The commerce in life is rarely so simple and never so just. The appreciations are more short-term in life; there isn't the same impetus to see it through. There is in fact no selection in life – one takes opportunities and amusement where one can – it's accumulative, if you like, piecemeal' (Brookner, 1985: 66). Brookner's fiction concentrates on the contingent, on the 'accumulative' and 'piecemeal' nature of the experiences to which her heroines are subject.

Hotel du Lac, like all Brookner's novels, explores the question of 'what behaviour most becomes a woman'. In particular, the novel explores the ideology of romantic love, which is endorsed by the heroine (and by Brookner herself, in interview), but which is shown in the novel to have profoundly damaging effects. This ideology offers a script for women in which only the young and attractive can find happiness and fulfilment: unattractive or older women have no significant place in the scheme. Accordingly, Edith is pushed to the margins of her lover's life because she is not sufficiently attractive to tempt him to leave his wife. Rejecting two other men, she risks looking 'a bit of a fool' as an ageing, unmarried woman. She is not the only miserable woman staying at the punningly named Hotel du Lac. All the other women are neglected or dispossessed in some way. The beautiful and glamorous Monica has been banished there by her aristocratic husband because she has been unable to produce an heir. If she fails to 'get herself into working order' she will be 'given her cards and told to vacate the premises' so that her husband can make alternative arrangements. Monica responds by developing an eating disorder, punishing the body which has let her down. Monica is sympathetically presented, as is Mme Bonneuil, lame and deaf, forced out of her home by her son and his wife, condemned to a life of loneliness and alienation. The reader feels sympathy even for the greedy and selfish Mrs Pusey, who at seventy-nine manages to keep herself going only by maintaining an appearance of youthful femininity. When Edith first sees her she strikes a note of 'unexpected glamour ... a lady of indeterminate age, her hair radiantly ash blonde, her nails scarlet, her dress a charming ... printed silk' (Brookner, [1984] 1995: 17). However, even Mrs Pusey betrays a fear of death which she must distance 'until her momentary weakness is clearly seen as being *someone else's fault*, and in that way the shadow of her mortality will be exorcised' (Brookner, [1984] 1995: 143).

Brookner's novel does not so much 'teach lessons' as explore the tension between Romantic/romantic ideals and the messy contingencies of life. Edith Hope is imbued with ideals about love which are explicitly connected with the Romantic movement in painting. When she first meets her lover, David, and he speaks of getting back to 'the Rooms' (his auction rooms), Edith thinks of Delacroix: 'She turned the amazing sentence over in her mind, conjuring up vistas of courtyards with fountains trickling and silent servants in gauze trousers bringing sherbet. Or possibly large divans in whitewashed houses shuttered against the heat of the afternoon, a dreaming, glowing idleness, inspired by Delacroix' (Brookner, [1984] 1995: 56). Edith's Romanticism is echoed by Mrs Pusey's romanticism, offering a debased and parodic version of Edith's ideals: ' "Yes," she went on ... "I'm afraid I'm a romantic." ... Here we go, thought Edith, swallowing a tiny yawn. "Love means marriage to me," pursued Mrs Pusey. "Romance and courtship go together. A woman should be able to make a man worship her"' (Brookner, [1984] 1995: 73–4). Against these ideals, Brookner sets the contingencies of bodily, material life, showing the disjunction between ideal representations of the feminine (as in the 'harem' paintings of Delacroix) and the actual experience of female embodiment (the problems of infertility, ageing and so on). Against the 'lessons' of great books she offers, perhaps, a woman's realism. Asked whether she minded being described as a 'woman's novelist', Brookner had this to say in an interview:

Not in the least. Women have devoted themselves to a certain kind of storytelling, which is extremely valid and extremely absorbing; mainly to other women, but to men as well, I think. It's quite a different genre. It does limit itself, but it tends to go deeper. Also it's full of information. Women tend to read novels for information – and to learn about other women, so the novel fulfils a particular function if it's written by a woman for other women. (Brookner, 1989: 22)

Brookner is happy to align herself with a separate tradition of the 'woman's novel', conveying information and dealing with experience which is not represented elsewhere. While her work does not address the problems of working-class women or women of colour, within its white middle-class confines Brookner's fiction, like that of Byatt, persistently questions the elitism of 'high' art from a gendered perspective.

Notes

1 See Wilson, Elizabeth (1992) 'The Invisible Flaneur', *New Left Review*, 191; Wolff, Janet (1985) 'The Invisible Flaneuse: Women and the Literature of Modernity', *Theory, Culture and Society*, 2:3.
2 See Beauman (1983), pp. 173–4.
3 See Wilson, Elizabeth (1980) *Only Halfway to Paradise: Women in Postwar Britain, 1945–68*, London: Tavistock Publications.

References

Beauman, Nicola (1983) *A Very Great Profession: The Woman's Novel 1914–39*, London: Virago.

Brookner, Anita ([1984] 1995) *Hotel du Lac*, London: Triad/Panther.

——— (1985) 'Interview' in John Haffenden, *Novelists in Interview*, London: Methuen.

——— (1989) 'Interview' in Olga Kenyon, *Women Writers Talk*, Oxford: Lennard Publishing.

Byatt, A. S. (1985) *Still Life*, London: Chatto & Windus.

——— ([1991] 1993a) *Passions of the Mind: Selected Writings*, London: Vintage.

——— (1993b) *The Matisse Stories*, London: Chatto & Windus.

Clark, Suzanne (1991) *Sentimental Modernism: Women Writers and the Revolution of the Word*, Bloomington, Indiana: Indiana University Press.

Coward, Rosalind ([1980] 1986) 'Are Women's Novels Feminist Novels?', repr. in Elaine Showalter (ed.), *The New Feminist Criticism*, London: Virago.

Drabble, Margaret ([1973] 1983) 'A Woman Writer', repr. in Michelene Wandor (ed.), *On Gender and Writing*, London: Pandora.

Fowler, Bridget (1995) 'Literature Beyond Modernism: Middlebrow and Popular Romance', in Lynne Pearce and Jackie Stacey (eds), *Romance Revisited*, London: Lawrence and Wishart.

Lessing, D. (1962) *The Golden Notebook*, London: Michael Joseph.

Liddell, Robert (1986) *Elizabeth and Ivy*, London: Peter Owen.

Quinton, Anthony (1959) review of Elizabeth Taylor 'The Blush and Other Stories', *London Magazine* 6:6.

Radner, Hilary (1989) 'Exiled from Within: The Woman's Novel', in Mary Lynne

Broe and Angela Ingram (eds), *Women's Writing in Exile*, Chapel Hill and London: University of North Carolina Press.

—— (1995) '"Out of Category": The Middlebrow Novel', in *Shopping Around: Female Culture and the Pursuit of Pleasure*, London: Routledge.

Scott, Bonnie Kime (ed.) (1990) *The Gender of Modernism: A Critical Anthology*, Bloomington and Indianapolis: Indiana University Press.

Taylor, Elizabeth ([1949] 1950) *A Wreath of Roses*, London: The Reprint Society.

—— ([1945] 1988) *At Mrs Lippincote's*, London: Virago. (The 1953 *New York Herald Tribune* interview is reprinted in Virago's 1988 edition of the novel.)

Woolf, Virginia (1942) *Death of the Moth and Other Essays*, London: Hogarth Press.

5

Her brilliant career: the marketing of Angela Carter

Elaine Jordan

That writing is, or is not, 'a woman's business', can have several meanings. It was Angela Carter's business because she lived by it in a variety of ways including journalism, reviewing, editing, and of course her long fictions and short tales, radio plays, film and TV scripts, children's stories, even the draft of a libretto for an opera, *Orlando* (Glyndebourne chose *The Tales of Beatrix Potter* instead). Like her circus star, Fevvers, in *Nights at the Circus*, she turned her head and hand to what the market offered, and could take of her gifts. In Japan, she had worked as a bar-hostess, and wrote later, in *New Society*, 'In Japan, I learnt what it is to be a woman and became radicalised' (*Nothing Sacred* 1982: 28).

It is sometimes complained (even by people writing academic theses, which she never did) that her writing is for an academic élite. This is a mistake. She was very much in the literary marketplace, needing to sell her work. She also loved reading, and watching, whether what she read or watched was 'élite' or 'popular'; from early on she read Freud, and things that followed from that, with interests in cinema, surrealism, socialist cultural theory, and so on. As a 'writer in residence' or teacher of creative writing at universities in England (Sheffield and East Anglia), in the USA (Brown) and Australia (Adelaide), she was always the writer from outside the academy, not an academic. In the USA, at the beginning, no-one had read her work. It was not an easy or secure living. Her career achieved its most brilliant peak posthumously – stocks of her work sold out within days of her death in February 1992, and have since been republished by anyone with a claim to do so; and everyone, it seems, wants to write about her work. The 'Angela Carter factor' has become a modern myth for the British grant funding agency:

in 1993–94 the British Academy were saying that for every three people who wanted to do a thesis on eighteenth-century writing, there were forty who wanted to write on Angela Carter. She is a warning as well as a beaconing star to anyone who might want to make writing their business, which may well be an even more difficult and compromising matter now. The tangle of kinds of work Carter did (always involving, however, particular aesthetic and socio-political commitments and principles) may be typical of the working lives of most writers who do not have other adequate sources of income.

This chapter is not about the publishers' policies for marketing Carter (she had seven primary publishers for her major works alone, finding some kind of a home base with Virago in the late 1970s: the reference section of this chapter suggests some of the complexities of her publication and reception). As a reader, I am interested in the different ways her work could and can be encountered. Notoriously, publishers and booksellers irritate writers by segregating 'popular fiction' and 'serious literature'. She wrote anxiously to Lorna Sage about how *The Passion of New Eve* was presented in 1977: 'I suspect Golly's have buggered it by inventing a new category - Gollancz Fantasy and the Macarbre [*sic*] – for it; it seemed a good idea at the time but may precipitate the novel into a reviewer's limbo' (Sage 1994a: 31–2).

Her second and third novels, *The Magic Toyshop* (1967) and *Several Perceptions* (1968), had won literary prizes, but with works like *Heroes and Villains* (1969) she also had a following outside the literary mainstream (in which she wanted to be taken seriously), and different from later academic interest in her work, particularly in the areas of feminism, gender studies, and postmodern, or post-structuralist, theory. She was read by enthusiasts of fantasy, Gothic, science fiction, and the experimental interzone named by one of its inhabitants or travelling practitioners, Samuel Delany, as 'speculative fiction' (see the chapter by Roz Kaveney, in Sage 1994b: 171–88). It is important to remember that Carter found a big but not 'mainstream' readership here, along with J. G. Ballard and Michael Moorcock, two other British writers who fused popular with experimental fiction, and had (and perhaps still have) a long haul to be recognised for the range, intelligence, and adventurousness of their writing. This distinctively sets her apart from other British women writers who were well reviewed in the same period.

Her late 1960s feminist radicalism involved doing what Conrad said women could not do, being 'man enough to face the darkness', going with the wild boys into rough and weird territories where no girl had gone before. Hence the antagonism between Carter's ways of working and more repressive, neo-conservative, modes of feminism. At one US campus she was boycotted by Women's Studies staff and students, a cultural shock which intensified her reservations about the 'language of sisterhood' (Michaels and Ricks 1980: 226–34). She was not, of course, alone in wanting to walk on the wild side, though now lesbian or gay-identified writers appear to have done more of this (for example, Joanna Russ, Pat Califia, Poppy Z. Brite); and now tough bad boy writers like Irvine Welsh write good feminist novels (*Marabou Stork Nightmares* 1995). It is notable that Harold Bloom can put Jeanette Winterson somewhere in his canon of writers who matter to writers (perhaps because of some occult connection to Camille Paglia) but not Angela Carter: maybe she had not yet acquired a sufficient body of interested supporters in the USA. This is the only reason I can think of why Winterson should be included and Carter excluded. Lynne Segal has complained that after the sexual radicalism of the late 1960s and 1970s it actually became more difficult to write about women's heterosexual desire, while all the exciting work was played out in the lesbian field (see the introduction to McIntosh and Segal 1992). Carter, however, continued to write about women's heterosexual desire, as a feminist.

Uncertainties about how to place and present Carter's fiction are reflected in paperback covers of originals and re-issues over nearly three decades from 1966 to 1993. Penguin editions published in the USA have mildly coloured sketches whose whimsical elegance recalls Ronald Searle's leggy Girls of St Trinian's: the angelic carthorse Fevvers becomes a sylph. Book covers suggest something about origin and destiny, they are a kind of signature, and have an effect on what we think we are reading. They sometimes want to suggest classic status – like a Penguin Classic. The hardback dust jacket of *American Ghosts and Old World Wonders* (1993) reproduces Georges de la Tour's *The Wrightsman Madonna*, on which Carter writes in this posthumous collection of stories and essays. It shows a sleek, full-bodied, apparently pregnant woman with a skull in her lap, gazing at a mirror which reflects only the candle flame by which she gazes. It is 'classy' as well as appropriately strange and suggestive, and no doubt the choice was also economically acute: if it is the cover picture, no need for the illustration to be provided for the essay. It contrasts strongly with two earlier covers.

Carter's first novel *Shadow Dance* was reprinted in the USA as *Honey-*

buzzard (1966); the Pan Books cover of *Honeybuzzard* shows a doctored photograph of a pretty china doll face, half of which is lank-haired, eyeless, with a slashed and stitched cheek like the heroine Ghislaine. The back cover promises 'Dark glasses, casual lust and violence ... a decided touch for the grotesque scene, the nightmarish atmosphere' (*The New Statesman*). [1] Dark glasses figure on the cover of *Several Perceptions* (1970). These dark glasses are jollier in their signification – the head which wears them and rounds the scene is a Beatle-type, maybe Lennon, more like George Harrison, full of innocent Sergeant Pepper images, with a little bit of hellfire. It is brightly coloured against black.

Two fantasy versions of the British 1960s: the disfigured dolly bird, the jokey young man, both offering something a bit raffish, a bit villain-ous. Yet *Shadow Dance* and *Several Perceptions*, together with *Love* (1971), are rightly described by Marc O'Day as realist accounts of a particular 1960s scene of provincial bohemia, of junk and recycling, a reality which *was* weird. Post-war demolition, and the reconstruction of large houses as flats, made ripping the insides out of old houses and selling off their ornamental or quaint bits a new British industry in the 1960s, in which students participated. Now we take all this recycling (or reproduction of 'notions' and 'past-times') as normal, but then it marked a distinctly new style, more exciting as well as more cynical than that of 1950s Britain. Recycling for a new age is very obviously part of Carter's deliberate style, and mimes the history within which and about which she writes (Sage 1994b: 24–58); Marc O'Day's account of Carter's 'Bristol trilogy' was underlined and confirmed by Paul Barker and Lorna Sage at the York 'Fireworks' conference on Carter in September 1994.

King Penguin and early Virago paperback covers of Carter's work usually suggest the avant-garde with surreal artwork, both visceral and machine-like: virulent and fleshy fruits, flowers and snakes cut off from any whole body or environment. Posthumously, the Virago covers were startlingly updated to catch a youthful 'postmodern' taste: contrast for example the modernist image of shifting female faces and eyes on their 1982 edition of *The Passion of New Eve* (after Picabia's *Hera*) with the 1992 cover, a starry Julian Clary look-alike. The most striking contrast is between three editions of Carter's enigmatic stories collected in *Fire-works*. Quartet's 1976 paperback features a naked near-coital couple, chained and semi-masked, in a futuristic jungle landscape (see figure 9). The blond man wears some kind of metal headset and gazes into the distance while absent-mindedly clasping the woman's breast, which looks a bit detachable; she is brown, with a leopard mask on her head which also looks rather like an octopus. She grimaces away from him, and one of her hands is a leopard claw clutching for a knife, whose sharp steel-grey blade echoes the spikes of his headset. A small blue bird seems to be biting at the chain which binds them. The effect, especially the foregrounding of her oiled buttock and thigh, is a pornography that depends on the conjunction of nature and technology. The 1987 Virago cover is cleanly Japanese in style (preferring a focus on the stories which derive from Carter's time in Japan, 1969–72), all streamlined, with vivid primaries and pastels in contrast to the soft greens and browns of the Quartet cover (see figure 10). It features a motorway and a high-speed train, with cornered blossoms formally counteracting the hard-edged diagonals. These two covers are absolutely inverse, in representing flesh/metal; nature/culture; curves/straight lines. A more recent Virago

9 The profane: nature and technology. Cover of Angela Carter's *Fireworks: 9 Profane Pieces*, by Bob Foulke (Quartet, 1974).

10 The classic: stylish lines. Cover of Angela Carter's *Fireworks*, by Hiroshi Mauabe (Virago, 1987).

cover also cleans and smartens up the 'ancient and modern' cross-cultural act: a vaguely Japanese woman's face in a Parisian hat. What would be the right 'visual identity' for a work by Carter? The diversity, the not-quite-rightness, seems appropriate, a comic cultural history. The trend seems to be towards faces, so I would have put some Hollywood image, Greta Garbo probably, on the new cover of *The Passion of New Eve*; or else an image of the bearded Queen Hatshepsut from Pharaonic Egypt.

I knew Carter's work first through *The Passion of New Eve* (1977) which Dr Jane Heath, better than I at keeping in touch with the feminist publishing scene, had set for a course on 'Women and Ideology in Literature' which we taught together at Essex University. (Carter later wrote to me that *The Passion of New Eve* was her favourite, because it was her most ambitious and 'hopelessly flawed' novel.) Carter's scandalously bold 'exercise in cultural history', *The Sadeian Woman* (1979) was supplementary reading, and *The Bloody Chamber and Other Stories* (1979) soon followed these onto the course, so this must have been around 1982, when paperbacks would have been available for students. My pleasure in undertaking this course, which had been set up by graduate students, was in teaching modern writing by women in ways which allowed discussion of what actually and directly concerned students' thinking about their lives as women (later, some men came into the discussion too), as well as my own life and that of other women from different cultures. This may be a basic and banal way of putting it, but for me it was a crucial animation and redirection of my training and teaching practice, a new honesty, in the sense that the 'important questions' had always been ones suggested to me by the academy, and not much related, apparently, to more pressing concerns of a personal life within a wider public life. It was through focusing on 'women's issues' through discussion of writing by women, that other ethical, political, cultural and theoretical questions became genuinely important to my work – including of course ethnic difference, different sexualities, and thinking about gender both more broadly and more specifically. The way to anything that might become accepted 'universally' is through an enquiring and active concern with particular and diverse interests, demands, and struggles for rights.

But what we discussed on this course tended, to some extent, to be dominated by socio-political and ethical arguments. I wondered what had become of my old aesthetic and intellectual delight in technical skill, in surprise and complexity (or direct simplicity), in the sheer inventiveness of writing, its ironies and freedoms, its allusive or 'intertextual' significances, the new paths and patterns it could make. Carter was quite a find: she was not the only 'real writer', but the one who most delighted me, partly perhaps because of our closeness in age and cultural background. I could recognise intelligent and imaginative calculation, celebrate subtle or explosive reworking, while keeping close to what this meant in thinking about actual lives and sexualised culture. Reading Carter renewed for me the new awareness she described: 'I can date to that time ... and to that sense of heightened awareness of the society around me in the summer of 1968, my own questioning of the nature of my reality as a *woman*. How that social fiction of my 'femininity' was created, by means outside my control, and palmed off on me as the real thing' (Wandor 1983: 70).

Students in the 1980s tended to be shocked (but fascinated when not baffled) by *The Passion of New Eve*, *The Sadeian Woman* and some of the stories in *The Bloody Chamber*. Now, in the 1990s they often startle me by how little I need to argue about gender, sexuality, deconstruction in a broad sense, or about revisionary writing and political intervention in discourses, as distinct from a blunt commitment to 'women telling their own story in their own authentic voice'. The possibilities suggested by her work are still felt to be exciting, to open new horizons, for students from around the world. Carter helped make this new consciousness and sophistication possible, rather than jumping in with a pre-existing 'militant orthodoxy' (as John Bayley claimed in his review of her work at large, which read as if it were designed to blight and prune her posthumously blossoming reception as soon as possible). [2] Her feminist conversion, quoted above and often cited, remained crucial in her work, and chimed well with her previous 'bloody-minded' questioning of pieties, her attraction to socialist, psychoanalytic, surreal or situationist challenges to dominant rationalisations, while keeping a sceptical eye on them too (see for example 'Elegy for a Freelance' in *Fireworks*, or *Nights at the Circus* throughout, especially the arguments between Fevvers and Lizzie).

It is important, however, not to redogmatise her work, which was always 'written to the moment', however archaic some of its materials. Consideration of it should not be restricted to feminist revisionary writing (though that was, and still is, an important moment), or to the fantastic and Gothic – anti-realist (and therefore anti-phallic?) – modes. Her experimentalism, as I have said, coincided with that of others crossing the borderlines of 'high' and popular forms, informed by modernism, by university and literary educations, impatient with the limits of these and the market's distinction between popular and serious writing. Maybe coincidentally, or in 'friendly plagiarism', they form an argumentative community, trying things on. It would be interesting to read Carter's speculative fictions in relation to those of the gay black writer Samuel Delany. As a fan buying his 'sci fi', or Octavia Butler's, you wouldn't know those identities, any more than you would know them on the Internet. Or read her in relation to the British writers Michael Moorcock and J. G. Ballard: read the sex and violence, psychotic and utopian ideals, and especially the winged beings, light aircraft, and film studios, in Ballard's *The Unlimited Dream Company* (Cape 1979), with *The Passion of New Eve* (1977) and *Nights at the Circus* (1984); as well as her earlier *The Infernal Desire Machines of Dr Hoffman* (1972) and her later *Wise Children* (1991). Carter's writing is not limited by one political position, or by one genre, though she is always highly conscious of genre and style, and always politically engaged, in her own particular relation to Marxism and feminism. [3]

At the York 'Fireworks' conference there was a distinct contrast between those, often speaking from the platform, who were more or less of Carter's generation or from her literary/publishing milieux, and younger scholars producing academic theses. Already when Carter was a quite unhappy Arts Council Fellow at Sheffield University between 1976 and 1978 (not unhappy so far as I know because of Sheffield, where she seems to have found good company, but because her years in Japan from 1969 to 1972 had cut away any foothold she had earlier gained on the metropolitan literary scene, as well as ending her earlier marriage), students used to ask her 'What was it really like in the sixties?', and this was uncannily echoed in 1994 at the 'Fireworks' conference. Frankly my dear, it's not that I don't give a damn, but that I don't really know: do the research. If you are working on Carter and pornography, or on *The Infernal Desire Machines of Dr Hoffman* (1972), read the stuff she and her readers had been reading on liberatory desire, Marcuse and Reich, for example, with the mixture of enthusiasm, scepticism, illusion, disillusion, captured in 'Elegy for a Freelance'.

There was a difference, embodied and enacted at York in 1994, between those of us who were able to look forward to what Angela Carter might unpredictably say in her journalism and reviews (and on the phone, a medium in which, unrecorded, she gave of her extraordinary best), and do in her fiction, and those who are producing a scholarly paper about an author irremediably distanced by her too early death. (You can say what you like about dead authors, but you will be more circumspect about living authors – they might bite.) The future undoubtedly belongs to younger scholars more than to those who cannot help but mourn a particular loss, and remember a particular history in a personal way. The business of reading Carter now floats free of her generation and culture. But I would want to ask that it not be closed up into the second death of discrete categories, considering 'porn' or 'sexuality' or 'fantasy' outside time and the historical determinations on which she always insisted.

Carter's work has aroused international interest both as translatable story telling and in relation to the cultural and critical theory which has become a *lingua franca* in the study of the humanities for good reasons. Her work responded to the fusion of Marxist and psychoanalytic thinking, and to linguistic, literary, and structuralist/post-structuralist theory. She was always interested in how cultures, myths, psyches and symbolic orders get constructed, and can be changed. 'Wolf Alice' in *The Bloody Chamber*, for example, can be read as a handbook for reconsidering Lévi-Strauss and Lacan from a feminist perspective: how nature becomes culture in an unsustainable but unavoidable opposition, how the 'mirror phase', seeing oneself outside oneself, becomes the basis for language and its differentiations. She wrote fiction as literary criticism and as argument, without losing a passion for the peculiar working of narrative and style, or her own 'curious room' (*American Ghosts and Old World Wonders*, 127). It was all ripe for use, because she was an early independent reader of much of the material required for theoretically-oriented courses. The York conference was such a celebration of Carter that it was quite difficult for those who, like her, wanted to ask questions, critically. For an oldie, like me, many of the workshop presentations seemed too machined. Ten minutes on theory of pornography, gender, sexuality or fantasy, ten minutes on its application to one of Carter's texts – there was something of that hygenic, aseptic, over-careful academicism, a new orthodoxy, rather than troubled or chancy questioning. (This impression was no doubt exaggerated by the routine twenty-minute limitation for presentations.)

Carter, however, did not write primarily to be discussed in the academy. She wrote fiction that attracted a diverse audience, and she was also a cultural journalist, and a reviewer of books. She was a commentator on the life of her times, and in her lifetime was at least as well known for this work, in Britain, as for her fiction. It is this which is in danger of being forgotten, if we think of her as a feminist only, or as a 'fantastic' writer only. Paul Barker commissioned work from her, as literary editor and then editor of *New Society*, beginning with 'Notes Towards a Definition of Sixties Style', and in talking of this at York ranked her essays on contemporary culture (including what lipstick, knickers and bruises may signify) with those of Orwell, and hinted that he rated this aspect of her work higher than the later novels (Barker 1995). She was not someone you would ask to do routine journalism, he said – she would suggest an area she wanted to work on, and after a while they would talk about it on the phone, then she would send it in: she could not spell for toffee and sentences in her typescripts might start off one way then charge off in another. This seems odd for such a stylishly conscious writer, which she was – she had her own particular poetics as you can see most readily in the syntax of some of the stories in *The Bloody Chamber* – but this element of chaos in first drafts and personal letters is part of the way in which she was always revising herself, part of the bold dynamics of her writing. 'The vigour of her best essays came from a collision between her stylishness and her radical eye on the world. They were important in keeping her in touch with a reading public' (Barker, 1995: 16).

'I learned how to look at things in the sixties, and I have carried on looking' – one of the headnotes in the first collection of her essays, *Nothing Sacred* (1982) which was largely drawn from *New Society*. 'England, Whose England?' is the post-D. H. Lawrence, post-Orwellian, title of another section. Though Paul Barker knows more about Carter and the time in which they worked together than he does about different possibilities within feminism, I value his recall of her cultural journalism, of her thoughtfulness about significant details, of that in her fictions which is not easily checked-off as *merely* allegorical, and his resistance to the current tendency to prefer Carter's last two novels over earlier ones. Posthumous tributes, including panel discussions at the York conference, tended to stress a benevolently affirmative fairy godmother Carter, especially the *Wise Children* Carter, at the expense of more risky, exploratory, critical, earlier work, such as *The Passion of New Eve* and *The Sadeian Woman*. I am happy enough to see *Nights at the Circus* and

Wise Children as working out from and through her earlier concerns, but not to see this as a 'growing-up' which would remedially cancel out the serious imaginative questioning of earlier work. Against Paul Barker's apparent preference for cultural comment over allegory, I would say that the opposition is a false one. Carter's cultural interests and analyses cannot be opposed to her 'fantastic' writing, because they share the same concerns and work in similar ways.

In *Nights at the Circus*, for example, the apes organise their escape from the circus by study and organisation. They are one example of several other modes of escape from systems dominated by the interests of others. In *New Society* in 1976 Carter thinks about nice zoos (London and Verona) and nasty zoos (Turin): 'The nastier the monkey-house, the more exemplary the quality of ape life, the more they seem to be staging some sort of primates agitprop.' The essay complicates rather than inverts analogies between human culture and animal nature, the nice and the nasty. The zoo animals acculturate themselves to what humans impose on them while providing for them as an exhibition of the natural: 'They order their monkey-houses more existentially than we do, in Turin; grief, despair, degradation, defiance, hopelessness. A pecking order. A lice-picking order. Easy to see what *these* chaps are thinking of - such a pitch of rage they'd never be fobbed off with a Habitat lounge-suite ...' (*Nothing Sacred*, 120). 'At London Zoo, of course, there are only invisible bars in the monkey-house; the apes live in a nice, low-rise, brick-built complex and their apartments have huge picture windows in which visitors can see their own reflections almost as if moving about inside the apes' lovely homes, with their Design Centre exercise bars, their Habitat stylishness' (*Nothing Sacred*, 116). The essay ends with a story of 'a very nice black gibbon with a white beard' who keeps himself in shape at 'a lovely zoo in Verona': appealing for contact (which might prove to be nasty if it came) and then pretending that he never wanted it anyway. 'The nicer the zoo, the more terrible.' Carter is certainly writing about the cultural practices of zoo-keeping and zoo-visiting, and about the real difference of animals, their radical strangeness to us, for example a mandrill with a face 'like a tropic flower': 'A luscious snout of the tenderest red; white, bulbous, blue-veined cheeks like the calyx of a pitcher plant; and delicate, pointed, leprechaun ears almost hidden in a foliage of speckled fur. He is the most magnificent, the least human-looking, therefore superbly dignified' (*Nothing Sacred*, 118) Carter's imaginative construction of this uncanny plant-animal inverts the usual zoo-visitor's pleasure of seeing animals behaving 'like' humans (which confirms our sense that they are only comically like us), and also the traditional hierarchy by which the human rather than the animal was regarded as superior. At the same time she uses the kind of analogies that TV nature films do, which affirm human culture as the standard for judgement, understanding, knowledge. This mandrill is a 'patriarch', he 'patrols the perimeter of his enclosure', he is manly, like the gibbon doing press-ups; but also Carter wants to affirm that he is something else entirely, and does that through an aestheticising gaze – he is a flower, a leprechaun. She is complicating the available languages for looking at and thinking about animals, human and not human; looking without innocence even while yearning for something natural, beyond culture. Simultaneously she is writing about culture, ethics, politics, beyond zoo practices. She implies that the 'agitprop' provoked in the baboons by the nasty zoo is fuller of revolutionary possibility (for human beings) than the nice habitat of the London mandrills ('after all this time, we couldn't really cope with the wild again, could we?'). I wish not to argue with her politics (I have reservations about thinking of bad conditions as promising change, or the provision of better conditions as conservative), but to say that *how* she writes throws into question the way we look and think. There is no radical difference between her cultural journalism and her fiction. In allegory she found some play for imaginative freedom, and also a way to write about political and cultural hopes as well as actualities, which were local to her time and place, and remain broader than that. [4]

Notes

1. Thanks to Dr John Sears of Manchester Metropolitan University for sending me a photocopy. Angela Carter refused to show me a copy of *Shadow Dance* in the 1980s, though she could have done; at that time she didn't want it reprinted, and people like me commenting on it: it has now been reissued.
2 *New York Review of Books*, 23 April 1992.
3 A community of readers, and people talking about their reading, lives on the edge of the academy and the publishing, reviewing, bookselling business. I am indebted to an itinerant second-hand bookseller, Marc Williams, for getting me to read Ballard by trusting me with his copy of *The Unlimited Dream Company* (1979) which he didn't want to sell. I am indebted to John Muckle, commissioning editor of *The New British Poetry* (1988) and of *Active in Airtime* (contemporary fiction and poetry, edited from 24, Regent Road,

Brightlingsea, Essex) for the term 'friendly plagiarism', and for lending me books by Delany, Moorcock and Ballard. I am also indebted to discussions with Marc O'Day, and with Lorna Sage and Angela Carter.

4 A day after I wrote this up, I received a copy of Christina Britzolakis's essay 'Angela Carter's fetishism' (*Textual Practice* 9:3, 1995), based on her paper at the 'Fireworks' conference. I recommend it, especially (in the context of this volume), pp. 469–70, on 'professionalism and masquerade'.

References

For further details see Lorna Sage's *Angela Carter* in the British Council's Writers and their Work series (details below). The bibliography, prepared by Kate Webb, does not go beyond 1994, and I have not attempted to list translations or later editions.

Novels by Angela Carter

Shadow Dance (1966), London, Heinemann; (1968) reprinted as *Honeybuzzard*, NY, Simon and Schuster; London, Pan.

The Magic Toyshop (1967), London, Heinemann; (1968) NY, Simon and Schuster; (1981) London, Virago.

Several Perceptions (1968), London, Heinemann; (1970) NY, Simon and Schuster; London, Pan.

Heroes and Villains (1969), London, Heinemann; (1981) NY, Simon and Schuster; Harmondsworth, Penguin.

Love (1971), London, Rupert Hart-Davis; (1987) revised edition, London, Chatto and Windus; (1988) NY, Viking Penguin; London, Picador.

The Infernal Desire Machines of Doctor Hoffman (1972), London, Rupert Hart-Davis; (1982) Harmondsworth, Penguin; (1977) reprinted as *The War of Dreams*, NY, Bard/Avon Books.

The Passion of New Eve (1977), London, Gollancz; NY, Harcourt Brace Jovanovich; (1982) London, Virago.

Nights at the Circus (1984), London, Chatto and Windus; (1985) NY, Viking; London, Pan.

Wise Children (1991), London, Chatto and Windus; (1992) NY, Farrar, Strauss and Giroux; London, Vintage.

Short stories by Angela Carter

Fireworks: Nine Profane Pieces (1974), London, Quartet Books; (1981) NY, Harper and Row; (1987) revised edition, without subtitle or afterword, London, Chatto and Windus; (1988) London, Virago.

The Bloody Chamber and Other Stories (1979), London, Gollancz; (1980) NY, Harper and Row; (1981) Harmondsworth, Penguin.

Black Venus (1985), London, Chatto and Windus; (1986) London, Pan; (1987) reprinted as *Saints and Strangers*, NY, Viking Penguin.

American Ghosts and Old-World Wonders (1993), London, Chatto and Windus; (1994) London, Vintage.

Non-fiction by Angela Carter

The Sadeian Woman: An Exercise in Cultural History (1979), London, Virago; reprinted as *The Sadeian Woman and the Ideology of Pornography*, NY, Pantheon.

Nothing Sacred: Selected Writings (1982), London, Virago; (1992) revised edition, London, Virago.

Expletives Deleted: Selected Writings (1992), London, Chatto and Windus; (1993) London, Vintage.

Other sources

Barker, Paul (1995) 'The Return of the Magic Story-Teller', *The Independent on Sunday*, 8 January, 14–16.

Bayley, John (1993) 'Fighting for the Crown', *New York Review of Books*, 39:8 (23 April), 9–11.

Bloom, Harold (1994) *The Western Canon*, New York, Harcourt Brace.

Britzolakis, Christina (1995) 'Angela Carter's fetishism', *Textual Practice* 9:3, 459–76.

McIntosh, Mary and Segal, Lynne (eds) (1992) *Sex Exposed: Sexuality and the Pornography Debate*, London, Virago.

Michaels, L. and Ricks, C. (1980) *The State of the Language*, Berkeley, University of California Press.

Sage, L. (1994a) *Angela Carter*, Plymouth, Northcote House.

Sage, L. (ed.) (1994b) *Flesh and the Mirror: Essays on the Art of Angela Carter*, London, Virago.

Wandor, M. (1983) *Gender and Writing*, London, Pandora Press.

II

Theorising the marketplace

6

Simone de Beauvoir and the intellectual marketplace

Kate Fullbrook

A recent visit to one of London's largest and most comprehensive academic bookshops disclosed some interesting (and, I think, telling) information on the reception of Simone de Beauvoir's work. Her writing is still significantly in demand, at least among her English-speaking readers, nearly ten years after her death, and nearly fifty years after publication of some of that writing. Equally, it looks as if Beauvoir is not only holding her place as an icon, as Toril Moi puts it in her excellent recent study of Beauvoir, 'the emblematic intellectual woman of the twentieth century',[1] but, more importantly, she is still widely read (at least in Britain, at least in translation). Booksellers and publishers have registered her purely economic value for what is now half a century. A selection of her writing has been continuously in print since it first appeared, and there exists as well a significant and still growing secondary body of commentary on this work from literary critics, biographers, writers of memoirs, feminist theorists, cultural historians, and straightforward enthusiasts. Despite Michèle Le Doeuff's melancholy (and somewhat frustrated) admission that, with the exception of her own fine analysis and that of a few Beauvoirian colleagues, interest in Beauvoir in France is currently moribund, at least among dominant feminist intellectuals, and despite Mary Dietz's account of the equivocal reception and marginal influence on feminist politics in the United States in the 1992 special Beauvoir issue of *Signs*, Beauvoir is still very much functioning in the marketplace.[2] She shifts units; and continues, in the shape of posthumously published letters and journals, to deliver product.

What I am interested in is this split: Beauvoir's retention of a wide readership (with largely popular but also professional components), and her peculiarly ambivalent reception by the international intellectual community, where she seems to be treated largely either with a kind of uncritical and unanalysed affection as a classic modern icon or else dismissed as a source of ideas, with the attitudes toward her work by those who reject it displaying a range of responses which run from indifference to hostility. I have two chief concerns here: the first has to do with *which* Beauvoir is visible in the general marketplace, the second with her place in the less tangible, but ultimately equally ferocious intellectual marketplace of the dominant ideas of the post-Second World War period. These two markets are, of course, not only co-existent but joined: both encompass various economic and social factors (sales, salaries, prestige, and at least limited power of many kinds) as well as more intangible factors such as loyalty to variant ideas and the development of operative worldviews.

To begin to address my first question, I want to go back to my London bookshop. There were roughly eighty books (covering roughly twenty titles) by or about Beauvoir on the shelves, though they weren't in one place. Looking for the scattered parts of her corpus became a rather amusing treasure hunt. There was a cache of Beauvoirs in the fiction section: five of her texts were available there. The biography sector contained a real trove of material: all her memoirs, several volumes of letters, and three separate biographies of Beauvoir were on the shelves. The former women's studies section (with its new, more fluidly transgressive and less womanish title of 'gender studies') contained several volumes on her work as well as copies of *The Second Sex*. I found more copies of *The Second Sex* as well as *Old Age* in an area devoted to general social commentary and popular sociology. The literary criticism section threw up a number of monographs on her novels and short stories. Most interesting for my purposes, however, was where Beauvoir was not. As on all my sporadic visits to the same bookshop over the last twenty years the philosophy section offered nothing whatsoever on Beauvoir: in this category she has had, and, it seems, continues to have, no existence whatsoever. This is not simply a case of the passing of the intense interest in mid-century French existentialism: Merleau-Ponty still figured on the shelves. There were, in addition, roughly fifteen titles either by or about Sartre (including, ironically, my and my co-author's recent study of the Beauvoir–Sartre partnership, *Simone de Beauvoir and Jean-Paul Sartre: The Remaking of a Twentieth-Century Legend*,[3] which, despite Beauvoir's being the lead name in the title, and the book's major concern to question the reception of Beauvoir as a philosopher, still wound up captive in the shelving territory of her much-beloved life-long companion, while the space which could have, indeed should have, been hers remains, as usual, empty).

That this should be the case, that the marketplace should have no place for Beauvoir the philosopher, while it retains a good deal of space for Beauvoir the novelist, the essayist, the feminist, and the cultural icon is perhaps not surprising. Beauvoir's major philosophical works are not, and have never been, readily available for the English-language reader. *The Ethics of Ambiguity*, her main traditional philosophical production, published in 1947 and translated by Bernard Frechtman in 1948, is only intermittently in print. Another essay on ethics, *Pyrrhus and Cinéas* from 1944, Beauvoir's second published work, which came out in the wake of her deeply philosophical novel, *She Came to Stay* in 1943, has never been translated in its entirety, though selections from it appeared in translation in *Partisan Review* in 1946 and, more recently, additional extracts have appeared in *Social Text* in 1987 (headed by the editor's hope that 'this elegant and pertinent essay will soon be translated into English': it hasn't).[4] *L'Existentialisme et la sagesse des nations* (1948), which contains major essays on ethical idealism and realism in politics, on literature and metaphysics, and on justice, has never, to my knowledge, been translated at all, in whole or in part. From Beauvoir's collection of essays, *Privilèges* (1955), only 'Must We Burn Sade?' has been, again, intermittently available, while 'La pensée de droite aujourd'hui' and 'Merleau-Ponty et le pseudo-sartrisme' remain inaccessible. Beauvoir's additional essays written for *Les Temps modernes*, her and Sartre's famous journal of which she was, in fact, the chief editor for many years, have never been collected, much less translated. It is, I think, highly curious that the most purely intellectual part of the body of work by 'the emblematic intellectual woman of the twentieth century' does not in fact have a place in the market, might just as well in fact not exist.

That such a curious case should indeed *be* the case is perhaps, in many ways, not overly surprising. 'Philosopher', as Michèle Le Doeuff (among others) points out with blinding obviousness, is not a category which easily admits that awkward category, 'women'. Equally, and even more curiously, Beauvoir herself took great pains to dissociate herself from her own philosophical production and her own philosophical originality. Her reasons had to do with her experience of the intellectual marketplace, though the accounts she gave of her rejection of the appellation 'philosopher' have their own fascinating edge. That Beauvoir *was*, in fact, a philosopher, and one of major importance, is something of which there can be no doubt (and I will try to explain why later in this chapter); that Beauvoir herself regarded being a philosopher as her most scandalous personal secret in a life whose last half was lived very much in public is even more interesting. The 'philosophical' was a category from which she insisted she be excluded during her lifetime, and that she should do so is, I think, a matter of extraordinary interest.

In *The Prime of Life*, the second volume of her memoirs published in 1960, Beauvoir looked back on herself in 1935 and gave the following account of her decision not to devote herself to philosophy, despite her clear talent as a philosopher. Margaret A. Simons provides a new translation of this crucial aspect of Beauvoir's autobiographical self-presentation:

'Why not try my hand at philosophy?' she asks herself in 1935. 'Sartre says that I understand philosophical doctrines, Husserl's among others, more quickly and more exactly than he ... In brief, I have ... a developed critical sense, and philosophy is for me a living reality. I'll never tire of its satisfactions.

'However, I don't consider myself a philosopher. I know very well that my ease in entering into a text comes precisely from my lack of inventiveness. In this domain, the truly creative spirits are so rare that it is idle of me to ask why I cannot join their ranks. It's necessary rather to explain how certain individuals are capable of pulling off this concerted delirium which is a system, and whence comes the stubbornness which gives to their insights that value of universal keys. I have said already that the feminine condition does not dispose one to this kind of obstinacy.' [5]

Throughout her public career, Beauvoir took pains to separate herself from the title of 'philosopher'. The statement just quoted is one of many such denials. Her readers have tended to take her at her word, without noting the idiosyncratic definition she uses for this term. A clue is given in her comment, just noted, on philosophy consisting of a 'concerted delirium which is a system'. Another clue is contained in her remarks in an interview with Margaret Simons in 1985, where the topic of discussion was the omission of much of the philosophical apparatus from H. M. Parshley's translation of *The Second Sex*:

Well, I think it's very bad to suppress the philosophical aspect because while I say that I'm not a philosopher in the sense that I'm not the creator of a system, I'm still a philosopher in the sense that I've studied a lot of philosophy, I have a degree in philosophy, I've taught philosophy, I'm infused with philosophy, and when I put philosophy into my books it's because that's a way for me to view the world and I can't allow them to eliminate that way of viewing the world, that dimension of my approach to women, as Mr. Parshley has done. I'm altogether against the principle of gaps, omissions, condensations which have the effect, among other things of suppressing the whole philosophical aspect of the book. [6]

'Philosopher', it should be clear by now, is a term which Beauvoir uses with extraordinary precision (and the shelves of the philosophy section in the bookshop would be thinly stocked indeed if this definition was generally operative. We could, for instance, start by clearing the Wittgenstein material and carry on backwards through the alphabet from there). I want to cite one more statement by Beauvoir to make it utterly clear what she was doing when she rejected this term for herself. In another interview with Simons, this time in 1979, after insisting that her 'field is literature' and that she has never 'created a philosophical work', she explains further to Simons, who mentions *The Ethics of Ambiguity* as an indubitably philosophical production, that

For me it is not philosophy; it is an essay. For me, a philosopher is someone like Spinoza, Hegel, or Sartre; someone who has built a great system, and not simply someone who likes philosophy, who can teach it, understand it, and who can make use of it in essays. A philosopher is somebody who truly builds a philosophical system. And that, I did not do. When I was young, I decided that it was not what I wanted to do. [7]

After this clarification, I think we can safely say that, using Beauvoir's terms, the bookshop philosophy shelves would have to be stripped almost bare. With Beauvoir, we are dealing with a very special, and strikingly limited, definition of philosophy. (And I must, as an aside, note how utterly charmed I am by the confidence, indeed arrogance of Beauvoir's rejection of her place among those who had surrendered to the 'concerted delirium' of abstract systems building to whom she alone grants the title of 'philosopher': 'I decided', she says, 'that it was not what I wanted to do.' Without a shred of doubt about her ability to have constructed her own systemic edifice, Beauvoir sees herself, rather splendidly, as having simply chosen not to do it.)

While it does not take much thought to realise why the general reading public has not clamoured, *en masse*, to recognise Beauvoir as a significant philosophical force (and I think I need only nod here to the still unusual idea of the 'female philosopher' to make the point), Beauvoir's consistent rejection of the classification (and her equally consistent appeal to a most unusual definition of the term) demands further comment. A clue to her adamancy in this matter must be linked to her own first forays into the marketplace as well as to her already noted statement that 'the female condition does not dispose one to this kind of obstinacy', that is, to the 'concerted delirium' of philosophical systems building.

For it would be wrong ever to underestimate Beauvoir's shrewd understanding of her own place in the intellectual market. She was always a woman with her living to make and her first attempts to break into publication carried lessons which she never forgot. In *Memoirs of a Dutiful Daughter* (1958) and *The Prime of Life* (1960), the first two volumes of her autobiography, Beauvoir repeatedly underscores her commitment to the literary life which, indeed, had been hers for over fifteen years by the time she began writing her memoirs in the mid-1950s. But the woman who had published three novels, *The Second Sex*, *The Ethics of Ambiguity*, and a great deal of journalism as well as a moderately successful play in the 1940s, who had won the Prix Goncourt in 1954 for *The Mandarins*, and who had been at the centre of the international existentialist craze for over a decade, was in a very different position than she had been in the late 1930s as an unpublished author. In 1938, as a thirty-year-old secondary schoolteacher, desperate to break into print, Beauvoir failed abjectly in her initial attempt to publish. The publication in question was her first serious fiction, a collection of short stories later entitled *When Things of the Spirit Come First*, which did not appear until over forty years later, in 1979. In the mid-thirties, during the two years she worked on the stories, Beauvoir said she 'was sustained by the hope that a publisher would accept them'. [8] Sartre had books of philosophy published in 1936 and 1937; *Nausea* had been accepted by Gallimard and was about to appear to instant acclaim. The couple were desperate for success for their writing, success which would lift them out of lives as schoolteachers with which Beauvoir was now bored, and which looked to her too enclosed. Those 'past nine years began to look rather threadbare', she explained; she wanted, she said, 'something to happen to me from the outside, as it were, something new and different'. [9] In *The Prime of Life*, Beauvoir treats the rejection of her volume of stories by two publishers offhandedly: the book, she said, 'was defective', her 'didactic and satirical aims were laboured far too heavily', it was a typical case of a beginner believing she had been original when she had been nothing of the kind.[10]

Beauvoir's autobiography blurs the disappointment which the rejection of *Things of the Spirit* caused. She had been so certain of publication that she had told her family and friends of the imminent appearance of the book.[11] And the rather anodyne account given in *The Prime of Life* for the stories' rejection takes on quite a different light when supplemented by the comments she made to her biographer Deirdre Bair:

> Sartre told me that [Brice Parain, the editor at Gallimard, said] it really had nothing to do with me or the quality of my writing, but that the house of Gallimard did not understand books written by women which were about the lives of women of my generation and background; that modern France and French publishing were not yet ready to deal with what women thought and felt and wanted; that to publish such a book would brand them a subversive publishing house and they couldn't risk offending all sorts of patrons and critics ... and he told me not to say anything negative about Gallimard, because they were so powerful and he needed them and perhaps with my next novel I would, too. So I kept my mouth shut and swallowed the hurt and told everyone the book was poorly written and because it dealt with silly girls it would probably not have sold anyway. [12]

Anyone who has received their first rejection after venturing into the marketplace can imagine Beauvoir's reactions. And the comments received in such vulnerable circumstances tend to influence their recipients in a way that no later criticism, made after any degree of success, can ever do. Sartre's mercenary but realistic warnings were an additional, difficult factor for Beauvoir. His pleas were also prescient. Beauvoir did, in the end, need Gallimard, who became the publisher of most of her books, including, with wonderful irony, *The Second Sex*, Beauvoir's most subversive treatise on the condition of women. Despite a bout of depression, Beauvoir let Sartre take her stories to another publisher, Grasset. The book was turned down again: she then refused to submit it elsewhere, despite Sartre's continued encouragement. In 1982, looking back on this initial defeat just before the English translation of the collection appeared, Beauvoir admitted just how hard she took these failures:

Two rejections were enough insult, enough humiliation. I was so naive then! If I had only known how many great writers are hurt by repeated rejection of their work, then I might have had the courage to try again with another publisher, but at the time I only believed that my work was inferior, undeserving of public attention. I saw myself as a failure and for a long time viewed myself as unworthy. [13]

If the market would not accept what one of the publishers' readers called her 'description of post-war young women influenced by the intellectual currents of their day' in stories laced through with 'intelligence' and 'the ability both to observe and to analyse' which gave accounts of 'certain contemporary milieus' and which were 'extremely accurate',[14] clearly, there would be no place for a woman who wished to take her place among the handful of thinkers over the centuries, who spent their lives constructing philosophical systems. The ambitious writerly neophyte who was Beauvoir at the end of the 1930s listened carefully to the voice of the market. She would tell her stories of intelligent women in the certain intellectual milieus she best knew, but from now on, she would give the market what it wanted as well. The door to success in philosophy, even if it had been the one against which she most wanted to push, must have looked utterly closed to this humiliated school-teacher.

If this young woman, 'infused with philosophy', had good reason to believe that the market did not want what she had to give in terms of textual treatment of either women or philosophy, she nevertheless was outstandingly successful in finding ways to write her way into the market in ways that allowed her to exercise her philosophical drive and to report on the condition of the women of her generation. And she found her way through the closed doors remarkably quickly. *She Came to Stay*, the novel on which she was working while the rejections for *When Things of the Spirit Come First* were received, is deeply informed with a profoundly original treatment of the problem of the Other, which found a way out of the impasse of Hegel's master/slave dialectic onto the open ground of situated existential reciprocity as well as offering exactly the kind of commentary on the problems faced by twentieth-century intellectual women which had so disturbed Gallimard in Beauvoir's first manuscript. The philosophical content of *She Came to Stay* is treated so deftly that this particular aspect of the novel has only recently received extensive analysis.[15] The novel, published in 1943, marked Beauvoir's first secure entry into the market, and the fiction was received as the kind of sex, scandal, and confessional commodity with which the market has rarely had problems. For the most part, these are still, overwhelmingly, the terms within which it is read. As I noted above, it is unwise to underestimate Beauvoir's shrewdness with regard to the market once any particular lesson had been learned.

Beauvoir's personal disavowal of the title 'philosopher' (and one might add here that she tended to be wary of all labels; a good example is her refusal of the 'feminist' tag until late in her life), however, goes only a small way toward explaining her absence from the philosophy shelves. To understand this, I think it is necessary to look at the trajectory of post-war French thought and at its influence on English-speaking readers. We are dealing here with trails of intellectual fashions and, while it seems to me to be too simple to invoke the double clichés of Anglophone empiricism versus Francophile abstraction, and French intellectuals' tendency often to adopt German philosophies as their points of departure, I think there is enough truth in these received views to map the territory I want to cover. (For example, Tom Rockmore, in his excellent study *Heidegger and French Philosophy: Humanism, antihumanism and being*, mentions Nietzsche, Heidegger, Marx and Freud as the German thinkers who most significantly underpin post-war French thought. I think it is difficult to argue with this observation, though like Rockmore, I think it is only fair to add two more German thinkers, Husserl and Hegel, to the list.)[16] What is of crucial interest in the case of Beauvoir are the ways in which the French intellectual post-war swerve to varieties of neo-Heideggerianism has served to obscure her work as a philosopher, and the ways in which this direction has occluded her thought even for those who might be judged most receptive to it.

It strikes me as continuingly bizarre that for the past fifteen years one can scarcely move in the study of literature in England or America without tripping over some (usually partially-assimilated) variety of neo-Heideggerian thought. Derrida, Lacan, Foucault, Gadamer, Lyotard, Irigaray: the Heideggerian line of irrationalist writers are, and have been, the power-names to invoke in order to signal intellectual depth and currency. Neither deconstruction nor the Lyotardian version of postmodernism are conceivable as intellectual formations without their Heideggerian roots. The attacks on (and often simply sneers at) rationality and humanism which are now so commonplace in literary studies as to have become orthodox are also directly attributable to the influence of this intellectual lineage (though the strong presence of Nietzsche filtered through both Heidegger and neo-Heideggerians must also be mentioned as important to these developments). Convinced as I am of the (at the very least) compatibility between Heidegger's philosophy and Heidegger's Nazism, it is scarcely surprising that I belong to the group which regards this development with more than regret.[17] However, that is another (very large) argument. What I am interested in here is the intellectual market's investment in the Heideggerian topics of Being and Dasein, in his attempt to find a way out of the Cartesian philosophical line, and in the ways in which, as Richard Rorty remarks, for neo-Heideggerians, '"Language" [has] become the latest substitute for "God" or "Mind" – something mysterious, incapable of being described in the same terms in which we describe tables, trees, and atoms.'[18] These dominant ideas, which seem to me to constitute a faithfully Heideggerian attempt to reinstate the ineffable as a respectable category in non-theological European imagination (whether this is identified by the Heideggerian name of 'Thinking' or some other term, and which seems to comprise a curious attempt to move to a post-metaphysical position by the invocation of the utterly unknowable), have affected the continuing lack of space in the intellectual market for Beauvoir as a philosopher.

Some of the factors which have blocked serious consideration of the philosopher Beauvoir are outlined succinctly by Rockmore, who intelligently follows the work of Pierre Bourdieu on the sociology of knowledge in France. For example, the French tradition of the philosophical 'master-thinker' presented a role which Sartre filled only too well in the immediate aftermath of the Second World War and the early 1950s. In some ways, there was no getting past him during his lifetime and the strong interest in Sartrian existentialism which was a feature of British and American intellectual life in the 1950s and 1960s represented part of the international response to this peculiarly French phenomenon. I think it is useful to note certain continuities here: Bergson had a similar effect in English-speaking countries during the modernist period; Derrida, Lacan, and Foucault (with Heidegger in the background as the meta-master-thinker) seem to be sharing this role at the end of the twentieth century. It seems as necessary for the functioning of French intellectual life to overthrow master-thinkers as to establish them, and the eclipse of Sartre, after the waning of his period of most profound influence, bears a distinct similarity to the treatment of Bergson's reputation earlier in the century (and the minor Bergson revival of the late 1990s is interesting in this light). The turning away from Sartre to Heidegger outside of France, however, presents another kind of case. There are good historical reasons why the Heideggerian line, which ultimately privileges the self as sovereign, and which allows no grounds for discussion of ethics, of the good, should have become so widespread from the 1970s to the present in English-speaking countries, but that, too, is another argument. There are many reasons why the political right should be quite satisfied with this circumstance: it is more puzzling why neo-Heideggerianism should find such favour with the political left, though here one can cite factors such as a generous tendency to conflate the new with the avant-garde and the avant-garde with the progressive, and a willingness to interpret some descriptions of repression as attacks on it.

One minor factor in the rise of Heideggerian anti-humanism has to do with Beauvoir and Sartre's own strong misreading of Heidegger. Their interpretation of Heidegger left their existential humanism (which is so important for Beauvoir's treatment of the problem of the Other, and therefore, for her treatment of women, the old, the oppressed) relatively undefended against neo-Heideggerian attacks. Sartre's misreading of Heidegger was signalled early, and very publicly, in his wildly successful popular lecture of 1945, 'Existentialism is a Humanism', which builds on Beauvoir's notions of reciprocity and his own work on authenticity and which stresses the importance of action. Sartre's ideas were savaged by Heidegger in his 'Letter on Humanism' of 1947, which became the main text through which French intellectuals had access to Heidegger.[19] Heidegger proposes a post-metaphysical 'humanism', related not to the biological nor to the anthropological nor, indeed, to any material activities of suffering existents, but rather to the thought of being, the forgetfulness of which has led, in Heidegger's view, to the 'homelessness' and alienation of 'modern man'.[20]

This philosophy of the ineffable seems so far from the notions of engagement espoused by Sartre and reciprocity espoused by Beauvoir that it is most curious that both French philosophers believed themselves to be working the same philosophical ground as Heidegger. For example, in *The Second Sex*, Beauvoir, in explaining her discussion of the body as a situation as opposed to a thing, writes that this must be seen in terms of the 'perspective [she is] adopting – that of Heidegger, Sartre, and Merleau-Ponty'.[21] These fellow-philosophers are claimed as members of her own, coherent group of thinkers. Discussing the need for a new translation of *The Second Sex* in 1982 and in 1985, the year before her death, Beauvoir lamented H. M. Parshley's mistranslation of 'la réalité humaine' as 'human nature' in the English edition of the book:

> you tell me that [Parshley] speaks of human nature whereas I have never believed – nor Sartre either, and on this point I am his disciple – we never believed in human nature. So it's a serious mistake to speak of 'human nature' instead of 'human reality', which is a Heideggerian term. I was infused with Heidegger's philosophy and when I speak about human reality, that is, about man's presence in the world, I'm not speaking about human nature, it's completely different. [22]

This is a fascinating response as 'réalité humaine' is itself a highly problematic French translation of Heidegger's 'Dasein', which suggests the inclusion in the Heideggerian category of the particular, social ways in which human beings exist and have existed, which are exactly what Heidegger wants to exclude from his ontology, and exactly where he locates the corruption of being which his thought is designed to purify. [23]

The 'réalité humaine' which exercised Beauvoir, as one of the key ethical philosophers of her age, had nothing to do with an ontology which severs itself from experience, and everything to do with questions of agency, freedom, rights, and justice, in short, with the identifiably modern project which Charles Taylor describes in terms of a historically modern identity which implicates us 'in a sense of self defined by the powers of disengaged reason as well as in the creative imagination, in the characteristically modern understandings of freedom and dignity and rights, in the ideals of self-fulfilment and expression, and in the demands of universal benevolence and justice.' [24] Heidegger himself found the idea of the modern encapsulated by these terms entirely bankrupt, and it was precisely to avoid the poison of modernity that he asserted the need to take thought back to the notions of the Pre-Socratics, which erase, among other things, the modern notion of the subject. This unease with the subject, with agency, with freedom, is a standard marker of the current intellectual marketplace. The neo-Heideggerian projects which, again as Taylor remarks, are grounded on a view of the 'subject who is enfolded in language which he can neither oversee nor escape' or locked in transmutations of paradigms of psychological or social and political power which simply play themselves out as self-governing systems, which 'disclaim any notion of the good' [25] are antithetical to the entirety of the Beauvoirian project.

The intellectual marketplace

Beauvoir's absence from the philosophy shelves begins to look overdetermined, especially as major lines of feminist work (which have been instrumental in keeping her work alive, and which still provide the major forum for discussion of Beauvoir) become more deeply immersed in the neo-Heideggerian stream, and move away from a defining interest in justice and onto the blurred terrain of gender as performance. The intellectual marketplace of the moment is not a friendly place for Beauvoir the philosopher, with her passion for justice, her insistence on responsibility, her obsession with freedom, her attention to material conditions, and her ethics of reciprocity. And I think that, for the moment, the place that is undeniably Beauvoir's on the philosophy shelves in the London bookshop is likely to remain empty. But not forever.

Notes

1 Toril Moi, *Simone de Beauvoir: The Making of an Intellectual Woman* (Oxford, Blackwell, 1994), 1.

2 See Michèle Le Doeuff, *Hipparchia's Choice: An Essay Concerning Women, Philosophy, etc.* trans. Trista Selous (Oxford, Blackwell, 1991) and Mary G. Dietz, 'Introduction: Debating Simone de Beauvoir', *Signs*, 18: 1 (Autumn 1992), 74–88.

3 Kate Fullbrook and Edward Fullbrook, *Simone de Beauvoir and Jean-Paul Sartre: The Remaking of a Twentieth-Century Legend* (Hemel Hempstead, Harvester Wheatsheaf, 1993; New York, Basic Books, 1994).

4 See Simone de Beauvoir, 'Selections from Towards a Morals of Ambiguity, According to Pyrrhus and Cinéas', trans. Jay Miskowiec; Introduction, Bob Stone, *Social Text* (Fall 1987), 135; and Simone de Beauvoir, 'Pyrrhus and Cinéas', trans. Christopher Freemantle, *Partisan Review*, 3:3 (1946), 330–7.

5 Margaret A. Simons, 'Two Interviews with Simone de Beauvoir', trans. Jane Marie Todd in Nancy Fraser and Sandra Lee Bartky (eds), *Revaluing French Feminism: Critical Essays on Difference, Agency, and Culture* (Bloomington, Indiana, Indiana University Press, 1992), 27–8. Peter Green translates 'concerted delirium which is a system' as 'conscious venture into lunacy known as a "philosophical system"'. See Simone de Beauvoir, *The Prime of Life*, trans. Peter Green (Harmondsworth, Penguin, 1965), 221.

6 Simons, 'Two Interviews with Simone de Beauvoir', 34.

7 Margaret A. Simons and Jessica Benjamin, 'Simone de Beauvoir: An Interview', *Feminist Studies*, 5:2 (Summer 1979), 338.

8 de Beauvoir, *Prime of Life*, 225.

9 *Ibid.*, 327.

10 *Ibid.*, 224, 327–8.

11 Deirdre Bair, *Simone de Beauvoir: A Biography* (London, Jonathan Cape, 1990), 206.

12 *Ibid.*, 207–8.

13 *Ibid.*, 209.

14 Quotations from the report of Grasset's reader, Henry Müller, which Beauvoir cites in *Prime of Life*, 327.

15 See Fullbrook and Fullbrook, *Simone de Beauvoir and Jean-Paul Sartre*, especially 97–127, and Kate Fullbrook and Edward Fullbrook, 'Sartre's Secret Key' in Margaret A. Simons (ed.), *Feminist Interpretations of Simone de Beauvoir (Re-Reading the Canon)* (Philadelphia, Pennsylvania State University Press, 1995). But see also the early recognition, by the distinguished Sartre scholar Hazel Barnes, of the philosophical dimension of the novel in Hazel Barnes, *The Literature of Possibility: A Study in Humanistic Existentialism* (London, Tavistock, 1959).

16 Tom Rockmore, *Heidegger and French Philosophy: Humanism, antihumanism and being* (London, Routledge, 1995), 14. The following discussion draws, in various ways, on this excellent new study of Heidegger's influence in France.

17 The key texts supporting this view are Victor Farías' controversial book, *Heidegger and Nazism*, trans. Paul Burrell and Gabriel R. Ricci, ed. Joseph Margolis and Tom Rockmore (Philadelphia, Temple University Press, 1989), which attracted enormous attention on its first, French, publication in 1987, and Richard Wolin (ed.), *The Heidegger Controversy: A Critical Reader* (London, MIT Press, 1993).

18 Richard Rorty, 'Introduction' to *Essays on Heidegger and Others*, *Philosophical Papers*, 2 (Cambridge, Cambridge University Press, 1991), 4.

19 See Rockmore, *Heidegger and French Philosophy*, 94–8.

20 *Ibid.*, 97.

21 Simone de Beauvoir, *The Second Sex*, trans. H. M. Parshley (Harmondsworth, Penguin, 1972), 66.

22 Simons, 'Two Interviews with Simone de Beauvoir', 33–4.

23 Rockmore, *Heidegger and French Philosophy*, 72–5.

24 Charles Taylor, *Sources of the Self: The Making of the Modern Identity* (Cambridge, Cambridge University Press, 1989), 503.

25 *Ibid.*, 487–8.

7

The business of a 'new art': Woolf, Potter and postmodernism

Maggie Humm

The major features of popular culture in the last decades are mundanely visible: an intensive reworking of past styles (whether bell-bottoms or the Beatles); an often jokey and intensive interreflexivity (the mutual cannibalism of advertisements and films); and a privileging of 'sight' in an overriding concern with surface. These phenomena are understood as postmodern and are deeply bound up with issues of commercialism and representation. You could argue that the *commodification* of post-modernism itself, both by the high street and by the academy, has been the business success story of the 1990s. Hardly a week goes by without a casual and often imprecise synaesthesia of 'postmodern' with 'pro-gress' and with 'pleasure'. For example the media critic Paul Morley often describes himself as a Sue-Ellen fan and a serious up-beat post-masturbator.

The other business success story preceding and continuing through the 1990s is, of course, the commodification of the sign 'Virginia Woolf'. She was first drawn as 'mad and asexual' by Leonard Woolf in his edition of *A Writer's Diary* (1953). Currently 'Woolf' appears in a welter of popular culture iconography including throw cushions, the *New York Review of Books* freebies, Channel Four's *J'Accuse*; Hanif Kureishi's 1987 film *Sammy and Rosie Get Laid*; the hard rock group Virginia Woolf as well as the more overtly feminist signs of sisterhood evidenced by Shake-speare's Sister and feminist tee shirts produced by Historical Products Inc. (Silver, 1992).

Radically disparate signs of contemporary culture, then (postmodern buildings and Virginia Woolf), sometimes take similar performative roles by apparently encouraging surface identifications rather than mat-erial change. Yet, perhaps perversely, my argument is that attention to surface as history is precisely what makes postmodernism a distinctive and potentially radical cultural enterprise and that this is 'reflected' both in Sally Potter's film of *Orlando* and in Woolf's original text. Both film and book suggest new ideas of subjectivity through a spectacular vocabulary of visuality. For example both book and film challenge *through the visual* modernist assumptions that characters 'own' their own identity in some progressive individual history. *Orlando* traverses the centuries from 1600 to Woolf's or Potter's present day. The eponymous hero favoured by Elizabeth I falls in love with Sasha, a Russian princess visiting the court, is spurned first as a lover by Sasha, and then as a writer by Nick Greene. Appointed ambassador to Constantinople by King William, Orlando changes sex and, now a woman, returns to the literary salons of eighteenth-century London. In Potter's film, Orlando loses her estate by giving birth to a daughter in the twentieth century, but in Woolf's biography Orlando retains her property with the birth of a son. Both book and film suggest new ideas of history and subjectivity through the visual by positioning the spectator/reader in new and interesting ways.

Now it is exactly this 'signature of the visible', the title of Fredric Jameson's collected essays about cinema, which so panics critics from the left (Jameson, 1992). Jameson's volume addresses the visibility of postmodern culture and within that, specifically film. Jameson's dis-ease with postmodernism is by now well known (McRobbie, 1994). The title of Jameson's book reveals this. It is a quotation from that text of high modernism, James Joyce's *Ulysses*, 'signatures of all things I am here to read', which stresses *scriptibility* rather than visibility. And it is *precisely* the visibility of particular postmodern films which so distresses Jameson. In his analysis of *Diva* (1981) directed by Jean-Jacques Beineix (whose motorbike rider hero illicitly tapes a famous diva), Jameson praises the extraordinary luminosity of *Diva*'s images – while deploring the very primacy of those images. It is because *Diva*, and other postmodern films such as de Palma's *Blow Out* (also 1981), insistently foreground the *processes* of reproduction exhilarating in a surface aesthetic, that for Jameson such films lack effect. Now feminist critics might also deplore *Diva*, although for very different reasons than those chosen by Jameson. As Toni Cade Bambara points out, the film's young white male steals both voice and clothing from the African-American opera star Wilhelmina Wiggins and this, Bambara rightly suggests, is a 'theft-of-the-Third World shadow text' (Bambara, 1993: 137).

Jameson conceives of postmodernism as a 'litter of cultural artifacts' like a 'great junk pile of video cassettes' (Jameson, 1992: 203). What Jameson particularly fears, of course, is postmodernism's representation of history as 'surface'. The ransacking of preceding culture Jameson calls the 'culture capital' of the postmodern and its 'new forms of cultural credit' (Jameson, 1992: 157). The real distinction between post-modernism and classical modernism, for Jameson, is that modernism has truth value, an 'authentic vision', while postmodernism is text, sheer surface and superficial (Jameson, 1992: 75). In short, what Jameson most deplores in postmodern film is an obsession with the 'society of the spectacle' (Jameson, 1992: 217).

From another direction, the American feminist critic Jane Marcus shares Jameson's anxiety about spectacle and uses oddly similar termin-ology in her savage attack on the film *Orlando* in *The Women's Review of Books*. Again titles are revealing. Marcus's 'Tale of Two Cultures' disparages *Orlando* in order to praise *Modern Fiction Studies'* academic essays about Woolf. The film of *Orlando*, Marcus claims, is 'blancmange' and (curiously simultaneously) 'tapioca pudding' (perhaps Marcus is confused about British puddings) ... 'a sweet white movie taken to the toothache level' ... 'ridiculously bad' ... 'the filmmakers didn't know of the novel's cult status in lesbian and gay culture' (this claim would surprise both Swinton and Potter). And finally the 'film slobbers' and 'I had to apologize', Marcus says, 'to my husband' (in an interesting in-sertion of the circumscriptions of heterosexuality) (Marcus, 1994: 11).

The recognition of a more positive relation between spectacle, women and consumerism in the context of postmodernism is the much keener-eyed focus of feminist critics of the postmodern such as E. Ann Kaplan in America and Meaghan Morris in Australia. In 'Things to Do With Shopping Centres', Morris makes connections between spatial stories (Morris is here in debt to the anthropological writings of Michel de Certeau), the surface displays in Australian shopping centres and women's memory and local history whose admixture is a potential site of social conflict and therefore social change (Morris, 1988). Similarly, in 'Feminism/Oedipus/Postmodernism', Ann Kaplan argues that trans-gressive strategies such as non-narrative devices and the surface repetitions of some rock videos might be potentially feminist and post-modern (Kaplan, 1988).

Following Morris and Kaplan, it is precisely *Orlando*'s representation of history as surface, as consumerism, in both book and film, which marks both not only as postmodernist but, for me, as offering a perception of a new rhetoric of difference. Yet it is important to realise that the aspect of postmodernism that now seems in many ways to characterise it – the attention to surface – is of recent gestation. As a descriptive label, 'postmodernism' came to be applied to films and television only in the 1980s and first gained currency in America in literary criticism which made vigorous attempts to celebrate popular culture as much as the literary canon, projecting a powerful sense of literary and cultural change as the title of Fiedler's book *Waiting for the End* suggests (see Humm, 1994). Postmodern fiction, for example E. L. Doctorow's *Welcome to Hard Times*, is characterised by a knowing play with genres and a scepticism about realism and the values of high art. Indeed 'hyper-reality' became a common theme in the postmodern architectural criticism of Charles Jencks. Attempts to specify the postmodern features of contemporary culture – buildings, novels, television, film – involved critics in one major recognition. This was the idea that although culture was a multiple collection of many different forms, culture could be read or understood as *surface*. This stress on surface rather than on structure by the leading postmodernists Baudrillard and Lyotard is the most obvious change from post-structuralism to postmodernism.

Cultural critics return repeatedly to the idea of postmodernity because its theories help to explain changes in twentieth-century cultural practices. Hence the attempts to represent postmodernism as a coherent whole have inspired a plethora of writing including the now classic accounts by Jean-François Lyotard. Lyotard's *The Postmodern Condition* (1984) is regarded as the *ur*-text of postmodernism. The book gives economic and cultural explanations for the new dissolution of boundaries between high and low culture and for the way in which contemporary culture is recklessly able to synthesise and reconstitute any artistic formation. Lyotard's central claim is that the grand narratives, or theories, of Marxism and Humanism have ceased to work as explanatory paradigms because these 'narratives' do not help us to understand constant and contradictory cultural change. Lyotard replaces metanarratives with an examination of cultural *surface*; that is to say, he argues that the meaning of culture derives both from its visual *processes*, like genre formation in film, and from the visible contexts in which these processes take place (Lyotard, 1984).

In *The Language of Postmodern Architecture* (1977) the architect Charles Jencks adopts the term 'double-coded' from communication studies to describe how postmodernism incorporates differing codes including the styles of many cultural groups. 'The style is hybrid, double-coded, based on fundamental dualities' (Jencks, 1977: 5). Jencks argues that, rather than a 'metanarrative' of classicism, postmodern architecture is fragmented. 'Through our reproduction techniques ... we can reproduce fragmented experiences of different cultures' (Jencks, 1977: 5). Woolf's *Orlando* reproduces the diverse cultures of Constantinople, gypsy life and Elizabethan England. Fragmentation is the representational schema of Potter's *Orlando* whose filmic intertitles are neither summative nor introductory but offer the viewer scenic and Woolfian pauses for breath. Architecture is a 'verb', Jencks claims, 'an action where the image of a city becomes inchoate, the architecture evasive' (Jencks, 1977: 91, 104).

'Inchoate' street scenes are commonplace in Virginia Woolf's novels. An important part of Orlando's characterisation comes from Orlando's reflections on the surface detail of urban scenes. Orlando pursues his locomotor pleasures as a man in Constantinople and, as a Victorian woman, equally enjoys the restless detail of London's department stores and the Old Kent Road. Urban journeys allow Orlando the space of narrative self-reflection. Rather than a panoptic eye, Orlando has the optical point of view of a Hollywood camera.

'Nothing could be seen whole or read from start to finish. What was seen begun – like two friends starting to meet each other across the street – was never seen ended' (Woolf, 1992: 293). In *Illuminations* Walter Benjamin flags 'fragmentation' as a key feature of cinematic form. The 'tactile quality' of Dadaist art, Benjamin argues, 'promoted a demand for film' in which 'no sooner has [the spectator's] eye grasped a scene than it is already changed' (Benjamin, 1973: 240). The street matches the epistemology of the cinema. In a revealing footnote Benjamin remarks: 'the film corresponds to profound changes in the apperceptive apparatus – changes that are experienced on an individual scale by the man in the street in big city traffic' (Benjamin, 1973: 252). Potter similarly stages Woolf's scene as an image of fractured experience by transferring Orlando from a motor vehicle to a motorbike and side car, and by placing the spectator in intimate close-up (see figure 11).

Orlando's active acquisition of knowledge *through* the spectacular in the Old Kent Road finds a ringing reproduction in Benjamin's essay. Similarly Sally Potter's almost fetishistic dedication to mirroring Orlando's states of mind with external objects, for example house facades

11 Tilda Swinton and Jessica (her niece) in *Orlando.*

and garden topiary, matches Woolf's: in the Old Kent Road after 'twenty minutes the body and mind' (an interesting emphatic material reversal of the usual mind and body) 'were like scraps of torn paper tumbling from a sack' (Woolf, 1992: 293). Woolf's anthropomorphising of the urban (its litter) is endorsed in postmodern theory. Jencks often describes buildings as actively human, 'dressed' with faces.

Orlando's picture of the Old Kent Road is the moment when a consolidation of spectacle and consumerism *as knowledge* is dramatically vivid and postmodern. At this point in the book what had been a continuous narrative by Orlando in first person becomes fragmentary, split into cinematic points of view. Like contemporary American cinema the narrator favours medium shots and close-ups rather than long shots. For example, and very uncharacteristically for Woolf, the passage explodes into extremely short sentences clicking from still to still.

'People spilt off the pavement. There were women with shopping bags. Children ran out' (Woolf, 1992: 292). An irresistible testimonial to the power of shot-reaction-shot follows. 'When this happened, Orlando heaved a sigh of relief, lit a cigarette, and puffed for a minute or two in silence' (Woolf, 1992: 293). What Woolf achieves, through Orlando's survey of the surface territory of South London, is the illusion that surface movement can be a simulacrum of knowledge. Jencks's description of postmodernism as a 'Chinese garden space' which 'suspends the clear, final ordering of events for a labyrinth, rambling "way" that never achieves an absolute goal' (Jencks, 1977: 134) is a perfect analogue both to Orlando's enjoyment of the surface incoherence of the Old Kent Road and to Sally Potter's equally inventive scene of Orlando's race through centuries following rapid impetus of a twisting garden maze.

Postmodern texts often transcend gender binaries. For example, Potter characterises the feminine as masquerade with Quentin Crisp's homosexual, cross-dressed performance as Queen Elizabeth I. Woolf's *Orlando* pastiches gender categories in the episode of the Crystal Palace by exposing the arbitrariness of bourgeois gender binaries 'whiskers/wedding cakes', 'cannons/Christmas trees', fully clothed males and 'partly draped' females (Woolf, 1992: 222). If one tries to read *Orlando* simply as a modernist text, as the narrative of an alienated intellectual for example, you miss its foregrounding of gender instabilities. There are multiple Orlandos. 'Then she called hesitatingly, as if the person she wanted might not be there, "Orlando?".' For if there are (at a venture) seventy-six different times all ticking in the mind at once, how many different people are there not – Heaven help us – all having lodgement at one time or another in the human spirit? Some say two thousand and fifty-two' (Woolf, 1992: 293–4).

If Woolf's novel is so clearly marked by its grappling with a postmodern gender instability *avant la lettre*, from where does this come? *Orlando* is profoundly shaped by Woolf's immediate antecedent essays. Woolf wrote *Orlando* between October and December 1927, completing the final third in March 1928. In the same year, Woolf explored ideas about biography, gender and the visual in 'The Art of Biography'. 'Biography will enlarge its scope by hanging up looking glasses at odd corners. And yet from all this diversity it will bring out, not a riot of confusion, but a richer unity' (Woolf, 1961: 167). Woolf's intense interest in the relation between refractions of light and the representation of character is a continuing theme in *Orlando*. The year previously, Woolf had recognised that correspondence in an essay directly about film, 'The Cinema', published in *Arts* in New York in 1926. Woolf's persistent attention to the surface appearance of characters is the theme of that essay (Woolf, 1978). Leslie Hankins argues that Woolf's essay draws on film theory of the twenties (Hankins, 1993). Far more striking are Woolf's descriptions of cinema as an abstract space, perhaps the first British essay to describe avant-garde cinema. Woolf has a unique and singular focus in her theme of spectacle, avidly responding to *Dr Caligari*'s expressionist perspectives and new angles and shapes. Woolf claims that these surface representations offer a new visual aesthetic.

'The most fantastic contrasts could be flashed before us with a speed which the writer can only toil after in vain ... we get intimations only in the chaos of the streets, perhaps, (a point echoed later by Benjamin) when some momentary assembly of colour, sound, movement suggests that here is a scene waiting a new art to be transfixed' (Woolf, 1978: 185–6). That 'new art' was *Orlando*. In an interview in 1993, Potter suggested that her own attention to surface is a similar and integral part of the *script writing* process because she 'reaches out viscerally through the senses, through a feeling of seeing things for the first time. There's a sense of the abstract, almost the metaphysical' (Dargis, 1993: 42).

In the novel, Woolf depicts Marshall and Snelgrove both as a commodity spectacle *and* a space where Orlando *positively* reprises her life 'a vision of innumerable coloured stuffs flaunting in a breeze ... she remembered the feel of rough rubies running through her fingers' (Woolf, 1992: 287). Orlando is able to turn from the plate glass mirror of retail capitalism to her *own* 'little looking glass and a powder puff' (Woolf, 1992: 288). By the end of the novel the house has become 'like a scraped new photograph' with 'a loudspeaker *condensing* on the terrace a dance tune' (Woolf, 1992: 288; my emphasis). As Lyotard suggests, the changed status of knowledge brought about by information technology designates the state of postmodern culture. In *Orlando* lifts and loudspeakers condense and intensify Orlando's knowledge. Information technology also marks the end of the film *Orlando*. In characteristic postmodern fashion, Potter parodies the demands of corporate publishing – the setting is the *Observer*'s Marco Polo building – 'providing you rewrite a little' Orlando is told 'you know develop the love interest and give it a happy ending' (Potter, 1994: 59). History is circular, not progressive, with Jimmy Somerville's hovering golden angel harking back to his song for Queen Elizabeth at the beginning of the film. The reference is, of course, to Walter Benjamin's *Theses on the Philosophy of History*, also taken up by another postmodern artist, Laurie Anderson, in her album *Strange Angel* in the shared image of history as an angel being blown backwards into the future (Benjamin, 1973; Anderson,

1989). The feminist historian Sheila Rowbotham has drawn attention to this postmodern perception most significantly in the title of her book *The Past is Before Us* (Rowbotham, 1989). As Rowbotham explains, 'the past has gone by and is already evident for scrutiny. It is after all the future which is behind us. For with all our gazing and peering we cannot see what is not yet' (Rowbotham, 1989: xi).

Similarly, Potter continually exposes the artificiality of recorded history. Potter defines 'women's time' as active looking (confirming Jameson's worst fears). 'It is time for women to take up our inheritance, an inheritance of a different kind. That is why the daughter is at the end playing with a little movie camera' (Dowell, 1993: 16). Like Woolf, Potter deflates the grand narrative of imperial history by ironically framing Orlando's receipt of the Order of the Bath in the arch of an Islamic mosque, watched by an audience merely of a few courtiers. History becomes a series of scenes. 'I have tried to subvert what is being set up', Potter claims, 'that seemed to me a useful way of looking at British history ... In each scene, in each frame even there is an element of contradiction' (Francke, 1993: 5).

The acquisition of knowledge is not progressive. History is not traditionally linear. The film's intertitles 'Love', 'Death', '1510' and so on replace the traditional periodisation of British history. Instead objects, surface and music become crucial signifiers of meaning, not linear narrative. Texture and very precise colour coding (the film is resolutely *not* all blancmange!) replace the cause and effect of narrative. Each period has a very precise palette: Elizabethan black and white, in Constantinople blue floods into costume and background objects (the Khan's blue cuffs and Khiva's blue tiles). As Potter says, framing is the 'magic key' to understanding (Donahue, 1993: 12). And Potter's framing is very precise. For example, in the scene where Orlando loses her house, the door opens into an apparently endless hole. A metaphorical mapping of objects, for example, the jokey topiary tea cups of the nineteenth century, do the work of linear narrative. Instead of the film offering a transparent window onto an Elizabethan or Victorian world, the film is *perspectival*, commenting continually on its own process as if the world is seen at an angle. This notion of angle of vision is a recurrent metonymy in Woolf's novels, of course, for sexual difference. And when asked about the lesbian politics of her earlier film *The Gold-Diggers* Potter replied 'those ideas were there, but stated at an angle; like everything else in the film' (Ehrenstein, 1993: 3). Potter's continual use of doubles in *Orlando* (Elizabethan double portraits, two child pickpockets in Constantinople) encapsulates this theme (Glaessner, 1992: 15).

Where Lyotard envisaged the social-psychological androgyne as a goal of postmodernism, Potter is more critical, aware that androgyny does not address repressive gender roles (Lyotard, 1984). Potter claims to have retained Woolf's 'notion of the androgynous mind and dissolving gender boundaries' but characterises this as 'polymorphous sexuality rather than specific sexual identities' (Florence, 1993: 283). The arbitrariness of gender is a specific focus of the film. For example, the library scene juxtaposes a gay, falsetto singing voice with an unusually deep-voiced woman. Potter parodies the artificial catachresis 'truly feminine' with Orlando's absurd and exaggerated eighteenth-century blue dress hindering her unwieldy passage through the picture gallery. Again the sound track provides dissonance and irony as an exotic peacock's cry parallels Orlando's walk. In the film, gender is always performance – most transparently in the brief scene where Orlando watches *Othello* whose actors are necessarily male but model women's 'treachery' and the horrific consequences of 'compulsory heterosexuality' (Rich, 1980).

Potter disarticulates gender fixities primarily by usurping the masculine gaze. The artificiality of gender construction is matched by the open artificiality of *Orlando*'s camera shots. Tilda Swinton encouraged Potter to allow Orlando direct speech to camera. In rehearsal, Swinton first spoke her lines to Potter and the intimacy of that address is reflected in her performance. The subject/object hierarchy of conventional spectatorship is deconstructed as Orlando, with her daughter, turns to camera: 'this really is a good film'. Potter describes her aim which is 'to weave a golden thread between Orlando and the audience through the lens of the camera' (Donohue, 1993: 10).

Swinton's extraordinarily luminous and unmarked complexion and studied performance of a non-masculine yet non-feminised male draws attention to the instability of traditional gender motifs. Swinton's physical beauty connotes femininity (slight, fine-featured), throwing into relief the performative quality of her masculinity. The association of whiteness with female desirability has a long cinematic history. Marilyn Monroe, Richard Dyer suggests, similarly acted as a 'visual analogue for a basic conception of female sexuality as itself formless' (Dyer, 1987: 58). Monroe, Dyer claims, anticipates the vaginal imagery of feminist art of the 1970s because her 'image is reaching out to embody an experience [the

Irigarayan two lips] that does not in fact exist' (Dyer, 1987: 66). As Dyer suggests, stardom is an unstable phenomenon which is never constant and hence can never be successfully mapped onto a particular and confirmed sexuality. Significantly Swinton next looks into camera when invited by Queen Elizabeth into the royal chamber, allowing the Queen to 'kiss his forehead sensually' and concludes '(*To Camera*) very interesting person' (Potter, 1994: 9).

The scene highlights the possibility of reforging sexual preferences since Quentin Crisp's 'Queen' would undoubtedly admire a young beautiful boy, but the historic Queen may have favoured both sexes. The direct address of the gaze is of course, in the pornographic tradition, an expressive, specularized relation to the spectator *qua* spectator. Potter dialectically contrasts Swinton's *masculine* control of the gaze with the *feminine* quality of her 'to-be-looked-at-ness' fragile female beauty. Swinton is *both* the fetishistic object of *our* gaze *and* actively governs the camera gaze. The doubling of vision is a metonymy of the doubling of gender. Swinton's use of direct address and epigrammatic, often touchingly conversational, asides to camera momentarily freezes the narrative *and* encourages us as *spectators* to be sensitive to the activity of gazing.

In some senses Potter, quite radically and with originality, shows same-sex desire between Sasha and Orlando (in that the audience knows Orlando is the female actress Tilda Swinton) without Orlando being fixed to a stable gender identity. The effect is not a naturalistic portrayal of a positive androgynous model, or at least not only this. Orlando's gender, in biography and film, is free – Swinton *negotiates gender* in performance lacking any consistent and core gender identity.

In a letter to R. C. Trevelyan about *Orlando*, Woolf felt herself to be decentering historical and gender perspectives. 'Of course the effort to break with strict representation is very unsettling, and many things were not controlled as they should have been ... but the method was not so much at fault as my ignorance of how to do it psychologically ... I'm sorry about the obscurity' (Woolf, 1976: 588). Jane Flax argues that the common ground of feminism and postmodernism is precisely this new theory of subjectivity which can draw on memories, on the unconscious to construct new social subjectivities (Flax, 1987).

Woolf's fragmented punctuation, for example the use of ellipses, frequent question marks and parenthesis, shows a breakdown in the master narrative of biography. *Orlando* took on a life of its own. 'After two days entirely gave up my time chart and abandoned myself to the pure delight of this farce' (Woolf, 1953: 117). 'How extraordinarily unwilled by me but potent in its own right, by the way, *Orlando* was! as if it shoved everything aside to come into existence' (Woolf, 1953: 120).

As Jeanette Winterson wittily suggests 'Woolf wanted to say dangerous things in *Orlando* but she did not want to say them in the missionary position' (Winterson, 1995: 68). Woolf's investment (and Potter's active endorsement of that investment) in gender transitivity presages postmodernism. An acutely critical view of heterosexuality is a crucial part of some postmodern theory. Victorian patriarchy, on the other hand, assumes Orlando to be 'dead and therefore could not hold any property whatsoever; (2) that she was a woman which amounts to much the same thing' (Woolf, 1992: 161). Woolf deflates the binary opposites of gender most famously in her description of love which has 'two faces: one white, the other black; two bodies: one smooth, the other hairy ... Yet, so strictly are they joined together that you cannot separate them' (Woolf, 1992: 112–13).

Orlando was written and published at a time of crisis in the legitimising categories of gender. The first decades of the twentieth century witnessed a feminisation of the urban scene and a specific masculine fear of a loss of identity, in the face of women's advancement (Huyssen, 1986; Nava, 1996). Following the First World War's swingeing decimation of the male population, suffrage challenges combined with the demographic crisis were perceived to delegitimate Victorian sexual mores. Havelock Ellis and Radclyffe Hall had added a third sex, or Uranians, to existing binaries based on Ellis's research into sexual phenomena and identities. The *grands récits* of contemporary masculinity and femininity were in crisis, Vita Sackville-West and Virginia Woolf organised support for *The Well of Loneliness* and Woolf agreed to appear at Radclyffe Hall's obscenity trial.

'The red of the cheeks was covered with peach down; the down on the lips was only a little thicker than the down on the cheeks ... the ears small ... eyes like drenched violets, so large that the water seemed to have brimmed in them and widened them' (Woolf, 1992: 15). Here is a feminised transcendence of masculinity. The mixture of water and violets for Orlando's eyes suggests the possibility of cross-genders. Orlando's indeterminable gender is an issue of costume and performance. The engendering of gender is in the surface ecology of dress. 'He – for there could be no doubt of his sex, though the fashion of the time did something to disguise it' (Woolf, 1992: 13). *Orlando* consistently foregrounds the mismatching of dress and identity.

Similarly we need to note the historical moment in which the film *Orlando* enters a particular social discourse of gender. Following second-wave feminism, new gender identifications matched the progressive economic liberation of contemporary women. As Susan Faludi notes, the annual sales of women's business suits rose by six million units between 1980 and 1990 and, in a less trivial gesture, a historic House of Lords ruling the year before the completion of *Orlando* enabled the British judiciary for the first time to sentence a man to imprisonment for raping his wife (Faludi, 1992). The film reflects that newer terrain outside of motherhood, the family and heterosexuality.

Potter's choice of Derek Jarman, and Mick Jagger's costume designer Sandy Powell, the performance of Quentin Crisp, one of Britain's leading queens, and the choice of Tilda Swinton, known for her cross-gender performances, matches Potter's attack on the catachresis of true womanhood and true manhood when Orlando and Shelmerdine agree their doubled gender. Shelmerdine: 'You might choose not to be a *real man* at all ... say if I was a woman' (Potter, 1994: 54). Potter suggests that, for her, *Orlando* is 'not so much about femininity and difference as about Virginia Woolf's notion of an essential self that lies beyond gender' (Glaessner, 1992: 14). Like Potter, Marjorie Garber argues in *Vested Interests* that to appropriate the cross-dresser as one or other of the two sexes is to underestimate the object of cross-dressing which offers a 'challenge to easy notions of binarity' (Garber, 1992: 10). Cross-dressing is, to Garber, a 'third term', a space of possibility (Garber, 1992: 11). *Orlando*, like Woolf's hope for the future of cinema, represents gender subjectivity as *process*.

Both book and film of *Orlando* share that postmodern aim to reframe gender by reframing history as surface, and finally share postmodernism's key feature which is the extensive use of parody. Woolf parodies her own writing style of intrusive biography as well as Ariosto's *Orlando Furioso*, nineteenth-century romance and Shakespeare's *As You Like It*. As Potter suggested in interview, these literary parodies would not work at the level of cinema: 'Because the book is almost a running commentary on the history of literature as a vehicle for consciousness there had to be a cinematic equivalent to what happened to that consciousness post war. In other words the fracturing of her consciousness and the arrival of the electronic age' (Donohue, 1993: 12). Potter parodies her mentor

Michael Powell's palette of colours (to whom the film is dedicated), as well as high art when Botticelli's *Birth of Venus* is echoed in Orlando's recognition of herself as a woman. In addition Potter parodies those films she selected for a National Film Theatre season to complement the release of her film *The Gold-Diggers*: *Queen Christina*'s close-ups, and Eisenstein's *Alexander Nevsky*'s battle on the ice (British Film Institute, 1984).

In *A Poetics of Postmodernism* Linda Hutcheon suggests that historiographical metafiction (in which category we might include both versions of *Orlando*) 'use[s] parody not only to restore history and memory' but also at the same time 'to put into question the authority of any act of writing' (or viewing) (Hutcheon, 1988: 136). One of the effects of this pluralising, Hutcheon claims, is to give new value to the 'ex-centric'. The move to gender deconstruction, to new meanings of history, the whole impulsive charge against those metanarratives of patriarchal, naturalised sexual divisions makes *Orlando*(s) perfectly postmodern. So, to circle back to my beginning, there is little doubt that while the signs of postmodernism and Woolf are big business, Orlando, as Woolf said in her diary 'keeps the realities at bay' (Woolf, 1953: 136).

References

Anderson, L. (1989) *Strange Angel*, London, Warner Bros.

Bambara, T. C. (1993) 'Reading the Signs, Empowering the Eye: *Daughters of the Dust* and the Black Independent Cinema Movement', in *Black American Cinema* (ed.), M. Diawara, London, Routledge.

Benjamin, W. (1973) *Illuminations*, Fontana, London.

British Film Institute (1984) *National Film Theatre Programme* (May), 2–8.

Dargis, M. (1993) 'Sally Potter: A Director Not Afraid of Virginia Woolf', *Interview*, 23:6 (June), 42–3.

Donohue, W. (1993) 'Immortal Longing', *Sight and Sound*, 3:3 (March), 10–14.

Dowell, P. (1993) 'Demystifying Traditional Notions of Gender: An Interview with Sally Potter', *Cineaste*, 20:1, 16–18.

Dyer, R. (1987) *Heavenly Bodies: Film Stars and Society*, London, Macmillan.

Ehrenstein, D. (1993) 'Out of the Wilderness: An Interview with Sally Potter', *Film Quarterly*, 47:1 (Fall) 2–8.

Faludi, S. (1992) *Backlash: The Undeclared War Against Women*, London, Chatto and Windus.

Flax, J. (1987) 'Postmodernism and Gender Relations in Feminist Theory', *Signs*, 12:4, 621–43.

Florence, P. (1993) 'A Conversation with Sally Potter', *Screen*, 34:3 (Autumn), 275–85.

Francke, L. (1993) 'A Director Comes in from the Cold', *Guardian*, 11 March, 5.

Garber, M. (1992) *Vested Interests: Cross-Dressing and Cultural Anxiety*, Harmondsworth, Penguin.

Glaessner, V. (1992) 'Fire and Ice', *Sight and Sound*, 2:4 (August), 12–15.

Hankins, L. (1993) 'Woolf's *The Cinema* and Film Forums of the Twenties', in D. F. Gillespie (ed.), *The Multiple Muses of Virginia Woolf*, Columbia, University of Missouri Press.

Humm, M. (1994) *A Reader's Guide to Contemporary Feminist Literary Criticism*, Hemel Hempstead, Harvester Wheatsheaf.

Hutcheon, L. (1988) *A Poetics of Postmodernism*, London, Routledge.

Huyssen, A. (1986) *After the Great Divide: Modernism, Mass Culture, Postmodernism*, Bloomington, Indiana University Press.

Jameson, F. (1992) *Signatures of the Visible*, London, Routledge.

Jencks, C. (1977) *The Language of Postmodern Architecture*, London, Academy Editions.

Kaplan, E. A. (1988) 'Feminism/Oedipus/Postmodernism: The Case of MTV', in E. A. Kaplan (ed.), *Postmodernism and its Discontents*, London, Verso.

Lyotard, J.-F. (1984) *The Postmodern Condition: A Report on Knowledge*, trans. G. Bennington and B. Massumi, Minneapolis, University of Minnesota Press.

Marcus, J. (1994) 'A Tale of Two Cultures', *The Women's Review of Books*, 6:4 (January), 11–12.

McRobbie, A. (1994) *Postmodernism and Popular Culture*, London, Routledge.

Morris, M. (1988) 'Things to do with Shopping Centres', in S. Sheridan (ed.), *Grafts*, London, Verso.

Nava, M. (1996) 'Modernity's Disavowal: Women, the City and the Department Store', in M. Nava and A. O'Shea (eds), *Modern Times: Reflections on a Century of English Modernity*, London, Routledge.

Potter, S. (1994) *Orlando*, London, Faber and Faber.

Rich, A. (1980) 'Compulsory Heterosexuality and Lesbian Existence', *Signs*, 5:4, 631–60.

Rowbotham, S. (1989) *The Past is Before Us: Feminism in Action Since the 1960s*, Harmondsworth, Penguin.

Silver, B. R. (1992) 'What's Woolf Got to Do With It? Or the Perils of Popularity', *Modern Fiction Studies*, 38:1 (Spring), 21–61.

Winterson, J. (1995) *Art Objects: Essays on Ecstasy and Effrontery*, London, Jonathan Cape.

Woolf, V. (1953) *A Writer's Diary*, London, Hogarth Press.

—— (1961) *The Death of the Moth and Other Essays*, Harmondsworth, Penguin.

—— (1976) *The Letters of Virginia Woolf: Volume 2 1912–1922*, ed. N. Nicholson, New York, Harcourt Brace Jovanovich.

—— (1978) 'The Cinema', in *The Captain's Death Bed and Other Essays*, New York, Harcourt Brace Jovanovich.

—— (1992) *Orlando*, ed. R. Bowlby, Oxford, Oxford University Press.

8

Performing hysteria: Anne Sexton's 'business' of writing suicide

Elisabeth Bronfen

Adrienne Rich began her commemorative address for Anne Sexton at City College in New York in 1974, with the strong statement 'Anne Sexton was a poet and a suicide', only to continue by offering her own counterstance: 'Many women writers, learning of her death, have been trying to reconcile our feelings about her, her poetry, her suicide at forty-five, with the lives we are trying to stay alive in. We have had enough suicidal women poets, enough suicidal women, enough of self-destructiveness as the sole form of violence permitted to women' (Rich, 1979: 122). While I fully agree with Adrienne Rich that women should explore other expressions of violence than those turned solely against themselves and that an attraction to death should not be considered the privileged ground and vanishing point of the feminine poetic voice, I also believe that we may not yet have had enough critical attention paid to the interface of suicide and poetry, especially when it comes to the issue of women writing and performing in public spaces such as the writer's marketplace. In response to the outrage that arose when the press discovered that Anne Sexton's therapist, Dr Martin T. Orne, had released the tapes recording his sessions with the poet to Linda Gray Sexton, so that these could be used in the biography she had commissioned, the daughter confirmed 'my mother was a dramatic woman, an actress, a publicity hound and wise in the way of business' (Sexton, 1991: 20). I want, therefore, to talk about Anne Sexton as a public figure, as a woman whose business was poetry and suicide, in order to explore the contradictions, the eccentric disregard of propriety, the anguish, the fatality but also the resilient power contained in that strange equation.

I had initially worked on Anne Sexton in conjunction with Sylvia

Plath, as part of my interest in the way twentieth-century women writers adopt but also transform a cultural narrative I came to call 'the dead beloved serving as muse for poetic inspiration and creation' (Bronfen, 1992). Both Plath and Sexton had made it their business to repeatedly invoke their own suicide attempts, their fascination with and desire for death in their work and in their discussion of each other. Indeed, in her article 'The Barfly Ought to Sing' Anne Sexton describes how she, Sylvia Plath and George Starbuck used to go drinking together in the lounge-bar of the Boston Ritz after their poetry workshop with Robert Lowell, to talk at length about their first suicides, 'as if death made each of us a little more real at the moment ... we talked death and this was life for us, lasting in spite of us, or better, because of us, our intent eyes, our fingers clutching the glass, three pairs of eyes fixed on someone's – each one's gossip' (Sexton, 1966: 90). At the time I was struck with the way that for Sexton, using poetry to turn an experience of death and a desire for death into one's business meant thriving on an aporia. For, even while she describes the burned-up, quasi-erotic intensity with which they talked death, she insists that 'suicide is, after all, the opposite of the poem. Sylvia and I often talked opposites' (Sexton, 1966: 90).

I then became intrigued with Anne Sexton a second time after I had been asked to review the German edition of Diane Wood Middlebrook's biography (Bronfen, 1994), precisely because she introduces a provocative new element into the equation that Adrienne Rich offers between suicide and poet, namely that of Sexton's public performance of the stellar female poet. For, throughout her compelling presentation of Anne Sexton's life, Diane Middlebrook suggests that the transformation of frustrated, indeed mad, suburban middle-class housewife into successful poet, for which this biography has become so famous within the archives of twentieth-century women's writing, was sustained precisely by virtue of the fact that the poet herself actively worked at fashioning herself into a marketable image (Middlebrook, 1992: 401 ff.). During the eighteen years that she published and presented her poetry, starting with *To Bedlam and Part Way Back* (1960) Anne Sexton earned almost all of the important awards available to American poets, including the Pulitzer prize and the Shelley prize. She saw her play *Mercy Street* produced off-Broadway, was published in major literary and mass market magazines and newspapers, including *Esquire* and *The New York Times*, and became a regular contributor to *The New Yorker*. At the end of her life she was among the best-paid poetry performers in America, monitoring the fees offered to James Dickey so as to set her own fees. A creature of contradiction to the hilt, she would launch her complaint at the misery of American middle-class women, even as she would insist on doing so in the elegant attire, gesture and style of precisely this class. Similarly, she could live the contradiction of presenting her poem 'Little Girl, My Stringbean, My Lovely Woman' at a read-in against the Vietnam War at Harvard in 1966 while, in what would seem to us today to be incompatible with this, she also accepted the invitation to write her poem 'Moon Song, Woman Song' for a commemorative ceremony, celebrating the Apollo moon landing in 1969.

Middlebrook describes her as both a shrewd businesswoman and a successful teacher, who was offered honorary doctorates from several American universities and who rose to the rank of Professor at Boston University even though she had been skimpily educated. Particularly intriguing about her is, of course, the fact that she was able to conduct this business as poet even though she was suffering from a mental disorder that, eluding diagnosis, could not be cured, and whose symptoms were suicidal self-hatred, addiction to alcohol and pills. For the split that ran through Anne Sexton's personality was such that even as she seemed to lose utter control over her psychic behaviour, falling into trances or epileptic fits while at home, in the midst of her family (the suicide), she was also an expert at selling herself and her work to the public, perfectly adept at producing calculated radio and magazine interviews, completely self-conscious when she encouraged herself to be photographed as well as to have recordings and films made of her readings. Middlebrook confesses that she was initially rather hesitant about accepting Linda Gray Sexton's offer that she become her mother's official biographer precisely because she did not like Sexton's public persona. At the same time she admits that the compelling force and resonance of Anne Sexton's writings, indeed her legacy, is very heavily based on the power her physical presence had on her audience, an aura that has been preserved beyond her death in the many photographic and sound recordings of her highly stylised manner of self-presentation (Middlebrook, 1991: xx).

In other words, to look at Anne Sexton as a cultural phenomenon, as I suggest we could, means addressing the fact that she was one of the first American women writers to perfect the writing and presentation of poetry as a performance that would even appeal to poetry-avoiders;

that over and beyond the controversy her writings provoked, what has entered into public memory is her physical beauty, and along with it the flamboyant and provocative, almost exhibitionist manner so perfectly controlled, with which, in Maxine Kumin's words, 'she bared her liver to the eagle in public readings where almost invariably there was standing room only ... Her presence on the platform dazzled with its staginess, its props of water glass, cigarettes, and ashtray. She used pregnant pauses, husky whispers, pseudoshouts to calculated effect. A Sexton audience might hiss its displeasure or deliver a standing ovation. It did not doze off during a reading' (Kumin, 1981: xxi).

In an article published 1973 in the *American Poetry Review*, entitled 'The Freak Show', Sexton articulates all the contradictions inherent in a public staging of intimate poetic expression, while skilfully leaving her own position opaque. While she explains that she writes for an audience of one person, that perfect reader who understands and loves, she realises that the moment she performs her poetry, she turns into a freak, an actor, a clown, an oddball. The act of performance emphasises what is implicit to all intimate poetic writing: that writing turns the intimate into something exterior, draws a boundary between experience or feeling and expression, creates a distance between the speaker and the persona or self-representation articulating the speaker in the process of poetic transformation. But in so doing, the *self-conscious* performance in fact implicitly uncovers this underlying contradiction. 'Poetry is for us poets the handwriting on the tablet of the soul. It is the most private, deepest, most precious part of us. Yet somehow in this poetry biz, as one of my students calls it, we are asked to make a show of it' (Sexton, 1973: 35).

What is so compelling for me in Anne Sexton as public performer of femininity is the fact that, in the course of her extravagant, flamboyant, mannered self-presentation, she seems cannily to have staged a psychoanalytic and a deconstructive truth, namely the fact that the most interior part of the psyche has, as Jacques Lacan argues, a quality of exteriority, of being Other, like a foreign body, a parasite, a state for which he coined the term 'extimacy' (Miller, 1988). In other words, her performances of her poetry externalise the fact that as a woman, born and raised in a particular cultural space, she is performatively constructed by a particular discourse and a particular psychic make-up. If we recall that linguistic speech act theory designates the performative as an utterance that constitutes some act, especially the act described by the verb of a sentence, Anne Sexton in her gesture of presenting herself other than she is – as an actress, speaking lines she has constructed for herself, recasting sentences or stories handed down to her by her relatives or lines that have come to her by inspiration, but in all cases lines that are explicitly marked as not being natural – insists that the act of self-representation is the verb of her public performance. She seems to say, I am a performance, indeed, I am only *as a performance*, as the knotting together of languages, of languages that have determined me, be it the forbiddances of my parents, the cultural texts they have endowed me with, be it the constraints and phantasmas of the culture I was educated in (its fairy tales and myths), be it my unconscious, that speaks to me a knowledge I have no direct access to.

Indeed Sexton has herself been quite vocal about the alterity of the unconscious, explaining in an interview with Barbara Kevles, 'Sometimes, my doctors tell me that I understand something in a poem that I haven't integrated into my life ... The poetry is often more advanced, in terms of my unconscious, than I am. Poetry, after all, milks the unconscious. The unconscious is there to feed it little images, little symbols, the answers, the insights I know not of' (Sexton, 1974: 85). I will return to the notion that intimate psychic truth was conceived by Sexton as radically Other later on, when I will develop a set of analogies between her psychic disturbances, her therapy and her creative acts. At this point I simply want to emphasise that, in the case of Anne Sexton, the issue of the female poet's public self-display is, in fact, two-fold, and it is above all this duplicitous doubleness, this splitting of the poet into substance and performance of poetic speech, which makes her such a compelling case for any discussion of the equation of suicide and poet for the woman writer in the marketplace.

For on the one hand, like many of the poets of her generation, though perhaps more boldly so, Sexton writes so-called 'confessional poetry' about intimate aspects of the feminine condition – the sexual assault inflicted upon her by her father, the madness that would overpower her, her own transgressive sexual desires, such as incest or adultery, along with explicit descriptions of the feminine body, such as the infamous celebration of her uterus, her poems on menstruation, abortion, masturbation and drug addiction. On the other hand, her resilience as a poet resided precisely in the fact that not only was her body the thematic subject of her poetry, but that she also used it as her poetic medium, staging it self-consciously as a vehicle for her self-display that was on a par with her words. And it is precisely because of the way she explicitly staged her presence within public space that Anne Sexton is, in fact, quite different from the other women poets politically committed to the situation of women in the 1960s and early 1970s like Maxime Kumin, Adrienne Rich or Muriel Rukeyser.

In a sense, one could say, her performances work in two directions. On the one hand, to invoke Teresa de Lauretis (1984), they enact the contradiction that any feminine self-representation, as long as it is informed by prevalent cultural expectations of femininity, indeed inscribed by these patriarchal constructions, does not coincide with the reality of feminine experience. In so doing her public self-representations perform the terms of the production of woman as text, as image, but by virtue of this performance also exceed the constraints, the inadequacy this transformation implies. Instead, her performances offer a jarring spectacle that both invites identification and defies it; they elicit, as I have already quoted, the hiss of displeasure or/and the delivery of a standing-ovation. On the other hand, her performances also stage the performative quality of gender, the parody of femininity, in the manner described by Judith Butler (1990), who argues that when a female subject assumes a particular gender position within a given cultural space, this is a performance, constituted by that which must be dislocated, in order for this position to hold. The female subject, she maintains, is constructed through a series of exclusions and choices. The 'I', the speaking and spoken persona, is not simply situated in an identity, autonomous and original. Rather, the subject is constituted through the discursive position that she chooses, in order to define herself, as well as through the family relations that determine her formation. In other words, the subject is constituted performatively; there is no easy equation between a feminine subject and its articulation, no transparent coincidence between the woman Anne Sexton and her self-representations, her public persona. Her truth is a foreign body inhabiting her, speaking from within, but finding articulation only through externalisations that are no longer true renditions of the feminine condition but are only true because the act of public performance performs them as truths.

In the coda to the second edition of her biography of Anne Sexton, Diane Middlebrook (1992) suggestively argues that we could see her as a precursor of the generation of women performance artists that has emerged in the 1980s, artists like Laurie Anderson, Patti Smith,

Diamanda Gallas or Madonna, and I would add, including the medium of visual arts, Cindy Sherman or Orlane. For in her insistence on exploring women's power within the public space by virtue of a highly contrived performance of femininity, Anne Sexton oscillates between using her body as the site over which those images of femininity privileged by a particular culture can be performed, even as the self-consciousness inherent to this pose serves to disclose the presuppositions of the implicit ideology. At the same time she illustrates, perhaps more poignantly and more fatefully than the generation of performance artists that come after her, how the act of public performance, exhilarating as it may be, also implies being subsumed by, indeed depleted by this transformation of the woman, speaking about her body, into the feminine body as medium of its own self-expression. In the same interview with Barbara Kevles she also explains that a public reading took three weeks out of her life; 'a week before it happens, the nervousness begins and it builds up to the night of the reading, when the poet in you changes into a performer. Readings take so much out of you, because they are a reliving of the experience, that is, they are happening all over again. I am an actress in my own autobiographical play' (Sexton, 1974: 109). In other words, in the act of performance, the poet and the suicide conflate precisely because the speaking woman transforms into an image of herself, repeating an intimate scene, but at another site, at another temporal moment, no longer authentic, Other. While Sexton always understood writing poetry as the movement through death into a new life, 'inherent in the process is a rebirth of a sense of self, each time stripping away a dead self' (Sexton, 1974: 86), her performances augment this dialectic by staging a wilful splitting into self and representation of the self, staging the performative constitution of the female poet, insisting that her existence is *as* an actress, *on* a stage, *in* a play scripted by her life.

A seminal difference between Sexton and her performing daughters, one could argue, is of course the fact that the second generation performs femininity within and in explicit reference to a cultural context informed by twenty years of feminist theories dismantling the presuppositions underlying traditional gender constructions. To speak of self-conscious staging in the case of Anne Sexton implies something far less self-assured. Though her gestures are also calculated, controlled and self-reflexive, they do not come from the position of one who can ironically distance herself from the discourse that has constructed her, but rather one who can only make her implication within this discourse explicit. Anne Sexton, one could say, performs the constraints of the discourse within which she was formed in her gesture of making her intimacy external without, however, being able to extract herself from its fatality. Yet poignant, it seems to me, is that both generations of performance artists share sex, violence, mental illness, humour and passionate spirituality as their themes, as they also share the fact that they perform poetry articulating feminine intimacies publicly.

In so doing they above all share the fact that they make explicit the distance between the female poet, her body and her voice articulating this poetry, and the poetic text itself. They quite explicitly insist that they are not making a confession but playing at confessing. One could add, their gestures are fetishistic, in accordance with what Sarah Kofman (1985) has called the affirmative Woman, split between denying and affirming her construction as Woman, as a cultural text, a gendered construction. They can be seen as affirming femininity – a parody that accepts and deconstructs the feminine – because they oscillate between the gesture of incarnating a woman's truth and incarnating a deception of her truth; performing the reconciliation of incompatible attitudes to lack and integrity, to lying and telling the truth about one's intimacy. As Anne Sexton articulates this affirmative duplicity, 'Many of my poems are true, line by line, altering a few facts to get the story at its heart ... Each poem has its own truth ... But then poetic truth is not necessarily autobiographical. It is truth that goes beyond the immediate self, another life. I don't adhere to literal facts all the time; I make them up whenever needed' (Sexton, 1974: 103). In other words, what Anne Sexton shares with her performing daughters is that she seems to be telling the audience in one and the same gesture, you think you see a woman in all her intimacy, confessing to you her private desires, fantasies and anxieties, you do, but what you also see is her performing a representation of this woman; what you are also presented with is a text of feminine intimacy, a duplicitous representation of the feminine confession, in fact a self-conscious performance of the fact that we are performatively constructed according to the stories we are taught and the stories we live by.

Taking my cue from Middlebrook, I want to suggest that Anne Sexton's publicly-staged performances of the feminine confession and the feminine complaint allow us to theorise what is a truly spectacular contradiction in Anne Sexton's biography, namely the fact that she kept oscillating between public success and psychic disturbance, that she kept renegotiating the exchange between psychic illness as a result of the feminine condition and its therapeutic rearticulation through analysis and art. As I will explicate further on, it is quite significant that Anne Sexton was diagnosed as a hysteric, a malady which is traditionally connected with feminine dissatisfaction and symptomised as the wandering uterus, searching for nourishment, in the course of which it upsets normal bodily and psychic functions by settling in improper sites – the legs or arms that then become paralysed; the throat, resulting in suffocation, screams or voicelessness; the chest, calling forth epileptic fits; the brain, producing hallucinations, loss of consciousness. On a less poetic and more pragmatic level, however, this illness is above all characterised as one that has no organic lesions, and as such is entirely an illness by representation (Veith, 1965; Showalter, 1985; Micale, 1995). The body symptoms stand in for a disorder that cannot be located in the body, so that one can conclude the disorder is itself performative. The production of the hysterical symptoms – loss of consciousness, speaking in different voices, loss of control over bodily functions – are themselves the only possible articulation of the psychic disturbance, but a disturbance that uses the language of the body where it cannot resort to symbolic language: it says, 'I am caught in an emotional impasse' by resorting to a paralysis of the legs; it says, 'I cannot live with the constraints imposed on my desire for self-development' by resorting to a loss of self entirely or a split of the self into many roles.

We must not forget, however, that hysteria is also an illness by representation in so far as the hysteric is not only haunted by memories and stories she has incorporated and which she cannot shed, texts occupying her body as though it were their host, using her body to speak their alterity. Rather, the seminal definition of the hysteric is, furthermore, that there is a non-coincidence between her self-representations and the being she really is, but in such a manner that not only does she play roles, but her existence resides in the performance of these roles (Mentzos, 1980). The issue is not whether there is a true kernel of the self, which the hysteric is oblivious to or which she keeps hidden in the course of her public display. Rather, at stake is the fact that the public display is the only way she can articulate her true self, albeit knowing that this is a performance. If we recall the spectacular performances of the young hysterics in Charcot's amphitheatre during his *leçons de mardi*, where, at the end of the last century, he sought to exhibit to a heterogeneous Parisian audience the five-phase cycle of hysteria (Didi-Huberman, 1982), or if we recall the case histories told by Freud and Breuer in their *Studies on Hysteria* (1895), we will notice that hysteric self-display always meant the public staging of an intimate trauma, of intimate fantasies, a presentation of the self as 'an actress in an autobiographical play' (Sexton, 1974: 109). And it is here that the analogy between hysteria and Sexton's art of performance begins to unfold. For, like the classic hysteric, she too seems to have fallen into a sort of trance, both when she spoke during her interviews, and when she performed her poetry in lecture theatres; she too articulated traumatic truths by having recourse to other, foreign, extimate personae. To quote Sexton yet again, 'It's a little mad, but I believe I am many people. When I am writing a poem, I feel I am the person who should have written it. Many times I assume these guises ... sometimes I become someone else and when I do, I believe, even in moments when I'm not writing the poem, that I am that person' (Sexton, 1974: 193f).

What strikes me as so compelling about Sexton's public performances is then the way they ask us to consider how giving voice to alterity is a gesture that oscillates between being sincere and being contrived, how she may have had no regard for the private, as some have accused her, by turning all intimacy into a public self-display, but that this confession was always presented as an assumed role, a resourceful ruse. My point is not to belabour what seems obvious, namely that the spontaneity of confessional poetry is highly artificial, that the seemingly private is presented in an inextricably public guise, the seemingly autobiographical in fact the result of extreme artifice. As Sexton says 'I use the personal when I am applying a mask to my face' (quoted in Pollitt, 1991: 21). Rather, I want to suggest that there is a fruitful alignment that can be made between hysteria and feminine performance. For both the hysteric and the performance artist stage a scene where the woman being spoken of is someone other than the one speaking. They negotiate the issue of private and public, of the intimate being confessed and exhibited on the marketplace, precisely by virtue of the fact that to undertake an autobiographic performance always contains a contradiction, the act of performing, of representing, undermines any easy assumptions of authenticity inherent in autobiography. Put apodictically, the public performance is a hysterical gesture, even as hysteria articulates the split between a seemingly controlled public self-representation and the disturbances underlying and subverting any fixed notion of self-representation. Thus, when we confront Middlebrook's assessment that the horizon or story-line of much of Sexton's poetry is, 'of course, autobiographical, focused on Sexton's attraction to death' (Middlebrook, 1985: 313) with Sexton's own insistence that 'suicide is the opposite of the poem' (Sexton, 1966: 90), we are quite literally at the aporetic heart of the matter.

Sexton herself did not like to call herself a confessional poet, and preferred to be thought of as a storyteller. Indeed, as Middlebrook points out, Sexton always claimed that her career as a poet had the shape of a story, a story, furthermore, that opened not with the event of writing her first poem, but with the suicide attempt that separated her from a former life (Middlebrook, 1984: 7). The narrative she offered her public so as to explain this splitting and transformation of herself runs as follows:

> Until I was twenty-eight I had a kind of buried self who didn't know she could do anything but make white sauce and diaper babies. I didn't know I had any creative depths. I was a victim of the American Dream, the bourgeois, middle-class dream. All I wanted was a little piece of life, to be married, to have children. I thought the nightmares, the visions, the de-mons would go away if there was enough love to put them down. I was trying my damnedest to lead a conventional life, for that was how I was brought up, and it was what my husband wanted of me. But one can't build little white picket fences to keep nightmares out. The surface cracked when I was about twenty-eight. I had a psychotic break and tried to kill myself. (Sexton, 1974: 84).

Now, if we splice together the metaphor Sexton offers of a surface that cracks only to allow madness and suicidal desire to emerge, with Judith Butler's argument about the performative aspect of the gendered subject, we can interpret Sexton's psychotic break as an indication of the return of all that which had to be dislocated or excluded for the construction of the American middle-class bourgeois housewife to take place and to hold. Indeed, to stay with the metaphoric language of classic medical discourses on hysteria, the cracking of the surface, the psychotic break, is but another metaphor for the trope established within medical dis-course, the image of the breaking away of the uterus. As somatic initiation of disruptive dislocation, this cracking, this breaking loose took on, in the case of Anne Sexton, four performative modes.

1) The various expressions of madness; in her case particularly hallucin-ations, suicidal tendencies and a split into multiple identities, and her

tendency to fall into a self-induced trance and become unresponsive. As Orne suggests, 'it seemed likely that she used some of the trance episodes to play the role of dying, which perhaps helped her not to suicide' (Middlebrook, 1991: xvii). In so doing, she exhibited symptoms classic to the hysteric, a chameleon-like ability to adopt any symptom, concomitant with profound dissociation, and lesions of memory.

2) The scene of psychoanalysis, where Anne Sexton would take on several personae, invent roles for herself, create narratives about past traumas while in a trance that were not representations of actual events but fictitious versions; where she would speak from another place, indeed so completely give herself over to her unconscious, to the Other truth, the alterity within her psychic apparatus that at the end of her sessions she would become entirely unconscious. Owing to this, her therapist decided to tape their sessions and asked her to transcribe them, so as to get her to recollect what had passed and what her state of dissociation had demanded she repress.

3) The scene of writing, which she likens to a trance-like or a death-like state. We see here the resonant analogies emerging. Her therapist had encouraged her to write poetry, arguing for one thing that in the act of creation, she would discover truths about herself that were not available to her conscious self and for another, that her poetry might help others. Yet the trance-like state, the little deaths she experienced while writing, also, of course, hark back and mirror her psychic illness, her fascination with playing death. Then, too, in the state of writing she could repeat both the role-playing that characterised her hysteria and the production of explanatory fictions and personas within her therapy sessions.

4) Finally the performance of poetic writing, whose theme is madness, fascination with death, with taking on roles, with therapy and writing, imitating once more her dissociation, only now using it fruitfully for her public self-display.

What we have, of course, learned from feminist scholarship on hysteria is that in most cases, the hysteric's symptoms – inertia, over-excitation, role-playing, motoric functional disorders – in fact signal a recourse to body language so as to address the stifling social situation of women, the disillusionment of youthful hopes (Smith-Rosenberg, 1985). Mapping this social issue onto the pattern of hysterical performance delineated so far, we can embellish the four modalities. Anne Sexton's hysteric disorders are symptoms for the disorders of her culture in relation to women's position in it, and in fact perform the disorder and the feminine discontent with it. Her dissociations, her chameleon-like ability to take on any illness, her role-playing, can be seen as a desperate somatic parody of what was expected of the suburban house-wife and mother at the time: the vacuous smile, the perfect poise, the total submission to the myth about domestic bliss, integrity and har-mony (Middlebrook, 1991: 40). Her performances then repeat, by making completely public, this dialectic between the roles western cul-ture ascribed to mid-twentieth-century women and their assumption of these roles. The performative quality of Anne Sexton's public self-display, one could say, is like a chiasmic closure to the psychotic break of the shell, mirroring the two-fold aspect of hysteria. For in one and the same gesture her performance of hysteria serves both as a symptom of her discontent in relation to the discursive constitution of the feminine subject she found herself in and as a critical, albeit at times utterly self-destructive, display of this discontent.

I find it significant that Anne Sexton should have been diagnosed as a classic hysteric in light of Catherine Clément's (1979) comparison between performers and hysterics, given that she highlights the way they share the gesture of superlative simulacra, of pretence, of pure appearance, both reconstituting themselves daily in the spectacle of the roles they play, with life taking on the status of an intermission between performances. Both move from one assumed identity to another, appar-ently indifferent to any psychic reality. Each indifferent to her pain, both hysteric and performer can incite further stagings of pain and death-like states without ultimately killing a central point of resistance in their psychic makeup. Given that Anne Sexton in fact embodies both – the hysteric and the performer – her case allows us to explore the mutual implication of these two feminine gestures. Indeed what transpired in her early therapy is the following suggestive pattern. Initiating every-thing was the break-through of a traumatic truth, the psychotic break with her existence as a suburban housewife, an incursion of real psychic distress that served to disclose her previous identity as having been an illusory falsity, a lie, a mask. In therapy then, Sexton had recourse to several so-called false personae as means by which to give figure to her trauma, only to discover that they were 'truth crimes', 'lies' she had been treating as 'memories'. This hysterical performance of roles led her to fear 'I am nothing, if not an actress off the stage. In fact, it comes down to the terrible truth that there is no true part of me ... I suspect that I have no self so I produce a different one for different people. I don't believe me, and I seem forced to constantly establish long fake and various personalities' (quoted in Middlebrook, 1991: 62f).

Yet the sense that she was a 'total lie', which can be seen as her performative response to the lies her cultural context as well as her family structure had forced her to take on (that she should find utter and exclusive fulfilment in performing her culture's notion of wife and mother), found its chiasmic closure as she transformed the disempowered living of roles in her domestic everyday and in therapy into writing and performing her texts. The destructive hysteria of her day-to-day existence became a constructive hysteria once she actively used these masks and lies to consciously create and perform personas; 'Only in that funny trance can I believe myself, or feel my feeling,' she noted about writing. 'It is the split self, it seems to me, that is the mad woman. When writing you make a new reality and become whole ... It is like lying on the analyst's couch, reenacting a private terror, and the creative mind is the analyst who gives pattern and meaning to what the persona sees as only incoherent experience' (quoted in Middlebrook, 1991: 64). Poetry and its performance made these lies, these masks fruitful rather than pernicious, but precisely because it opened them to the public; 'Think I am a poet? false – someone else writes – I am a person selling poetry' (quoted in Middlebrook, 1991: 63).

My point, then, is not that writing and selling her confessions, transforming her sense of being an actress *off* the stage into an actress *in* her own autobiographical play, allowed Sexton to achieve a satisfying wholeness. Rather, I want to emphasise the performative that structures all four modes – the discontented housewife, the dissociated analysand, the tranced writer and the staged self-displayer; to be more precise, that each modality is a masking and demasking of the fact that femininity is constructed by the discourse in which woman finds herself emplaced. At the same time I want to hold on to the fact that each modality of the self-lie also performs the presence, albeit as an obscene underside, of a traumatic truth, at first entirely repressed, then articulated obliquely in the 'truth-crimes' in therapy, the tropes of her poetry, the personae of her public readings. For until the end, Anne Sexton also insisted, 'I'm hunting for the truth ... behind everything what happens to you, every act, there is another truth, a secret life' (quoted in Ostriker, 1982: 274), knowing full well that she would only have access to this truth once she had transformed it into a representation.

The point about hysteria is, of course, that it jars, that it performs such contradictions as those between confession and control, intimacy and extravagance, mental breakdown and public success, but flaunts its candour and its contrivance to such an excessive degree as to appear in bad taste. I would speculate that this is precisely why people disliked Anne Sexton. By performing the disease of her culture to its utmost extreme, to its turning point, she caused dis-ease in her audience. The hysteric, thus her message, won't be contained, not only because she makes public her private traumas, but because she performs these as contradictions. Unwittingly Lowell's disparaging comment 'She became meager and exaggerated. Many of her most embarrassing poems would have been fascinating if someone had put them in quotes, as the presentation of some character, not the author' (Lowell, 1978: 71) actually hits the mark. Under the auspices of her hysterical performance, her poetry was always meant to be seen in quotation marks. As Alicia Ostriker (1982) notes, her power as a poet resided precisely in her eccentricity, making external with force what is conventionally to be kept internal, her insistence on emotional intimacy, on unresignedness, on an explicit discussion of the feminine body against the poetic reticence and good taste traditionally valorised within the archive of modern poetry, even if this meant that she was a dazzling but not a 'fine artist'.

In a sense this flaunting of contradiction goes to the heart of the matter, namely that the hysteric must keep the question of identity open, oscillating between various self-fashionings, celebrating and affirming each, but as performances. She must remain not only alive to creation, as Diana Hume George notes, but also to the lived truth of terror, with panic always rumbling underneath joy (1987: 163). As Jacques Lacan argues in his discussion of Freud's case study on Dora (1951), the hysteric places herself in relation to a figure of paternity, sustaining his desire even as she ceaselessly questions the authority of his power. In Anne Sexton's poems this figure appears as the desirable and abusive father, as well as in the guise of her teachers of poetry, her therapists, and finally, in her late religious poetry, as God. But her position before this paternal law is contradictory, both accepting that the question of her existence can only be articulated in relation to this paternal figure and perpetually re-negotiating her relation to the Other. This exchange takes the shape of performing the question 'what am I?' concerning her sexual designation and her contingency in being. It means asking on the one hand, 'am I a man or a woman?', and on the other, 'am I or might I not be?' The enmeshment of these two paradigms, Lacan notes in another article, 'conjugates the mystery of the hysterical subject's existence, binding it in the symbols of procreation and death' (Lacan, 1955–6: 194). Thus the question of her existence, repeatedly performed in relation to the paternal figure, will bathe the hysteric, support her, invade her, tear her apart, and this is articulated in the various symptoms she produces; in the case of Anne Sexton, the repeated moments of psychic disorder, the dialogues with her therapists, her poetry and her public performance in her autobiographical play. The point to remember, however, is that this resilient, creative and destructive dialogue is one that is not only articulated in the Other but also articulates the Other. Crucial to the enmeshment of hysteria and performance, I argue, is the fact that Anne Sexton repeatedly staged her existence as the impossibility of deciding once and for all to be feminine or masculine, to live or to die, because she knew that her roles encircled not a self-kernel but a radical negativity. In the light of her autobiographical play, which she staged in public auditoriums as well as in the homes of her family and her friends, her epigraph to the collection *Live or Die*, taken from an early draft of Saul Bellow's *Herzog* – 'Don't cry, you idiot! Live or die, but don't poison everything' – can only be understood as the supremely ironic background for her insistence, 'I talk of the life/death cycle of the body' (Sexton, 1974: 109). The trace of poison is ineluctable.

So we return to the issue that Anne Sexton was a poet and a suicide, that her act of performing intimacy made suicide the opposite of the poem even as the horizon of the poem remained her attraction to death. For as poetry became her business, she learned to transform both the female complaint and the critique of her cultural construction, initially performed as an illness at her body, into a stardom we can interpret as a second-degree performance of the female complaint. In the course of her career, the poetic lament given voice through writing and staging was supported by another favoured narrative, as powerful as that of the psychotic break of the shell of middle-class integrity, namely her favourite palindrome, 'rats live on no evil star' (Kumin, 1981: xxx). In the uncollected poem 'An Obsessive combination of Ontological Inscape, Trickery and Love' she writes: 'Busy, with an idea for a code, I write/signals hurrying from left to right,/or right to left, by obscure routes,/ ... until, suddenly, RATS/can amazingly and funnily become STAR' (reprinted in Colburn, 1985, after the table of contents). In a letter to her analyst she plays with the same concept 'If I write RATS and discover that rats reads STAR backwards, and amazingly STAR is

wonderful and good because I found it in rats, then is star untrue? ...
I don't really believe the poem, but the name is surely mine so I must
belong to the poem. So I must be real ... when you say "words mean
nothing" then it means that the real me is nothing. All I am is the trick
of words writing themselves' (quoted in Middlebrook, 1991: 82).

The final psychic mapping I want, then, to suggest is that at the
beginning of her chiasmic narrative of her career, shaped like a story
that began with her suicide, tracing a trajectory from mad housewife,
through analysand, to stellar public performer is the rat, the Other in
her, the traumatic truth as alterity, for which Lacan has coined the term
extimacy. In the poem 'Rowing', Sexton invokes a 'gnawing pestilential
rat inside me' which she feels she must get rid of, her trope for what is
evil in her, for what she wishes to abject, for that internal Otherness,
for the archaic destructive *jouissance*, which she was able initially to
contain, by translating it into various hysteric symptoms, but which
ultimately broke the shell in the form of suicidal desire. Through the
experience of therapy-cum-poetry writing she fashioned herself into
'Anne', an identity that could keep oscillating between this unbearable
but true alterity, and the bearable versions of her self she could live with;
negotiating her constant performative recasting of the self, and its obscene underside, the knowledge that 'the real me is nothing'. The
chiasmic closure to this equation is then the star, coming out of, implicated by but also transforming, the rat. Thus she writes in her poem
'The Black Art', 'My friend, my friend, I was born/Doing reference work
in sin, and born/Confessing it. This is what poems are:/With mercy/For
the greedy,/They are the tongue's wrangle/The world's pottage, the rat's
star'. The point of Lacan's notion of extimacy, so perfected in the hysteric's performance, is that one can only oscillate between the rat and
the star, use the dislocation of the rat (hysteria's wandering uterus) to
produce stellar reversions of the self, but never truly sever the two.

Which forces me to close, nevertheless, on a disquietingly contradictory note. For if Anne Sexton's business was poetry, as the
transformation of her rats into herself as star, if her hysteric performance
was her way of living, with star the protection from the rats that were
inextricably written into her psychic apparatus, or if, as Kumin writes,
her art was that apotropaic device that protected her from succumbing
to the death baby we carry with us from the moment of birth (Kumin,
1981: xxix), we must not forget, her business was also death. Much
as the transformation of her contemporaries, Norma Jean Baker into

Marilyn Monroe, or the obese Maria Kalogeropoulos into the thin opera diva Maria Callas, meant a transformation in the course of which the discarded self could be recreated in a plethora of resilient performances of femininity, so too, taking on other voices, existing as the performance of texts implied a death of the self, or rather the recognition that the self is always plural, constructed over real negativity, traumatic Otherness, the archaic *jouissance* beyond any performative gesture. This impasse – to be a suicide and a poet – is an impasse we cannot have enough of because it is not solvable. For if rats can amazingly write star, the danger of reversal remains, lurking in the background, ready to strike back, when star suddenly and horrifically transforms into rats. With the image of Anne Sexton in mind, clad in her mother's fur coat, a whisky glass in her hand, slumped back on the seat of her car, finally giving in to those pestilential rats, to the death fumes, but performing to the last, which is to say, when all is said and done, what remains is the resonance of her text, the grain of its voice.

References

Bronfen, Elisabeth (1992) *Over Her Dead Body. Death, Femininity and the Aesthetic*, Manchester: Manchester University Press.
—— (1994) 'Zwischen Selbstinszenierung und Selbstaufgabe', *Neue Züricher Zeitung* (30/31 Juli), 55.
Butler, Judith (1990) *Gender Trouble. Feminism and the Subversion of Identity*, New York/London: Routledge.
Clément, Catherine (1979) *L'Opéra ou da défaite des femmes*, Paris: Grasset.
Colburn, Steven E. (1985) *No Evil Star. Selected Essays, Interviews, and Prose*, Ann Arbor: University of Michigan Press.
de Lauretis, Teresa (1984) *Alice Doesn't. Feminism, Semiotics, Cinema*, Bloomington: Indiana University Press.
Didi-Huberman, Georges (1982) *Invention de l'hystérie. Charcot et l'iconographie de la Salpêtrière*, Paris: Macula.
Freud, Sigmund and Breuer, Josef (1895) *Studies on Hysteria. Standard Edition II*, London: Hogarth Press, 1955.
George, Diana Hume (1987) *Oedipus Anne. The Poetry of Anne Sexton*, Urbana/Chicago: University of Illinois Press.
Kofman, Sarah (1985) *The Enigma of Woman. Woman in Freud's Writings*, Ithaca: Cornell University Press.
Kumin, Maxime (1981) 'How It Was', in *Anne Sexton. The Complete Poems*, Boston: Houghton Mifflin.
Lacan, Jacques (1951) 'Intervention on Transference', in Charles Bernheimer

and Claire Kahane (eds), *In Dora's Case. Freud-Hysteria-Feminism*, Ithaca: Cornell University Press, 1985.

—— (1955–6) 'On a Question Preliminary to any Possible Treatment of Psychosis', in Alan Sheridan (ed.), *Ecrits. A Selection*, New York: Norton, 1977.

Lowell, Robert (1978) 'Anne Sexton', in J. D. McClatchy (ed.), *Anne Sexton. The Artist and her Critics*, Bloomington: Indiana University Press.

Mentzos, Stavros (1980) *Hysterie. Zur Psychodynamik unbewußter Inszenierungen*, München: Kindler.

Micale, Mark S. (1995) *Approaching Hysteria. Disease and Its Interpretations*, Princeton: Princeton University Press.

Middlebrook, Diane Wood (1984) 'Becoming Anne Sexton', in Steven E. Colburn (ed.), *Anne Sexton. Telling the Tale*, Ann Arbor: University of Michigan Press.

—— (1985) 'Poet of Weird Abundance', *Parnassus*, 12–13 (Spring–Winter 1985), 293–315.

—— (1991) *Anne Sexton. A Biography*, Boston: Houghton Mifflin.

—— (1992) 'Coda', in *Anne Sexton. A Biography*, New York: Vintage.

Miller, Jacques-Alain (1988) 'Extimité', *Prose Studies*, 11.3 (December), 121–31.

Ostriker, Alicia (1982) 'That Story. The Changes of Anne Sexton', in Steven E. Colburn (ed.), *Anne Sexton. Telling the Tale*, Ann Arbor: University of Michigan Press.

Pollitt, Katha (1991) 'The Death is not the Life', *The New York Times Book Review* (August 18).

Rich, Adrienne (1974) 'Anne Sexton: 1928–1974', in *On Lies, Secrets, and Silence. Selected Prose 1966-1978*, New York: Norton, 1979.

Sexton, Anne (1966) 'The Barfly Ought to Sing', *Triquarterly*, 7 (Fall).

—— (1973) 'The Freak Show', in Steven E. Colburn (ed.) (1985), *No Evil Star. Selected Essays, Interviews, and Prose*, Ann Arbor: University of Michigan Press.

—— (1974) Interview with Barbara Kevles, in Steven E. Colburn (ed.) (1985), *No Evil Star. Selected Essays, Interviews, and Prose*, Ann Arbor: University of Michigan Press.

—— (1981) *The Complete Poems*, Boston: Houghton Mifflin.

Sexton, Linda Gray (1991) 'A Daughter's Story: I Knew Her Best', *The New York Times Book Review* (August 18).

Showalter, Elaine (1985) *The Female Malady. Women, Madness, and English Culture, 1830–1980*, New York: Pantheon Books.

Smith-Rosenberg, Carroll (1985) *Disorderly Conduct. Visions of Gender in Victorian England*, New York/Oxford: Oxford University Press.

Veith, Ilza (1965) *Hysteria. The History of a Disease*, Chicago: University of Chicago Press.

9

Marketing Black women's texts: the case of Alice Walker

Kadiatu Kanneh

'Did I mention my first sight of the African coast? Something struck in me, in my soul, Celie, and I just vibrated.' (Alice Walker, *The Color Purple*)

The marketing of Black women's texts in the late twentieth century is reliant on the particular and continuing viability of Black women as political subjects, on specific cultural and critical notions of Black female literary identity. Placing Black women's texts in a useful critical context must be, in a large measure, determined by the histories of eighteenth- and nineteenth-century traditions of authorship. These traditions persist in limiting the parameters of meaning within which the Black Woman Writer can be distributed as a marketable object.

Examining the marketing of Black women's texts, and the marketing of Black women as authors and spokespeople, becomes a *historical* pursuit. In this chapter, I will very briefly consider the historical and cultural location of Black women's texts within the marketplace and move on to examine the phenomenon of Alice Walker, whose commodification as spokesperson and cultural activist emerges from and has serious implications for the representation of Black female identity and authorship. I want to focus here, quite deliberately, on Alice Walker as an African-American woman writer due to the high profile of African-American writers as *defining* icons of Black identity – a situation which begs for particular historical, geographical and economic analyses.

There are specific reasons why Black women as authors occupy a significant, even radical imaginary. The packaging of texts by Black women writers in contemporary terms relies on the foregrounding of authorial identity, on emphasising the race and gender of the author to signal authenticity, a kind of autobiographical force behind the text.

What is needed is to trace what might be called a tradition of marketing effects around Black, and particularly Black American women writers.

Looking for the origins of a tradition takes us immediately beyond the current United States and into the eighteenth and nineteenth centuries. It takes us to a moment in between identities, in between Africa and the Americas. The importance of re-visiting the slave trade in these centuries is based not only on the fact of ancestry and what might be termed 'racial origins', but also on a more developed and historically significant notion of literary genealogies. The narratives provide the key to an early archive of Black self-identity, providing an early – often an originary – moment when the idea of a *Black* identity, of an *African* identity, and of a *Black American* identity become articulated. A reading of the slave narratives allows for an insight into two framing questions: What do Black women's texts define themselves within and against? How do questions of authorial identity and literary tradition impact upon questions of national boundaries, cultural definitions, distinct racial histories?

The singular importance of the slave narratives for a reading of what becomes identifiable as African self-consciousness in exile lies in the specific place these texts occupy as original literatures for the Black African diasporas. The peculiar conjunction of memory with writing creates a recognisable starting-point for a Black diasporic literary tradition – a starting-point which echoes the beginnings of pan-Africanist consciousness. Referring to the centrality of personal remembering for the history of Black people in the United States, Toni Morrison points to the slave narratives as key texts for tracing an early archive of Black self-identity:

> A very large part of my own literary heritage is the autobiography. In this country the print origins of Black literature (as distinguished from the oral origins) were slave narratives. These book-length narratives (autobiographies, recollections, memoirs), of which well over a hundred were published, are familiar texts to historians and students of Black history. (Morrison, 1990: 299)

The heavy emphasis placed here upon the individual act of private remembering and the weight given to these personal revelations in construction histories of Black identity in the West point to a concept of origins which relies on reflection, imagination, iteration. Morrison's understanding of herself as a writer – with the words, 'First of all I must trust my own recollection. I must also depend on the recollections of others' (Morrison, 1990: 302) – is reminiscent of the way in which slave autobiographical narratives re-write memory as a site for imagining the relationship between origins and identity. Exiled from an increasingly distant African origin through the trauma of slavery, the slave narratives increasingly, and often through contradiction, reconstitute the site of home from and in different places. The result is often that national belonging is rethought in imaginative and complicated ways that impact on the meaning of an 'African' identity through subtle textual inflections. The operation of memory and its link with projected, constantly renegotiated origins is described by Morrison's figurative reference to the longing of rivers, and her discussion acts as a valuable introduction to the significance of the slave narratives for pan-Africanist thought:

It is remembering. Remembering where it used to be. All water has a perfect memory and is forever trying to get back to where it was. Writers are like that: remembering where we were, what valley we ran through, what the banks were like, the light that was there and the route back to our original place. It is emotional memory. (Morrison, 1990: 305)

Reading the slave narratives, issues surrounding the concept of national or racial identity continually coalesce around discussions of freedom and its meaning. Freedom becomes projected backwards as either a historical or a personal memory in a way that allows a sense of future continuity only through a shifting perception of 'home'. The complicated relationship between home, origins and identity in the texts, and the peculiar set of pressures that come to bear on their meanings, have significant connections with late twentieth-century Black writing. Freedom is continually described in terms of travel and escape, and rarely in terms of return to an original African ancestral home. Return to Africa figures as the release of death rather than as the hope of a liberated future, and the ultimate return to sources. In this context, for example, the return to sources which suicide offers the slave is a direct expression of the impossibility of escape.

The association between travel and freedom in the slave narratives is crucial to the way in which the texts constitute an identity that is increasingly Western and metropolitan. And these tributes to movement and escape in, for example, the narratives of Frederick Douglass and Olaudah Equiano, are placed alongside the significance of literacy as one of the most important paths to independent self-expression and self-knowledge. The publication of the slave narratives makes the fact of literacy a profound and pivotal issue. Slave narratives typically begin with proof-statements as to the authenticity of authorship, with original title pages bearing claims to be 'written by himself/herself', or 'related by himself/herself'. The strategic importance of these proof-statements relates to the taboo on slave-literacy and self-expression.

While sharing the preoccupations of slave narratives written by men, the female slave narratives pay more sustained attention to sexual oppression and familial ties. Sexuality and sexual relationships are given central positions in the women's texts, where sexual abuse on the part of the slave masters and the denial of sexual choices on the part of their female slaves create a severe and lasting impression of the meaning of enslavement. Mary Prince, for example, is forced to choose between a lonely freedom in England and an enslaved marriage in Antigua (Gates, 1987: 212), while Linda Brent is forced to lose a 'love-dream' due to the sexual jealousy of her master, forced, even, to contemplate the prospect of liberation through marriage to her free Black lover, stating hopefully, 'my lover wanted to buy me' (Schomberg, 1988: 370–1, 369). Brent's argument against slavery is largely concentrated in her observation of the relationship between mistress and female slave, where the familial and maternal expectations of the one cancel out the human rights of the other: 'My mistress, like many others, seemed to think that slaves had no right to any family ties of their own; that they were created merely to wait upon the family of the mistress' (Schomberg, 1988: 370). The focus on nakedness, sexual abuse and physical violence in Prince's narrative clearly indicates her sense of the value of individual freedom. Her description of the sexual advantages taken by her master reveals the intimate relationship between violence and sexual depredation: 'He had an ugly fashion of stripping himself quite naked and ordering me then to wash him in a tub of water. This was worse to me than all the licks. Sometimes when he called me to wash him I would not come, my eyes were so full of shame' (Schomberg, 1988: 202).

Alice Walker's novels *The Color Purple* and *Possessing the Secret of Joy* can be read within the tradition of the female slave narrative. Both novels emphasise the significance of personal testament, of autobiography and self-expression. Both texts seek to make explicit the peculiarly female experience of sexual oppression and abuse, and the two narratives move towards a particularly American understanding of freedom and enlightenment via an ethnographic visitation to a static, tradition-bound and translated 'Africa'.

I want to read both texts in relation to their conditions of authorship and authority. As texts that are dedicated to the recognition and validation of African-American women's lives, to utopian resolutions of the oppression of Black women, they need to be situated within the literary history of the slave narratives, of pan-Africanist writings, of writing by Black American men and women. Contextualised in this way, the intertextual nuances and meanings of the novels are readable, as is the significance of the Black American author as a historical and political figure. Against this literary tradition, or, rather, in complementary agitation with it, there is a need to foreground the presence – re-read from *within* the texts themselves – of African sources or reflections. How does Alice Walker's position as American author impact on the novels' authority to read 'African' cultural meanings within a particular brand of American humanism?

The reverse journey by ship to 'the middle of Africa' in *The Color Purple*, communicated solely through the private letters of Nettie to her sister, acts as a journey of self-knowledge, of understanding the meaning of African-American identity. The pan-Africanist impulse that inspires the letters draws on an enlightenment vision of empowerment, where American ideals become undifferentiated in advance from those of Africans, purely on the grounds of race and ancestry: 'We are not white. We are not Europeans. We are black like the Africans themselves. And that we and the Africans will be working for a common goal: the uplift of black people everywhere' (Walker, 1983: 115).

This easy identification between African-American experiences of racism and cultural domination within the United States and the experience of colonialism in Africa, resulting in an advance vision of common purpose, already manipulated by American ideals, is one that remains unshaken at the end of the narrative. The mapping of freedom in *The Color Purple*, through the Olinkan Tashi's entry into the United States, read alongside Celie's liberation through capitalist enterprise, keeps the novel within expectations of American pan-Africanism. Africa's redemption through American capitalism, and the sustained superiority of the liberated African-American woman against the scarified African within the novel, comments on the greater cultural power and profile of the United States.

Tashi's exile from the Olinkan anti-colonial struggle, and her absorption into an American narrative that has already effaced the localised meaning of the scarification ceremony she undergoes, allows the novel to close down the *difference* of African cultural values in favour of the dominant story. Adam's scarification in sympathy with Tashi further neutralises the contextual location of the ritual into an *individualised* bond of love. This relentless move from a historical context to a neutralised individualism, reflected in the journey of liberation from Africa to North America, allows the difference between Black cultures to be effaced, or, rather, abandoned. Rachel Bowlby's comment is useful here: 'Unresolvable questions of racism, imperialism and cultural and sexual difference do surface, but almost always on the African side where they are left behind for the return to an implicitly accommodating U.S.A.' (Bowlby, 1985: 125).

This 'Africa read from San Francisco' (Bowlby, 1985: 118) as a damaged and finally abandoned continent is made culpable in its own decline in relation to precisely those liberating and enlightening elements of the slave narratives themselves: literacy, Christianity (or non-idolatrous spiritualism) and patriotism: 'Today the people of Africa – having murdered or sold into slavery their strongest folks – are riddled with disease and sunk in spiritual and physical confusion. They believe in the devil and worship the dead. Nor can they read or write' (Bowlby, 1985: 118).

The African insensibility to a responsibility that Nettie insists lies with them towards the 'stronger' Black Americans merits a stern reproval. Nettie's insistence energises the moral force behind an African-American 'common goal'. The reality of 'familial' indifference, repeatedly denied as in any way justified, remains as an underlying indignation within the text:

> 'It's worse than unwelcome,' said Samuel. 'The African don't even see us. They don't even recognise us as the brothers and sisters they sold . . . That's the heart of it, don't you see. We love them . . . But they reject us. They never even listen to how we've suffered.' (Walker, 1983: 201)

The bitter outcry to (or about) Africans for recognition and belonging resolves itself in the narrative by reinforcing the United States as home and final resting-place, where families become whole in a rural American idyll and, on July 4th, Africa itself *comes* to America.

Alice Walker's relationship as an author with her own narrative is analysed by her to be far more than one of simple imagination. For Walker, her role is profoundly spiritual, in which she communes with the 'spirits' of her characters. Her postscript, 'I thank everybody in the book for coming, A. W., author and medium', emphasises what she envisages as her position as communicator of the truth, as legitimate conduit for the ghosts of the past. This assessment by Alice Walker of her role as author is not limited to her profile as novelist. Her more recent ascendance into international cultural campaigner *for* African women relies on her un-examined position as spokesperson for Black women *in general*. This position, historically conferred and consolidated, allows her a prominent place in the Western media to comment on the rights and wishes of all Black Women.

Providing a reading of Alice Walker's *Possessing the Secret of Joy*, I want to explore how Black American feminisms and women's narratives can become implicated in oppressive forms of American nationalism, where a pan-Africanist feminism selects African women as objects for cultural reform. My reading is linked to the literary history of the slave narratives, as well as providing a discussion of the conceptual problems involved in African-American identification with Africa, and, in particular, as an interrogation of the political difficulties of Black feminist organisation across the boundaries of nation and continent. Walker's novel is a recent exposition of the variant cultural practices of 'female circumcision', or 'female genital mutilation', among particular African peoples. The text provides a framework for presenting the consciousness of a 'circumcised' African woman to the scrutiny of Western feminists.

The authority of memory and autobiographical fact that is asserted by the slave narratives re-emerges in Walker's modern text, where a Black Western consciousness operates as the site of translation, assessing, by virtue of its enlightened and subjective viewpoint, the meaning of freedom, of African traditions, and of American liberation. I would argue that *Possessing the Secret of Joy* works within the traditional framework of the eighteenth- and nineteenth-century slave narrative to the extent that it sees Africa as both origin and point of departure, and articulates a relationship to the Americas in terms of freedom and arrival at Western self-knowledge.

Possessing the Secret of Joy can be read, not only as a novel, but as a political commentary on a contemporary African condition. Moving on from *The Color Purple*, 'Africa' – still strangely homogenised and static, separated from its own varied political and historical contexts – is analysed in late-twentieth-century terms, and the novel has been marketed as a tool in a campaign against female genital mutilation and patriarchy in contemporary African societies. Before analysing the novel itself, it is important to situate the narrative, and Alice Walker, in the cultural interface between written text and film.

Whereas Steven Spielberg's filming of *The Color Purple* offers the text to a majority American audience, accustomed to Hollywood's sentimentality and the affirmation of family values, the film made by Pratibhha Parmar in conjunction with Alice Walker offers itself as an international feminist statement to viewers of British Channel 4. The film, *Warrior Marks: Like the Pupil of an Eye: Genital Mutilation and the Sexual Blinding of Women*, broadcast in 1993, uses a script by Alice Walker, written shortly after *Possessing the Secret of Joy*. The framing gesture of the film as a whole is Alice Walker herself and, here, the meanings attached to genital mutilation for African women emerge primarily from Walker's own childhood experience of an eye wound. Shot in the eye by an elder brother, Walker in her voice-over describes her own suffering as the result of 'a patriarchal wound' and the loss of her eye allows her to 'see' the meaning of genital mutilation. Walker's statement, printed in the text *Warrior Marks* (published in conjunction with the film), that 'It is the same with the vulva' (Walker and Parmar, 1993: 19) ushers in an exploration of genital mutilation that only makes sense with continual reference back to Walker as author and Western (American) feminist.

Walker's recognition of American cultural imperialism in her comment on the messages sent to African women by Michael Jackson's 'hair straightening and light skin' (Walker and Parmar, 1993: 14) is immediately erased by the superimposition of American femininity on the African scenes in the film. The opening to the accompanying text exhibits the picture of a Gambian child who Walker uses to represent 'the female child in Africa'. The reason for this choice is made explicit in the subsequent paragraph: 'It was exactly as if I were looking into a mirror but seeing my three-year-old self.' The film follows this pattern of 'reading' African women through American female sexuality by featuring an aggressively sexualised Black female dancer, who exhibits a body made dramatically present by a conical Madonna-like bra and bare legs in front of a screen depicting African women and girls covered by cloths and headscarves revealing only a few pairs of eyes. The dancer, miming the horrors of female circumcision, becomes the icon of liberated Western sexuality over the repressed and silenced African eyes.

Although the film has various locations in West Africa and discusses 'Africa' as a whole, it does not differentiate, either geographically or culturally, between the different forms of 'circumcision' that it discusses. The conclusion of the film in the House of Slaves on Goree Island, Senegal, where Walker discusses the horrors of slavery with Tracey Chapman, acts as the film's final closing commentary. The two women discuss their longing to bring the freedom they experience as Americans to African women. Walker's supreme position as cultural commentator and reference point is highlighted at the end of the accompanying text, where she announces in a final gesture of identification: 'It could have been me' (Walker and Parmar, 1993: 350).

Taking as its main character an African woman, Tashi, from Walker's earlier novel, *The Color Purple*, *Possessing the Secret of Joy* ostensibly presents a dialogue between the West and Africa through the inter-action of American, African and European characters. Tashi, from an imaginary African people, the Olinka, who are never given a location (though Walker mentions that the actress who played Tashi in the film of *The Color Purple* was Kenyan) (Walker, 1992: 267), allows herself to be excised and infibulated as part of her expression of cultural inde-pendence from British colonialism. What follows is an intimate description of physical and emotional pain expressed through the corre-sponding frames of European and American culture. The text insists on a collective female experience, possible through empathy, and given coherence through the wider and supposedly universal lens of anthro-pology and psychoanalysis. This collective female experience is proposed to exist within the identical and extra-cultural frame of the sentient female body, through which sexual identities and psychologies are as-sumed to subsist in a (spiritually) communal space of transparent femininity, beyond the artificial barriers of medical and familial cultures. In fact, Walker herself reveals a mystical and *physical* link with the character Tashi through the direct mediation of the body, presented in Walker's epilogue as the most tangible and truthful area of female bonding and sympathy: 'she also appeared to me in the flesh' (Walker, 1992: 267).

What results is an attempt to represent the practices of female circum-cision, not as only specific cultural practices, but as a metaphor for women's subordination and oppression on a global scale. In this way, the various operations of female circumcision can be culturally aligned with the Marquis de Sade, or Western 'slash' movies, as when Lisette, a French woman, is reported as saying: 'It's in all the movies that terrorize women ... only masked. The man who breaks in. The man with the knife' (Walker, 1992: 131). The presence of Jung, the Old Wise Man of Europe, as Tashi's analyst, to heal her of the psychological scars of her excision, allows for a communion between European and African cultures in such a way that the novel can resist difference. Jung, named in the novel as simply 'the doctor', or 'uncle Carl', is described as being surrounded by what are called 'tribal' furnishings. He is likened, by Tashi, to 'an old African grandmother', and he describes his relationship with Tashi and Adam (an African-American) in terms which form the basis of the narrative's insistence on absolute relativism and the possibility of a universal frame of cultural reference. 'Uncle Carl' says: 'I am finding myself in them. A self I have often felt was only halfway at home on the European continent. In my European skin. An ancient self that thirsts for knowledge of the experiences of its ancient kin. Needs this knowledge, and the feelings that come with it, to be whole ... A truly universal self' (Walker, 1992: 81).

The novel's celebration of the value of anthropology for understanding African culture, taken as a whole, and a human collective Unconscious, recoverable through sympathy, leads the narrative, in fact, to incorporate a vision of Africa within rigidly North American terms. 'Africa' emerges as a dying culture; both victim – through the ravages of AIDS and the suffering of circumcised girls – and as its own destroyer – due to the tyrannous collusion of female circumcisers with male sadism. The description of the AIDS floor in Tashi's African prison illustrates the novel's presentation of Africans, and particularly of African women, as passive victims of a continent which ravages its own people. Olivia, watching the crowds of emaciated and dying African sufferers from AIDS, comments on the lack of control, the lack of knowledge, from which they are also dying. From the assumed position of an informed observer, Olivia reports the reflexes of Tashi's liberated consciousness, freed and strengthened by the self-knowledge uncovered and narrativised by Jung's analysis, which encourage her to draw a contrast between her new self-awareness and that of the dying Africans:

> No one has any idea why he or she is sick. That's the most difficult thing. Witnessing their incomprehension. Their dumb patience, as they wait for death. It is their animal-like ignorance and acceptance that most angers Tashi. Perhaps because she is reminded of herself. She calls it, scornfully, the assigned role of the African: to suffer, to die, and not know why. (Walker, 1992: 233–4)

This image of inarticulate and bestial death is one which Simon Watney carefully uncovers in his reading of Western journalistic reporting of AIDS in Africa. Likening the metaphors and images of this journalism to Conrad's *Heart of Darkness*, Watney unravels the textual relationship between AIDS and Africa: 'It is as if HIV were a disease of "African-ness", the viral embodiment of a long legacy of colonial imagery which naturalises the devastating economic and social effects of European colonialism in the likeness of starvation' (Watney, 1990: 90, 91).

Walker's imaginary Olinkan state – a supposed paradigm, or microcosm, of the essential attributes of Africa as a whole – is close to Watney's reading of 'the language of metaphor that informs so much African AIDS commentary' (Watney, 1990: 92), being deeply saturated with ideas of a 'heart' of Africa. Tashi's idea in *Possessing the Secret of Joy* that AIDS has become a woman's disease in Africa through the transmission of HIV by 'the unwashed, unsterilized sharp stones, tine tops, bits of glass, rusty razors and grungy knives used by the *tsunga*' and that it has created a situation, peculiar to African countries, where 'there are as many women dying as men', leads to the sustained image of African women as sexually mutilated, sexually truncated victims of a sexuality to which they can get no access: 'A sweet-faced, woeful-eyed young woman has died. Her husband ... explained to Adam that although they had been married three years they had no children because he had been unable to sleep with her as a man does normally with his wife. She had cried so, and bled' (Walker, 1992: 236). Watney analyses the conflation in Western journalism of African women with AIDS by focusing on the contradictory reporting of women as dangerously and actively sexual, 'the author of her own destruction', and as the targets of White/Western male 'fascination'. Watney's interpretation of the commentary about Africa and AIDS targets precisely the generalising and totalising categories which Walker uses to discuss 'African culture' and cultural practices. As with the variant practices of excision, clitoridectomy and infibulation in various countries and among various peoples, AIDS also has a cultural diversity that needs attention in the struggle against its spread:

> In this respect the notion of 'African AIDS' already obscures the specific characteristics of the different AIDS epidemics in these countries, constructing them in the spurious unity of an 'Africa' which is immediately denied any of the cultural, social, economic and ethnic diversity which are taken for granted in Europe and North or South America. (Watney, 1990: 94).

Tashi's agony turns her against both the Olinkan nation-state and the Olinkan woman, M'Lissa – both victim and sadist – who circumcised her at her own request. Tashi's pain and what is called her 'resistance' are seen to be contained within the logic of Olinkan culture, whereas her affection, strength and salvation lie within Europe and the United States. Tashi's recurring expressions of her love for the United States leads to a vision of it as a microcosm of global empathy, representing and substituting itself for a damaged Africa. Tashi, as an African woman, is ultimately moved to see herself in an American reflection: 'An American, I said, sighing, but understanding my love of my adopted country perhaps for the first time: an American looks like a wounded person whose wound is hidden from others, and sometimes from herself. An American looks like me' (Walker, 1992: 200). Tashi's voluntary circumcision, brought about by the fervour of nationalist decolonisation and the need to be 'completely woman. Completely African. Completely Olinkan' (Walker, 1992: 61), allows the novel to reinscribe colonialism as the possibility of correspondence and unity between the West and Africa. Lisette's Paris becomes saturated with a paternalist or maternalist love of Algeria, symbolised by her son, Pierre, whose mixed race origins can be substituted for Algerian identity, and the novel's moral frame, concurring with the title – 'Black people are natural ... they possess the secret of joy' – is attributed to the wisdom of 'a white colonialist author' (Walker, 1992: 255).

Tashi's names, oscillating between, or being hyphenated by, European alternatives – Evelyn and Mrs Johnson – are clearly intended to allow her to represent – and be represented by – women of different cultures. She becomes the voice of Everywoman, articulated within the idealised terms of African-American womanhood, who, against the 'sliding gait' of broken African women, become icons of strength and power. The repeated use of Tashi's substitute names, and in the final section, as progressive points on the road to salvation – 'Tashi Evelyn Johnson Soul' – works to obliterate Tashi's allegiance to Africa, and, indeed, the validity or value of her African identity.

Walker's epilogue, 'To The Reader', is particularly significant for the structure and meaning of her novel. Discussing her use of fabricated 'African' words, the author claims: 'Perhaps it, and other words I use, are from an African language I used to know, now tossed up by my unconscious. I do not know from what part of Africa my African ancestors came, and so I claim the continent' (Walker, 1992: 267–8). This claiming or appropriation of a whole continent for Walker's American literary anthropology exposes the difficulties and dangers of a relativism that seeks to destroy, not just the significance of cultural difference on a grand scale, but the validity of contextualising and locating where one is speaking from, about whom, and with what egoism.

Possessing the Secret of Joy performs a simultaneous double move by insisting on the alien and deviant principles that dominate and construct African cultural practices, while also claiming the *universality* of patriarchy and female consciousness. Walker's use of Jungian psychoanalysis to ground her loosely ethnographic study of Africa allows her to recognise African cultural difference while at the same time denying the psychological implications of this difference. By upholding United States feminist consciousness as the ultimate destination for 'freed' African women, Walker presents an alternative slave narrative, with the United States as the territory of 'Northern' freedom. This use of slavery as the iconography of the text is made explicit in the words of Lisette, who aligns the oppression of women in general terms with the twin motifs of slavery and sexual violence: 'I recognised the connection between mutilation and enslavement that is at the root of the domination of women in the world' (Walker, 1992: 131).

The novel's intent to prove the existence of a universal feminine unconscious, indivisible by racial, cultural or historical differences, is expressed in this ultimate refutation of the American doctor's claim that 'Negro women ... are considered the most difficult of all people to be effectively analysed' (Walker, 1992: 17). Tashi's indignation at this point, at being so dismissively collapsed into the same category as Black Americans, seems to fit uneasily into the wider aim of the novel, which is to diminish the depth of the separation between African and African American women: 'Since I was not a Negro women I hesitated before hazarding an answer. I felt negated by the realization that even my psychiatrist could not see I was African. That to him all black people were Negroes' (Walker, 1992: 17). Re-reading Tashi's answer, however, her refusal of and anger at the doctor's dismissive generalisation that 'all black people' are Negroes rests more clearly on an irritation at the doctor's implicit denial that all Black people are *Africans*. The latent use of 'Negro' here as a racial category that slides over the geographical and historical origins of Black Americans, and which is used by the doctor as a racial slur – 'Your people like lots of kids, he allowed' – is presented as the problematic which the narrative tries to refute.

This underlying message, that all Black Americans are Africans, is clearly supported by Walker's epilogue, where she claims a familial relationship with Tashi: 'I suppose I have created Olinka as my village and the Olinkans as one of my ancient, ancestral tribal peoples. Certainly I recognise Tashi as my sister' (Walker, 1992: 268).

Possessing the Secret of Joy recognises the significance of colonial histories in perverting or creating cultural narratives and instigating grand battles between a supposedly coherent West and a holistic Africa. However, Walker's novel moves impatiently towards a modernity that can unproblematically include all peoples, all women, within a humanist framework that, via Jungian psychoanalysis, promises a terrain free of difference. Her claim on an Africa that is inherent to Black Americans manages to dismiss the dominating stance of the United States over Africa, and the social and imaginative inclusion of African-Americans in Western narratives of Africa.

The simplistic and one-dimensional representations of African women in Walker's text contrast sharply with the revolutionary women of Ousmane's novel *God's Bits of Wood* and with Ngugi's character Wanja in *Petals of Blood*. These female characters are represented as powerful women who, rather than become sexually and psychologically flattened by the African cultures in which they live, choose to redefine their roles in supportive and mutual relations with African men and families. The character of Wanja, although the survivor of a society that forces her into contradictory roles with conflicting expectations and values, many of which are oppressive and sexually exploitative, is allowed to emerge as that of an autonomous, decision-making being. Balancing the many images of her womanhood, as granddaughter of Nyakinyua, echoing the history of a clan, as the daughter of Christians, as an exploited city barmaid, a powerful woman in love, a fighter and mother, Wanja interprets and re-interprets her position as a woman in a rent and changing society, discovering that, like the different, twining, contradictory and repeating narratives around her, it consists of multiple masquerades, suffering and *choices*: 'She had carried dreams in a broken vessel. Looking back now she could not even see a trail of vanished dreams and expectations ... She had chosen. Everybody chose to accept or not to accept. The choice put one on this or that side of the line-up in the battlefield' (Ngugi: 328).

Walker's representation of Africa, fundamentally a Black American appropriation of Africa to highlight 'liberated' American cultural ideals, fails to acknowledge the infusion of American cultural patterns and self-understanding that has inevitably occurred amongst diasporic Blacks living in the United States. Walker's seamless and uncomplicated 'remembering' of her African origins in a mystical form of 'racial memory' does not take account of the dividing and transforming effects of diasporic movement on a people, the new allegiances that are formed and cherished, alongside the old and prior loyalties that remain to be dreamed. *Possessing the Secret of Joy*, while intent on dissolving the political barriers between women of different nations and cultures, does not analyse the poeticisation and narrativisation of a history which has continuously reinvented Black Americans from the time of slavery onwards. It is these necessary and radical reinventions, fused with the literary, political and practical energies involved with new approaches to and re-creations of the meaning of freedom, of national identity and of 'home', which have re-conditioned the role of Africa as trope, origin and destination for Black Americans. Walker's easeful crossing of oceans and time to embrace her imaginary African 'sister', ready to convert, to re-model her into an image of American femininity, shows no awareness of these political realities.

To return then to my discussion of slave narratives, it is important to emphasise that the struggles to which these narratives are witness involve the painful process of earning a place as Black and human in the West through the process of autobiography and authorship. The frequent re-visitation of Africa as an origin and 'possession' needs to be urgently and carefully re-thought within Black cultural politics, where Black American media predominance in Black letters remains significant.

References

Bowlby, Rachel (1985) 'Problems of the Progressive Text: *The Color Purple* by Alice Walker', in Taylor, Helen (ed.), *Literature Teaching Politics: Conference Papers*, Bristol: Bristol Polytechnic, Department of Humanities.

Gates, Henry Louis Jr. (ed.) (1987) *The Classic Slave Narratives*, New York: Mentor.

Morrison, Toni (1990) 'The Site of Memory', in Russell Ferguson *et al.* (eds), *Out There: Marginalization and Contemporary Culture*, Cambridge, Massachusetts: MIT Press.

Ngugiwa Thiong'o (1986) *Petals of Blood*, London: Heinemann, p. 328.

Ousmane, Sembene (1970) *God's Bits of Wood*, London: Heinemann.

Schomberg Library (1988) *Six Women's Slave Narratives,* The Schomberg Library of Nineteenth-Century Black Women Writers, New York: Oxford University Press.

Walker, Alice (1983) *The Color Purple,* London: The Women's Press.

—— (1992) *Possessing the Secret of Joy,* London: Jonathan Cape.

Walker, Alice and Parmar, Pratibha (1993) *Warrior Marks: Female Genital Mutilation and the Sexual Blinding of Women,* London: Jonathan Cape.

Simon Watney (1990) 'Missionary Positions', in Russell Ferguson *et al.* (eds), *Out There: Marginalization and Contemporary Culture,* Cambridge, Massachusetts: MIT Press.

III

Women in the business

10

Women writers as an unprotected species

Margaret Drabble

I have been in the marketplace for a long time now. I wrote my first novel in 1961–62 and have been publishing ever since, so I am able to speak, if not with objectivity, at least with first-hand knowledge of some areas of publishing. I want to focus on the subject of self-assertion as against protection, a subject which perhaps we all need to think about. Women generally are not thought to be very good at asserting themselves, but then neither are some men. I read recently, for instance, in Andrew Roberts's *Eminent Churchillians* (1995) that King George VI sat in a darkening room because he was too shy to ask the servant to come and turn on the lamp!

First, however, let's begin with some historical context. I went to university in the late nineteen fifties when the atmosphere between women was very competitive. Entry into university was still quite restricted so we had to fight to get in there at all. And when we arrived, we didn't espouse solidarity: we saw ourselves as being in competition, or at least that's how we thought we saw ourselves. Female friendships did prosper of course but they were not in any way recognised as being a creative force. They were just something that happened because you couldn't stop it happening. Certainly they were not given any particular status, as they are today. I remember speaking to Claire Tomalin about this issue when she read my novel, *The Radiant Way*, which is a story of three friends. She said, 'When I was at University we didn't have friends,' although she put it slightly more elaborately than that. There was, however, a feeling that women were fighting one another in the marketplace, a marketplace which then, of course, was not concerned with writing but with getting married, and I remember quite clearly that the triumphant way to leave university was to leave with a ring on your finger. It is pitiable, tragic even, that this should have been the case, but that was the atmosphere, although we were not particularly conscious of it at the time. It took until the early sixties for women to become conscious of the pressures to which they had surrendered. They had surrendered their honesty and their feeling of independence. They had been prepared to kick one another off the ladder, as indeed some of the more distinguished women of later years have also been keen to do.

Looking back on the climate of publishing and reviewing in the fifties is illuminating because some of the things that wouldn't have stood out at all then suddenly leap off the page at the eye. A paragraph from my biography of Angus Wilson (1995) illustrates the point perfectly and reveals something of the tenor of what was going on in the fifties in terms of the attitude toward men and women writers:

> The works of John Braine, John Wain, Kingsley Amis, John Osborne and Colin Wilson were aggressively masculine and frequently misogynist. Womanising was a popular theme, even with the older and relatively respectable William Cooper and C. P. Snow. Women's voices, in these post-war decades, were quiet and ladylike – still too much of the Mrs Miniver and Angela Thirkell for Angus's taste. (Of Antonia White's *The Lost Traveller* he wrote 'the middlebrow musquash fits Miss White all too like a glove' – *Listener*, 4 May 1950 – and in a review – *Time and Tide*, 5 July 1952 – otherwise full of high praise for his friend P. B. Abercrombie's first novel, *The Rescuers*, he had not hesitated to urge her to 'clear her purely descriptive passages of a number of high class women's magazine clichés'.) There was as yet little to signal the 1960s revolt of women against such categories and condescensions, but on another front protest was being organised, and impossible changes were being contemplated. (*Angus Wilson: A Biography*, 1995: 219)

The condescension in this passage is immediately striking, and moreover is typical of the tone of reviewing at that period. Of course Angus Wilson didn't like that particular school of writing very much and why should he? I think he would still have disliked Antonia White even after her resurrection by Carmen Callil, although I do not think he would have expressed himself in quite those terms but would have been obliged to defend his position in a very different way. I do acclaim Wilson as a proto-feminist before his time. It does, however, give some indication of what was happening in the fifties during the time I was at university.

When I left university, I wrote my first novel, *A Summer Birdcage* (1963), which I now see was about female choices. Many of us young women in the fifties thought we had achieved equality just because we got to university. We failed to realise how many others hadn't. We thought that because our mothers were back at home while we were out working or free to get a job, the battle had been won. Of course, we later realised that matters were not nearly so simple. Even today they are by no means simple, because when women have babies they find themselves back to square one, discovering that many of the problems which they thought had been solved by feminist theory are not solved by feminist practice. So my first novel was about career versus marriage. I sent it off in a brown paper parcel to publishers Weidenfeld and Nicolson, for the very good reason that I knew nothing at all about them except that they had published Saul Bellow, a writer whose work I admired.

After about three months of deadly silence, I thought I wasn't going to get anywhere with Weidenfeld and Nicolson, so I rang them up and asked, 'Please could you send me my typescript back?' and they said, 'Yes, of course.' I thought that was disappointing but couldn't be helped. About two days later I got a phone call saying, 'Well, no, we don't want to send it back. Why don't you come and have lunch?' Weidenfeld and Nicolson did publish that book but I still remember very clearly some of the remarks made by the woman editor who accepted the novel. She was a very acute reader and a good editor of fiction. She also had some money in the firm and therefore had some independence of choice. She said to me, 'Not everyone is going to like this book. There's a lot about girls and boys and men and sex and there's too much about clothes. Still, I like that bit about clothes. Why don't we leave it in?' I said, 'Fine. I liked it. That's why I wrote it.' In those days, however, the concept that writing too much about clothes was a deterrent to the male reader was very current – indeed it still is.

There is a passage in my biography of Angus Wilson, for instance, which aroused queries from my male editor. It's about a woman called Viva King, who was known as the Queen of Bohemia in the twenties and thirties. Viva was an amazing woman, bisexual, a great hostess who ran a salon, which was noted for its startling lack of respectability. In the nineteen twenties she married a man named Willie King, another highly ambiguous figure. Among other things, Viva was a dress designer, and this is a description of the dress she got married in·

I would have felt ridiculous in that symbolic panoply of white and a veil, so my dress was a dark blue charmeuse, a material which reversed crepe or satin. It was made on the crepe side with trimmings and belt of satin. It had a short pleated skirt and the top, which bloused over the scalloped belt, almost to my knees, was open in the front to show a pleated silk chemisette and a Peter Pan collar in the new *bois de rose* colour which was a subtle shade of rosewood pink. I wore a large blue petal straw hat down to my eyebrows, with a *bois de rose* ostrich feather threaded through the wide brim to the high crown, the curly end rounding my chin. (p. 159)

My male editor's comment was 'What's that in there for? Do we need so much of it?' Yet it's a wonderful portrait of a fetishist, which is what Viva was (she also collected royal underwear). It is also a wonderful description of an ideal wedding dress. I said that I wanted to leave it in. This is just one example of the way in which a writer does get inter-ference or support depending on the sex of the editor.

The editor of my last novel, *The Gates of Ivory* (1991), is a man whom I like and respect and whose judgement I think is good. He too, however, took exception to some passages in the novel. These had nothing to do with clothes, but verged on the more dangerous areas of taboo and censorship. Here is one of them; it's a woman speaking:

The moon is full again. It is pale, swimming gold as it rises. I can see it rising as I watch. My belly is swollen. It feels as though there were a fish hook inside me, pulling and pulling. An ache at the base of my spine, a swelling in my soft parts. I need to bleed. I am a day late.

As a matter of fact, there is a fish hook inside me. It's called an IUD. An intra-uterine device. It looks just like a fish hook. It is a fisher of men. (p. 245)

My editor didn't like that at all. It made him feel slightly queasy. Could I take it out? But my copy-editor, who was a woman, protested, because she had remembered this phrase with particular affection and wanted it to stay. So it stayed.

There has been an enormous change between the early sixties and the late eighties regarding the areas of protest and the freedom to write. There are very few areas now which writers would avoid entering, although we do sometimes have to think very hard about our tone when we do enter them. In the sixties, of course, female fiction became very fashionable. Magazines were still nervous about subjects such as cancer and orgasm, but eventually *Nova* and *Cosmopolitan* and *The Guardian* Woman's Page began to discuss much more openly subjects which had been hitherto taboo. At the same time, towards the end of the sixties, a body of serious academic feminist criticism began to see the light of day, stimulated by the publication of Mary Ellmann's first book, *Thinking about Women* (1968). Those of us writing at that time had an illusion – perhaps it was an illusion, perhaps it was a real sense of companionship in belonging to a group of writers who didn't necessarily know each other – that there was a great deal of change taking place in the area in which we were working. A feeling emerged that there were sufficient of us to say that we were there because the readers were there. I think that perhaps we became complacent about ourselves because we felt that we were occupying a large and significant area of territory.

We thought we had outnumbered the men, but of course once one began to reflect in the sober light of sociology, it soon became clear that we had not achieved anything resembling parity. When I read surveys today of, for example, how many women review for *The London Review of Books*, how many women operate at the top layers of publishing, how many women put in for senior management posts or how many women become university professors, I realise that the numbers just do not equate. I have recently been reading entries for the John Llewellyn Rhys Prize for writers under the age of thirty-five. This year there were thirty-three male entries and nineteen female entries. Nevertheless, as I was reading, I had the impression that the numbers of women and men were about equal. Because I was reading what I wanted to read, I was counting inaccurately. Women nowadays have become more alert to this phenomenon. They are no longer prepared to accept the token woman as an accurate representation of the whole picture.

Repeatedly, one has to stand up for oneself. Even after I had achieved the freedom to publish fiction, and to earn my living as a novelist, as a woman I still found it difficult to enter other areas of publishing. In 1979, I was approached by a representative of Oxford University Press as to whether I might be interested in undertaking the revision of *The Oxford Companion to English Literature*. When I tentatively said that I might be, I was told that I had to submit a proposal, meet the Board of delegates of Oxford University Press and be interrogated. I went to meet the Board, prepared with sample entries of people who I thought might be included in the next edition, plus various other proposals, such as the introduction of the terms of modern literary criticism, which included an updating of the whole framework of theory. I said that I thought we should, for example, have an entry on feminist literary criticism. With a look of dismay they replied to the effect of, 'That won't be necessary. You must realise that this is a reference book which will be around quite a long time and we don't want to include anything that will be only of ephemeral interest.'

I realise now how foolish I would have looked had I ignored this issue altogether and how useful it is to have a section on feminist criticism in *The Oxford Companion to English Literature*. Indeed, I feel sure that it is one of the entries that people refer to most frequently. I noticed how far the pendulum had swung when I recently saw reported in the press comments on John Vincent's *History* (1996), apparently de-commissioned by the Board because he had not sufficiently covered areas of social history and female development. It is a mark of how greatly the climate has changed and I am glad that I was in the right position at the right time to help effect that change, though I do not necessarily support Oxford University Press's decision with regard to Vincent's volume – which of course I have not seen.

In view, then, of the fact that one can win through, by arguing one's case and by persistence, is there really any need for protection for women in the literary marketplace? Some of the attempts at protection, such as creating a specifically female alternative to the Booker Prize, have obviously been worked out on the basis of the fact that women do not yet have equality or parity or anything remotely approaching it. But such attempts tend to backfire. One has to think extremely carefully before establishing alternative prizes which ghettoise women's fiction. The proposed Mitsubishi Prize, the first version of the Orange Prize, ran into trouble because a male journalist made fun of it in *The Times* and the Japanese backers consequently withdrew the money. This deplorable story illustrates incidentally how great is the need for independent Arts Council support for writers in addition to commercial sponsorship. Sponsors are clearly terrified of criticism or mockery in the press.

Do we, however, need any support of special affirmation as women who write? When I talk to women writer friends of my generation and older, we tend to say that we don't need protection. We, as a group, consider that we have done rather well: we would be prepared to get divorced, hit men on the jaw, bring up children single-handed or live on twopence halfpenny a week. In other words we prefer to see ourselves not as victims but as success stories. Admittedly we are all getting older and we have survived to the stage when we can afford the indulgence of sitting and reminiscing about our wonderful careers. But what about all those who do not have the luxury of getting together to reminisce because they never got there in the first place? The whole debate about marginalisation and victimisation is one that is very worrying to me because it can so easily be exploited by enemies. Candia McWilliam, a writer whom I greatly admire, has said that every baby costs you two books. For this she has been attacked by some feminists who argue vehemently that you should be able to have both babies and books. I remain anxious about this dispute and the question of the victim role within it.

I want to return to the subject of taboos and women's self-assertion with particular reference to my novel *The Millstone* (1965), which I wrote when I was in my mid-twenties. I notice that when I speak to young people now, my heroines are considered defeatist specimens who don't know how to cope with life and who can't even find their way to an abortion clinic. Young readers fail to realise that there were no such things as abortion clinics in the nineteen sixties and that abortion itself was illegal. There is a vast a-historical lacuna surrounding much of what I consider to be recent, common history and our perception of it.

Thinking too about taboos in the process of reading through the fascinating array of the John Llewellyn Rhys women's books, I have to admit that were I shockable I would have been shocked by some of the subjects that women write about nowadays. It is quite clear that Germaine Greer's remark about menstrual blood (to the effect that if you could not lick your own you were not a real woman) has gone to people's heads, hearts and brains in an amazing way. The material I came across was quite astonishing and much of it extraordinarily well written. My fish-hook pales into insignificance in comparison.

The extract from *The Millstone* which follows illustrates the progress that has been made. It concerns Rosamund Stacey whose baby has just had a heart operation in a National Health hospital. It is important to remember that in the nineteen sixties the NHS was much more hierarchical than it is now and the concept of female solidarity had not yet surfaced. In this extract Rosamund has just been told not to come back to see her baby until it has fully recovered because her visits are disturbing.

It was lunch time and I could not find the lady in white. There were a couple of nurses guarding her office who said she wouldn't be back until two.

'That doesn't matter', I said. 'It wasn't her I wanted to see. It was my baby. Would you take me to see my baby? She's in Ward 21G. Octavia Stacey, her name is.'

The two nurses looked at each other, nervously, as though I were a case. 'You're not allowed to visit in this ward,' one of them said, with timid politeness, propitiating, kind, as one speaks to the sick or the mad.

'I don't really care,' I said, 'whether I'm allowed to visit or not. If you'll tell me where it is, I'll get there by myself. And you needn't even say you saw me.'

'I'm afraid we can't possibly do that,' the other one said when the first speaker said nothing. Like her friend, she had a timid, undetermined note in her voice, and I felt mean to pursue my point. I did pursue it, however; I told them I had no intention of not seeing my baby, that I didn't think it would upset her at all, but that on the contrary it would cheer her up, and cheer me up, and was in every way desirable, and that if they didn't tell me how to find her I would just go and look for myself. No, no, I couldn't possibly do that, they both said at once, their voices hardening from personal timidity and embarrassment in the weight of authority. They had that whole building behind them, they knew, and I had nothing behind me at all except my intention. I have never been good at getting what I want; every impulse in me tells me to give up at the first breath of opposition. And yet this time I felt I would not be the only one to lose; somewhere Octavia was lying around and waiting for me. It was no longer a question of what I wanted: this time there was someone else involved. Life would never be a simple question of self-denial again ...

I screamed very loudly, shutting my eyes to do it, and listening in amazement to the deafening shindy that filled my head. Once I had started, I could not stop; I stood there, motionless, screaming, whilst they shook me and yelled at me and told me that I was upsetting everybody in earshot. 'I don't care,' I yelled, finding words for my inarticulate passion, 'I don't care, I don't care, I don't care about anyone, I don't care, I don't care, I don't care.'

Eventually they got me to sit down, but I went on screaming and moaning and keeping my eyes shut; through the noise I could hear things happening, people coming and going, someone slapped my face, someone tried to put a wet flannel on my head, and all the time I was thinking I must go on doing this until they let me see her. Inside my head it was red and black and very hot, I remember, and I remember also the clearness of my conscience and the ferocity of my emotion, and myself enduring them, and not breaking in two. After a while I heard someone shouting above the din, 'For God's sake tell her she can see the baby, someone try and tell her,' and I heard these words and instantly stopped and opened my eyes and beheld the stricken, confused silence around me.

'Did you say I could see the baby?' I said.

'Of course you can see the baby,' said Mr Protheroe. 'Of course you can see the baby. I cannot imagine why you should ever have been prevented from seeing the baby.' (pp. 131–4)

I do not see myself as a feminist writer because that implies you have only one agenda. I am a feminist and I am a writer, which is also, incidentally, presumably how Virginia Woolf would have described herself. Being a writer means that you do not have to adopt a single ideology but that you are able to communicate differing points of view. As a feminist I do support some affirmative action: I support equality of pay and equality of opportunity. The feminist discussion cannot be ignored, although the media can and do manipulate any term they choose, as is indeed the case with the word 'feminist' which has become pejorative in media terminology. The dangerous downside of feminism is the encouragement of a victim culture and the view that it is somehow dignified to be a victim. It is true that women tend to be self-deprecating. They apologise far too much. We should, however, never accept an automatically apologetic position. Rather we need to support one another, not unthinkingly, but for the strengths we have.

11

The contemporary writer: gender and genre

Maggie Gee and Lisa Appignanesi

One of the highlights of the 1995 conference was a writers' panel, which allowed authors to comment on their own, intensely personal experiences of the contemporary marketplace. Here, Maggie Gee and Lisa Appignanesi, two of the writers who took part in that panel, discuss some of the difficulties of being a 'woman writer' in a climate in which publishers and reviewers tend to place authors in pre-determined categories. The discussion that follows is taken from an edited transcript of the proceedings.

Maggie Gee

I went to an all-girls grammar school and then to a women's college at Oxford, so I had a very female education, but almost without noticing the fact. It was simply the way things were at the time – neither I nor my parents made conscious choices. Paradoxically, the effect was to make me very unaware of my gender. I didn't see boys doing one thing and girls doing another, so I felt I was free to do anything I wanted. Similarly, when it came to drawing inspiration from a literary tradition, I always perceived this unquestioningly as both male and female. My literary models were Dickens, Thackeray, Auden, MacNeice, Samuel Beckett and Kurt Vonnegut, as well as Jane Austen, the Brontës, Stevie Smith and Anna Kavan. I felt the same affinity with writers of both sexes. I lived their imaginary lives, dreamed their dreams – gender simply wasn't an issue. Now when I write, I feel both male and female. I write through male characters with as much ease and interest as I do through female characters (of course male readers might find my male characters less convincing – but they haven't said so, so far).

The contemporary writer

For me, the act of writing goes beyond physical gender, and so, ideally, does the act of reading. Writing and reading involve what Virginia Woolf called our 'unacted parts', the unrealised parts of ourselves, transcending our physical gender. It's partly because writing and reading are private acts, bringing with them the great luxury of being unobserved. When you're writing or reading, no-one is looking at you. And the consequence is that you are not limited by the classifying look, and can have a more generous, plural sense of what you are.

So much for the acts of reading and writing. The act of being published and going out into the marketplace is an altogether different thing unfortunately. My feeling about that has changed very much over the fifteen years during which I have been published. When I first began I rather naively thought that I would write and my books would be read as books by a writer, full stop. But more and more I have become aware that all women who write are perceived as *women* writers. And I'm afraid that in this instance women writers usually means 'lesser writers'. I'm sorry that this should be so, but I feel in literary terms it is still the truth for most women who write.

To take one example, my books are all very different from each other, and I have noticed that those of my books which deal with war or murder, which can be crudely categorised as male topics, receive far more attention and literary respect than those which deal with families or children or love or sex. Yet for me these are all great themes, themes from which you can make serious literary works, themes which demand the same careful attention to structure and form and style. Nevertheless, if I write a book about love, it is very likely to be reviewed in company with other books by women, and in a particular way. If there is 'love interest' in the foreground of a work by a woman, reviewers cannot see what else is there; immediately the book is categorised as women's romance. The act of reviewing is too often an act of domination or colonisation, and critics start to map their territory by categorising consciously or unconsciously in terms of gender.

In general, I have to say that I think women writers suffer from a lack of attention to style and even more particularly to form. Form is something that critics apparently only expect to find in the work of male literary writers (though to be fair, the standard of reviewing in Britain is not high, and sometimes literary journalists seem impervious to form and style in the work of male writers as well). However, I suspect that too often the whole category of literary writing is, without the critic being aware of it, predominantly a male domain. Women 'write *about*' – by which I mean that reviewers look first at our subject matter. Men simply 'write' – a primary, literary activity.

Now, these are terrible things to say, but they are observations drawn unwillingly from my own experience as a writer. In actual fact I have been relatively lucky because I have had some very perceptive reviews. Nonetheless, I have noticed that when a critic like (to take one example) Valentine Cunningham sets out to survey the literary scene, he will discuss literary writing on the one hand, and then discuss 'feminist writers' or 'women writers' as a separate category. He does not consciously think that 'feminist' is a negative category, but the effect is negative because 'feminist' is an alternative to 'literary'. I get categorised as a feminist writer because I'm a feminist – and yet my feminism has little to do with my writing. 'Feminist' is an adequate description for some of my opinions and actions in everyday life, but novelists write from levels that are more complex, as well as less conscious, than their opinions. I shudder when I hear myself described as a 'feminist writer', to be honest.

'Woman writer' is not much better, though the context varies. The term has its dangers on the lips of even the most well-intentioned man. I remember when I was a judge on the Booker Prize panel in 1989, and the male Chair of the panel, who was neither chauvinist nor narrow, referred to Margaret Atwood as 'one of the best women writers this year'. He was very surprised when I protested and said, 'Look, we're not talking about the best *men* writers this year.' There is often an invisible pressure on such panels to find a slot for a good 'woman writer' – but only one. In fact the 1989 panel ended up with three men and three women on their shortlist, but too often in recent years the Booker Prize shortlist has consisted of five books by men and one by a woman. So it is sometimes important to question this category of 'woman writer', because it doesn't help us when used unreflectively by men.

But it can also be used in other ways. A conference like this one consciously focuses on gender, and it celebrates the fact that women write, women read, women discuss. To me, as a feminist, that is exciting. I do not see it as ghettoisation. It is only a ghetto if we make it a ghetto by our own narrowness of outlook. I feel positive about any event that gets writing by women read and taken seriously, and that gives women a chance to talk. So much depends on who is using the categories, doesn't it? This conference is showcasing women writers in an eclectic, positive, liberating way, and among ourselves we use the term 'women writers' without negative connotations, but the phrase is still one to be wary of, for the literary-critical world is still basically a boys' world.

I love diversity. Categories are narrow things. Gender category, genre categories, marketing categories and academic and literary-critical categories are often merely strategies for avoiding thought. If you can categorise something, you don't have to think in too much detail about the specific book. The literary/commercial marketing divide in publishing is particularly bad news for writers, whatever their gender. If you're on the commercial side of the divide, you will get no serious review attention, and you are assumed to be uninteresting to intelligent people. If you're on the literary side of the great divide, your publisher will say, 'I don't want to publish you in April because we've got a big commercial book in April.' The implication of this at its most brutal is that your book is not intended to be sold, not intended to be read by many people. Yet good books should surely be available to everyone. Were Dickens and Jane Austen 'literary' or 'commercial'? I think the answer is 'both'.

The current chasm between the two kinds of book is not only the fault of publishers and critics; writers are also implicated. The difficulty of much twentieth-century literature does raise problems. My own view is that difficult language which shuts people out is intrinsically problematic, whether that language comes from academics or novelists. Of course there are contexts which justify difficulty, but the context has to be looked at very stringently. In my own work I have tried to make the surface of my writing more and more clear. That doesn't mean I put less work into the writing. I believe it is possible to create literary effects (which are not necessarily experienced as complex or literary) through form and structure, without using difficult language or arcane literary allusions. And I personally believe that serious fiction should speak at some level to the heart. If novels are purely cerebral constructs and have nothing to say about the things readers care about, people will surely defect *en masse* to biography or film. In the end I suppose we sink or swim in the marketplace, whatever its limitations. Without readers, writers are less than marginal.

The following extract comes from my novel *Lost Children*. It tells the story of a teenage girl who runs away from home, and links her to all the homeless children in Britain today, and also to the lost child in each of us. Alma, the mother, is forced to think back over her own forgotten childhood, and to realise how much her relationship with her own mother and father has affected her relationship with her daughter. She also starts to realise that her quiet, well-behaved son might be the real lost child – she has neglected him because he reminds her physically of her difficult father. So *Lost Children* is about the relation between the generations, which often swims into focus in middle age.

I have to settle accounts with Mother. There are no accounts … it can't be settled … but I have to make her talk to me. Or at the least, I'll make her listen. Maybe then I could love her properly. Maybe we could be close at last. If we could somehow be naked together … Alma sighed. She had never seen her mother naked. No, it was nonsense. She would never listen.

Her mother was encrusted, calcified. Alma would never know what lived inside. Exposed, it would be terrible; it *was* terrible, when Alma had tried.

But somewhere, thought Alma, she must be hiding. The child that my mother was. The one I could understand and pity. The one who could have been friends with me, when I was a child, when I was lonely.

But her parents forced her to hide away. And she hid so well that she can't be found.

She's somewhere, though, I know she is. If I had more patience. If I were kinder. If I could move outside myself …

Even the fathers, Owen, Jack. Were babies once. Needy, not bullies. Everything could have been different for them. They must have been pressed down a narrow path. Then suddenly it was all too late. And now they're dead – and they've done their damage. Whatever the details. Whatever they did. Things they did because they knew no better. Things they did because they could not stop. Things they did because they had been wounded in some deep place that they had forgotten … the secret place they could never find. So instead, they repeated. Passed it on.

Never to know. They had never known. The brilliant sand, dissolving, sifting.

They stretched down the beach, the rows of babies, separated by the dazzle of time, by the bands of sand between the generations which meant they could never touch each other. One row were parents, the next were children, and down that division sorrow flowered, the words unheard, the wounds untreated. From the power of the parents, sorrow flowered. From the needs of the children, sorrow flowered. The needs of the children, so new, so naked, crawling to their parents, infinitely hungry. As *they* had once crawled towards their own parents …

And then the sand blew across the picture. She could not remember, would never remember. And yet it was common, what had happened to her. She knew that much, that she held it in common. That everyone suffered, in the house of childhood. Perhaps there were further, more terrible rooms, but they interconnected, they were not separate.

And always the children became the parents. Owen and Jack were once those babies. My father is in my son's yellow hair. Perhaps that's why I could never love him ... But he was a child. He was innocent. My son, bearing the sins of the fathers ...

I have to love him. Now I can love him. If I can love him, I can break the pattern. That was the secret. Love allows ... love allows us to be ourselves.

Love might allow him to be himself.

Fade the past into a different future ...

[...]

What if nothing is lost, never lost entirely? – If time is a circle? – If love could return. And lack, and need; meek, mute.

If need crept back, and asked to be filled. If fear returned, to collide with courage. If we had time to feel, to listen. The impossible meeting would surely happen. The unimaginable could be imagined.

If only we could slip from the room for a second ...

Maybe we shall wake with the French windows flung wide and walk out into the landscape we have just dreamed, stretching away in every direction, perspectiveless, dazzling, unbounded, peopled.

Maybe the children are there already. Millions of them. The uncountable lost ones. Loud as life, running, laughing. Sun on the black, the ash-blonde, the auburn.

Myself, yourself, my mother, my father. Still young, still potential. All the lost children.

(*Lost Children*, Flamingo, 1994: 314–30)

It matters to me that my own voice can be very different from book to book, though it seems to annoy critics. One of the reasons why women have been attracted to writing is because we feel it offers us freedom to be ourselves. We can say things there that would not be listened to at home or in social contexts. In writing we can at last be authentic, and tell the whole truth in a way that is not possible when we are adapting our responses to individual speakers. Women are trained too well to adapt to other people, to be interested only in others, to say only what we think they want to hear. Writing makes us more powerful because when we write we are speaking to everyone, and so deferring to no-one.

I think that writing fiction is on the one hand a rather courageous activity, but on the other a very protected one. Novelists write alone, in private space, and enter public space only through the quiet channels of letter-boxes and editorial offices. I hope that in future women will write more for theatre and film than they have done in the past. I hope we'll be able to adjust to contexts where we have to work collaboratively and fight much more strenuously to be heard. Traditionally, women have had a hard time in theatre and film because you have to cross a lot of barriers to get plays on stage or find finance for films. Things are beginning to change, at last, though I don't believe women will ever stop writing novels. I hope we are slowly daring to emerge from the 'room of one's own' that half a century ago was our boldest dream, and filling bigger, more populated spaces with our visions and our voices. I hope some of those visions will show women and men able to realise all their different selves, crossing borders, shape-shifting, blissfully transgressing, plural and playful. And I speculate that that kind of playfulness, that kind of manifold expression, is also a dissolving of the rigid, repetitive categories of hatred and violence.

Lisa Appignanesi

A little perhaps useful background: I did a D.Phil in Comparative Literature and worked as a university lecturer for some years before I moved into publishing and then to the London Institute of Contemporary Arts (ICA), where I was deputy director. My first book was in fact my thesis, on Henry James and Proust. I have also written on the history of cabaret, on Simone de Beauvoir and co-authored a book, *Freud's Women* (with John Forrester), as well as edited and translated various other books. It was only in 1990 that I finally made the leap and decided to write full time. The fictions *Memory and Desire, Dreams of Innocence* and *A Good Woman* followed. Now, I think it may be quite clear, given who I am, my education, and my so-called career path, why I might choose to write on Simone de Beauvoir or on Freud's women, or indeed on various other literary and historical subjects. It is perhaps less clear – the matter of paying the bills aside – why I should choose to write women's popular fiction, what publishers categorise as best sellers, and what I like to think of as fiction – I hope intelligent fiction – as entertainment. And in the process have to put up with my friends' raised eyebrows, the occasionally derisive reviews in the literary supplements, and the fact that few of the people you know in fact read you.

When I look back on my professional life, however, this particular choice doesn't seem as discontinuous to me as it might appear from the outside. One reason for this is that I grew up in North America, where my reading was characterised by what we now call postmodern eclecticism. That very mingling of different things which co-exist side by side without much attempt being made to differentiate between them meant that as a teenager, I would quite happily read Georgette Heyer, Dostoyevsky and Tolstoy in the same week. It was all part of the same kind of reading experience. I have also always been interested in popular culture, whether cabaret, which in fact is a variety show hijacked by serious artists and satirists for their own ends, or at the other extreme, making high culture accessible. One of the many thrusts of my work at the ICA was to do precisely that, to mingle high and low, intellectual and popular culture in one space.

The final point is that as a reader I love the nineteenth-century novel, that 'great baggy monster' as Henry James tagged it, the novel which has a grand sweep through history or society, the novel of sentimental education, the novel which sets out to tell a story, and where that story is perhaps more important in the first instance than the fine tuning of language or the playing with structure or any overriding artistic ironies. In other words, I am attracted to the novel you can sink into, not a precise literary category, but a useful one.

In our own time, quite a lot of this kind of storytelling, with its concern for suspense, plot, intrigue and character, is most usually found in popular fiction, indeed in the popular media as a whole, including television and film. So I set out to write the kinds of novels that I like to read, stories where I think the language is effective but transparent, and subservient to the actual telling of the tale. Nonetheless, because you can only write, over any lengthy period of time, about what interests you, these books are obviously inflected with my own preoccupations. Perhaps it is a side issue, but I would suggest that in certain instances, the popular novel is a form of what is elsewhere called the novel of ideas, though of course when you say popular fiction, you are talking about a great many differences as well as similarities. It is a vast category.

So, just to tell you about some of my preoccupations, *Memory and Desire* was written while I was researching *Freud's Women*, although I had obviously done a lot of work on Freud before that. And in some ways I think of it as a parallel to *Freud's Women* in popular form. It is in many ways a play on its epigraph, which reads, 'memory is a past tense of desire'. In other words, we construct our memories, our pasts, so that we can live out our desires in the present or future. Or not. Popular fiction, as you know, is often cast in the form of the family saga.

I like to think of *Memory and Desire* as a family romance. It is about the way that romance and particularly the family romance structures the feminine. It is a novel about mothers and daughters and about fathers and daughters. It is also about the legacy of the Second World War. Put that way, it all sounds rather intellectual. But when you read the book, all this is of course subordinate to character and to story.

Dreams of Innocence, is, as I conceived it and thought about it, a book about excess. In this case, the excesses of purity. Whereas I like to think that in *Memory and Desire*, I focused on the feminine side of the equation, in *Dreams of Innocence* my intention was to look at masculinity, at what constitutes the masculine, at fathers and Fatherlands, brotherhoods and male fantasies. Naturally, perhaps, this book takes us to Germany in the period leading up to the Second World War. In the process, it is also a reflection on eco-fascism. Now, you could very easily read both these books and not inevitably notice the presence of these more intellectual preoccupations. Indeed, I hope that they are hidden, because for me part of the pleasure and the challenge of attempting to tell stories in a popular form is about how to work such preoccupations into the narrative, without either breaking the pace of the story or turning characters into mouthpieces.

As for the business of writing, I cannot say in all my experiences as a writer I have ever confronted any extraordinary difficulties with the publishing world. Perhaps this is because very early on I worked as a publisher, although in an alternative enterprise, The Writers and Readers Publishing Co-operative, which started out at the same time as Virago Press, and so I had an inkling of the problems which publishers face as well as those which writers face. Of course there have been the usual hiccups; about not enough publicity or marketing; about my book on Simone de Beauvoir, which I think is a fine book, getting lost in a series and never being appropriately reviewed because it only came out in paperback. It is very difficult when you have spent years on a project to see it disappear into inattention because it is just one of hundreds on a publisher's list or one of thousands available to a bookshop which can't be bothered to stock it. But for all the passing resentments, which all writers have, I don't think publishers are ogres. On the other hand, I do think that the tenor of reviewing in this country, the sloppy or spiteful showing off which is so much the name of the game, leaves something to be desired. I spent last year living in France and found that French reviewing habits were quite different. There, while reviewers are out to criticise, they are also quite genuinely trying to provide a sense of what goes on in books and do not simply try to show how clever they are at the book's expense. Maggie Gee has said that critics take her books more seriously when they are not about sex or love or children or the home. We see here that gender hierarchy which puts supposedly male concerns at the top of the cultural ladder and female concerns close to the bottom. This is particularly odd when one remembers that at the turn of the century, Henry James invented the novel of high modernism by going to school in the woman's novel. What are *The Portrait of a Lady*, *The Wings of the Dove* and *The Golden Bowl*, but stories of love, adultery and corruption? There is an irony here which would bear further exploration.

Unlike Maggie Gee, I have deliberately chosen a category in which to work, that of popular commercial fiction. The difference between this and 'literary' fiction has much to do with the way in which publishers categorise. They do this for very good reasons, not because they don't know the difference between one kind of writing and another. One difference between so-called popular fiction and literary fiction might be said to lie in expansiveness and compression. Where the literary novel leaps between moments and compresses time, the popular novel fills in gaps. Its montage isn't so radical. Another difference lies in story: in the popular novel there is a preponderance of story. This is not to say that there is no story-telling in literary fiction. A writer like Salman Rushdie deals in both story and history. But the elliptical quality, the emphasis on authorial voice and verbal pyrotechnics, takes equal place with story-telling.

I started to write initially for Mills and Boon because I desperately needed the money to pay for my son's school fees. A friend had suggested to me that one way to make money would be to try and write a Mills and Boon novel, so I went away and read some. I have quite a good ear for literary pastiche and although I hadn't read anything like that since I was about thirteen, I thought I could have a go. It's not as easy as it looks. Writing for Mills and Boon is very similar to the act of reading. There is little distance between the author's voice and the reading presence. Because of this, the voice of the book has to be completely right. Editors know immediately if the voice is slightly askew or if there is any attempt to ironise. It is all a very good literary exercise and I learned a great deal from it. I learned, for instance, how to handle point of view rigorously. It means imposing on yourself the constraint of writing only in a single narrow form so as to acquire technique, as if for example you said to yourself, 'I am only going to write sonnets until I have learned how to handle this particular poetic form, its rhyme, metre etc.' Anyway, I had an acceptance from Mills and Boon at my first attempt. After that I wrote four or five more until one day I sent one off which was returned. It was as if I had learned to do too many things and outgrown the form, which is a very simple one.

I do think, however, that that sort of writing provided a very useful training ground, especially for someone like me. I would certainly never have been able to write fiction in my own voice and under my own name from the outset. Then too, I have realised that I like writing what I am not. My own life has little to do with my fiction. Of course, my experience, my observation, forms a basis for my novels but fiction for me is about playing parts. It is not a confession or a search for an authentic self, if there is such a thing. Following on from Maggie, perhaps then one might say that one of the differences between literary and popular fiction as it has emerged in this discussion is this: that in literary fiction writers seek an authentic voice. I on the other hand, write in order to play out a masquerade, to set characters quite different from myself in motion, so as to explore what they might do.

12

Women, publishing and power

Judy Simons interviews Carmen Callil

J. S.: How did you begin in publishing?

C. C.: My own entry into the marketplace is a story which could never happen now. I came to England from Australia in 1960, when I was twenty-one. At that time I was doing the normal things young Australians did then, wandering around the world and seeing Europe. I put an advertisement in *The Times* which read, 'Australian BA, typing, wants a job in publishing'. I had three offers. I took one, and that's how I began in publishing!

I started at the bottom without knowing a soul. The job I took was as an assistant to an editor who acquired sponsored books for Hutchinson. He was a kind man, for it has to be said that I knew nothing at all, hardly even how to get to Great Portland Street in London, where the Hutchinson offices were then. A couple of other lowly jobs followed: sticking illustrations of ships or tatting into manuscripts, for example. Usually the publisher in question asked me to leave after a tolerant six months or so. Finally, the one person I knew in London, my cousin, met a blind writer called Sidney Bigman when she was on holiday in Portofino, and he got me a job with the publisher, MacGibbon & Kee, who passed me on to the paperback department of their group, which was Granada Publishing. Miraculously, they gave me a job as Publicity Manager, and once I started that job I never looked back. I loved it. Creating circumstances in which people – the public – were forced to hear about books and writers and encouraged to buy them, turned out be my forte.

How did Virago come into being?

Ultimately I tired of working for different publishers and I left books to do publicity for a newspaper, *Ink*. This was a paper started by Richard

Neville, another Australian, who also founded *Oz*. It was intended to be a link between the underground press and Fleet Street newspapers. Those terms themselves of course are virtually meaningless now. *Ink* folded after about two weeks, but on it I met two women, Rosie Boycott and Marsha Rowe. When *Ink* collapsed, Marsha and Rosie went on to start *Spare Rib*, and under their influence I decided to do for women's writing in book form what they were doing in journalism, so I founded Virago.

There was no great complication in this. I loved books and wanted more people to read them. When the ideas of the women's movement floated over the Atlantic in the late sixties and were disseminated in all sorts of ways – in newspapers, in conversations with women like Marsha and Rosie and many others – I immediately identified with feminist explanations of what had been and was my life. Feminism seemed absolutely natural to me, though it would be true to say I never was a feminist of the brutalist, radical, politically correct kind. I wanted to spread the message of the feminism I believed in to the widest possible audience of women and men. And I don't really like that word 'believe' there. Feminism is not a religion: it's a way of looking at the world and a woman's place in it. I was always interested in celebration rather than victimisation.

Rosie and Marsha became the first directors of Virago with me, although they never had time to do much work for it, being busy with *Spare Rib*. So for some years I soldiered on alone, with the help of my first secretary, Harriet Spicer, who went on, after many years, to become director of Virago herself. Many other women joined in the following years – Ursula Owen, Alexandra Pringle, Lennie Goodings, Ruthie Petrie, Lynn Knight and many more – as I got the financial situation under control, and the editorial plan under way. From a financial point of view, Virago was never a problem for me. I loved business, and I taught myself all the aspects of it I could lay my hands on. I did this by asking every friend I had for help: they all gave it to me, men and women alike. Of course there were many troubles, unsympathetic banks, times when we had to raise money and work like slaves to do it, but for the first years I supported Virago myself by working as an independent book publicist and using that money to keep myself and Harriet. There are many other financial stories to reveal about the starting of Virago: suffice to say for the moment that the business side of starting the company was fun and not a real problem, taking it as read that working twenty-four hours a day seven days a week was a *sine qua non*.

Women, publishing and power

What inspired you to start Virago?

There were two main reasons why I founded Virago. The first was ideological; the second was commercial. Virago was intended to publish books that celebrated and illuminated women's history, lives and traditions. What I really wanted to do was to make women's writing central to the canon of literary culture which was so absorbed by male writers, and when I look back at what has been achieved over the last twenty years, I feel that Virago has in some way been responsible for the improvements in that direction.

I never wanted Virago to be a collective or anything that would instantly fail. I wanted it to succeed so that it would give women something to be proud of. I also wanted to provide a place for women to publish and be published in a context where others understood what they were writing about. You must remember that all this took place in the 1970s when the issues of feminism were really hot news. Virago could never have been so successful had it not been for the extraordinary group of women and men of that decade who gave us so much help in every possible way, with ideas, suggestions, writing for little reward, listening on the telephone, etc. It was the result of an amazing outburst of group energy, to which my personal contribution was my literary taste, my business sense and my marketing skills. I wanted the books to look good and I wanted the work to be of high quality.

What is your view on the relationship between feminism and publishing?

Feminist publishing houses tend to be more concerned that work should be politically correct than about their authors and the quality of the writing they publish. This is why so many feminist publishers have failed. One cannot publish for an idea only. There are essential values required by the work itself and for the authors themselves. If you forget about standards and concentrate on political correctness then all is lost. This problem for feminist publishing was not properly addressed in the seventies and the whirlwind is being reaped now.

The market that I wanted to reach with Virago was not primarily feminist. Rather I wanted Virago to present feminism to a mass market, and certainly the presence of Virago in the bookshops is now as great as that of any other publisher and has been so for years. There are two quotations which best sum up what I was trying to do in those early days. The first is from Liz Calder, the Publishing Director of Bloomsbury,

185

who said, 'It seems to me that the most triumphantly feminist literature has always been that which is occupied rather than preoccupied by feminisms, shaped by feminist consciousness rather than encased in rigid structures.' The other comes from a friend who consoled me when a group of feminists was attacking me for something, and who said, 'If you think about it, the feminism of the 1970s was about changing people's lives: it was not about publishing a pamphlet for somebody who'd say to you, "What a wonderful socialist pamphlet".'

These days it's easy to put a name to what she was comforting me about. For many feminists it was okay to publish a socialist pamphlet (which might be interesting or not, as the case may be) but it was not acceptable to publish fiction which often did no more than shock or celebrate, illuminate the status quo or merely entertain. In that way I had terrible and continuing trouble with the Virago Modern Classics and often with covers. Angela Carter too often came in for this politically correct feminist narrowness. One of the downfalls of feminist publishing in general has been its overriding concern with ideological issues, and allowing these to come before the quality of the writing. This is a lethal fault for a publisher who must always put the author and the written word first.

How would you sum up the essential difference between Virago and other publishing houses?

In many ways it is an odd time to be addressing this question because the differences no longer exist to the same extent, and much of the work we did in the seventies is in abeyance. Perhaps the main difference was that Virago aimed to make women's writing the centre of a cultural scene. It was of course also important that we had an ideological message. In other ways, though, apart from the fact that it was smaller and couldn't pay authors so much, it was trying to be the same as mainstream publishers.

The press always like to bring up the subject of 'men' as a controversial issue in Virago's editorial policy, but in fact Virago always published men. Occasionally Virago didn't handle this issue well, such as the time when a parson wrote a novel under a female pseudonym, and when they found out, the management of Virago at the time refused to publish him. In my view this was a mistake. On the other hand, it's a lesson to publishers to meet their authors before they buy their books! But hostility to Virago was as vociferous as the praise. Because it was committed to an idea, it came in for more than average attention. Whatever the popular view, Virago has always published male writers. The difference was that we women were in control of all the choices, not men.

What in your view has been Virago's greatest achievement?

One of the greatest things that Virago achieved was the re-publication of a body of writing by women that had been neglected for years, and which became the Virago Classics list. Quite simply this boiled down to a matter of power. Before the 1970s, most editors who chose what the public would read were men. It wasn't that they disliked books by women; it merely never occurred to them that anyone would like them. Thus there existed an automatic power chain that went on year after year.

The choice of Virago's list sprung directly from the women's movement itself. Hundreds of women academics – and non-academics – who had studied various texts in universities would recommend books to us. One of the first of the non-fiction list with which Virago started was *Life As We Have Known It*, which was suggested by Jean McCrindle, a lecturer from Sheffield. *Round About a Pound a Week*, a book about the working lives of women in Lambeth, which has sold thousands of copies, was suggested by BBC Radio's Woman's Hour. Ros Delmar suggested *Testament of Youth* by Vera Brittain. The fiction side began much more straightforwardly. A friend gave me a novel by Antonia White, *Frost in May*, because I had had a wretched childhood in a convent and he thought I would enjoy reading it. After I read it, I felt I had to find a way of publishing it. The Virago Modern Classics grew from that. I merely published books I had read and liked.

Virago's greatest success, however, apart from the writers that we served, has been the fact that every single trade publishing house in Britain today now has a thriving list of women writers. Many of these are looked after by editors who are themselves remarkable young women, for publishing is a business where women can flourish. Those houses have now realised what a market there is for women's literature, and it was Virago which was directly responsible for that to a great degree. Our sales figures told other publishers that readers *did* want to read Rosamond Lehmann and Elizabeth Taylor: Virago sent them scurrying to their backlists.

Writing: a woman's business

What is your view now on the situation of women in today's literary and commercial marketplace?

The place of women in the marketplace today is a complicated issue. In 1992, I started a group of women who were in management in publishing. One of our first initiatives was to commission a research unit to undertake a statistical survey of book reviews. We analysed newspaper reviews of books in the literary and tabloid papers over a three-month period. The statistics that emerged presented a pretty grim picture. It is a fact that more women than men read books. Yet the results of the survey proved that overall only 24 per cent of books reviewed were by women, leaving the proportion of those by men at 76 per cent. An average of 23 per cent of reviews are written by women, while only half the newspapers carry less than 20 per cent of these reviews. Women tend to review female authors; men tend to review male authors.

When these figures emerged, we decided to examine how they related to the actual publication figures in trade publishing, where 64 per cent of all books published are by men and 36 per cent by women. Those figures, however, do not tell the whole story because they are also affected by publishers such as Mills & Boon and Virago, who publish almost 100 per cent women; Viking/Penguin is virtually the same; Bloomsbury's output is 80 per cent men and 20 per cent women. Chatto, of which I was Managing Director at the time, published 55 per cent women and 45 per cent men one year, and 45 per cent women and 55 per cent men the next. So we see that in the quality publishing, which constitutes our cultural core, the majority of work published is produced by men. It would be fascinating to know why this imbalance exists, and further research is needed on the subject. There is no acknowledged bias in the industry against women, and many women now have senior positions in publishing. The women editors are there and women buy and read books. Why then should this be the situation?

This leads on to the whole question of who runs the shop in publishing. The Bentinck Report [1995] on the situation of women in publishing shows that the boards of major publishing houses are almost entirely male-dominated, with very few women having seats on the board. There are, however, many important jobs in literary publishing which carry far more influence than does board membership. In fact the increase of women in positions of power in British publishing since I began has been extraordinary. The situation is of course by no

188

means perfect, but I feel strongly that the figures as presented in the Bentinck Report have been interpreted in a negative way. For example, the report states that 'macho cultures demand conformity to male mafia values' and that within publishing companies 'women succeed if they adopt an aggressive, larger than life persona, otherwise they are disregarded'. Now, as someone who was born with an aggressive, larger than life persona, I find this comment extremely patronising to women. It relies on the assumption that women's personalities are automatically different from men's. But I have worked with some very timid men!

The report also states that 'managers saw that commercial imperatives had replaced cultural values in publishing' and that 'women managers seemed more alienated by this shift'. Effectively, what this is saying to women is that they are no good at managing money in a time of economic recession, and that when everything turns rotten, it is their lovely, cultural, maternal values which come to the fore. It is true that publishing is in many ways a service industry, a caring profession. Editorial work, which includes nurturing authors, suits many women. We should not forget, however, that the relationship between editors and high-profile authors can give editors power. Publishers cannot afford to lose those writers. In all the agglomeration that has gone on in publishing houses in the last twenty years, many great editors have been sacked or have become so miserable under new management that they have left of their own accord. The big conglomerates gradually learned that if the editor left, many an author was likely to go too, if not immediately then very soon after. Or, if the authors stayed after the departure of the editor to whom they were originally committed, often the authors demanded twice as much money to stay on with the same imprint. Because loyalty had gone out of the window, they demanded money to remain on the list. *This* is the power of an editor with a good relationship with authors on the publishing list. These days management think twice before getting rid of high-calibre editors.

Do women authors have to fight harder than their male counterparts?

I don't think so. The marketplace for women in publishing is essentially a good one and further research needs to be done on why more women are not publishing. Women writers certainly have to fight for time, as Tillie Olsen's *Silences* makes abundantly clear. Every single woman on earth is born to make sure that a man can get on with *his* work.

Consequently, because they produce children, women inevitably write less. This is a fact, not a sob story.

The literary pages of national newspapers, however, remain a male ghetto. Most literary editors are men with only an occasional woman, such as Claire Tomalin, breaking the pattern. In the end this produces a jockstrap mentality which is ultimately boring. In 1995, three national newspapers appointed literary editors. I know that young men, who are in my view still in nappies as far as journalism is concerned, were considered for these jobs as well as at least one woman who is a very experienced literary editor. The experienced female literary editor did not get a job, even though one of the appointees was a woman journalist. But we are also into ageism here, and the wish of newspapers to treat books as news or events rather than as literature.

So do women writers get a bad deal?

Women's writing is central to all trade publishing today. In fact women have certain advantages over men as writers. Quite apart from any other considerations, they are immediately publicisable. Any publicity department can get you an interview if you're a woman because you can always talk about children, cooking, gardening ... If you're a man, you usually have nothing of interest to say other than about your work.

There are also certain literary categories that women seem to fall into naturally, such as crime writing or romances. Nothing, however, is inevitably closed to them. If, for instance, a book about war appears which is written by a woman, a publisher is thrilled because it is more commercial. A book about Japanese megalomaniacs, written by a woman financial journalist, is an immediately marketable proposition. I certainly don't feel that there are specific characteristics of women's writing which are immediately identifiable. Women write about the conditions of their lives, so there may be a tendency for them to write about similar subjects, but I could not identify whether a history book, for example, was written by a man or a woman.

What changes have you seen in the marketplace in the last twenty years?

In the last twenty years, the marketplace has undoubtedly changed beyond recognition. Thirty years ago, the publishing industry was run by gentlemen in trousers. It is not unkind to say that they were largely incredibly second rate. Almost all went bankrupt over a period of time and sold out to larger and larger conglomerates. The biggest single consequence of this culture shift has been that authors can now get more money. Consequently, publishers make less and they have to share services. Thus, while the climate has improved for writers as it has become more professional, publishers have less freedom. Conglomerates put the power to publish into the hands of management, not editorial staff: they *control* the editors. This means a different sort of editor is found in most publishing houses today – more obedient, less entrepreneurial – but I see no sign that these quieter editors are in any way worse for the authors they publish. Conglomerates arrived for economic reasons and because of the inefficiency of those people who were running the small British publishing houses in the fifties and the sixties.

Is, then, the concept of a women's publishing house outdated?

Any house that puts ideology before the quality of its writing is outdated. In addition, women's publishing cannot happen in isolation. Feminism today no longer needs to be separatist: it needs to engage in the society to which it belongs, keeping always that central core of women's culture, women's concerns as the driving force behind what is published. The reason is that I can see today no women's publishing house which appeals to young women and to older women as Virago did over twenty years ago. There is no point in trying to change the world unless you know what goes on in it, and I feel that a sense of the ghetto has fallen on the women's publishing houses of the last decade.

For authors, there is also now a very big question as to whether they need such a publisher. There are so many editors working in mainstream houses who are feminists or who understand exactly the issues and ideas involved. Most women writers today are happy on such lists and do not need a women's publishing house to give their voices utterance. On the other hand, it's an interesting question as to whether feminist publishers themselves would have kept these authors on their lists had they handled sales and marketing matters differently. To do that and remain a small publisher is a very difficult thing and almost always depends on the entrepreneurial nature of the publishers involved.

If you were starting again today, would you do anything differently?

If I were starting again, while the ideas of feminism would still provide my base, I now feel the need to move wider. The greatest lack in English language publishing today, and I include both British and American publishing practice here, is fine writing about ideas, political debates or contemporary issues. When I was working at Chatto, I published Edward Said, but one swallow does not make a summer. There also remains much material by neglected women writers to be rediscovered. The Virago Classics list is by no means exhausted, but quality and entertainment must remain paramount. My own sense of taste has always determined my choices over what to publish. The Australian writer David Malouf once explained to me that the Australian education system derives its base from the Scottish system, where the idea of a canon of literature is dinned into you. Essentially, I suppose I am a Leavisite, for Leavis, whatever you may have thought about his choice of books, maintained that English literature is important in terms of its moral imperatives. I am a child of the Empire and as a foreigner, I find it curious to observe that this tradition is not honoured in this country as it might be.

Index

Note: 'n.' after a page reference indicates the number of a note on that page.

Index

Index

Index

Index